The Seventeenth-Century Literature Handbook

Literature and Culture Handbooks

General Editors: Philip Tew and Steven Barfield

Literature and Culture Handbooks are an innovative series of guides to major periods, topics and authors in British and American literature and culture. Designed to provide a comprehensive, one-stop resource for literature students, each handbook provides the essential information and guidance needed from the beginning of a course through to developing more advanced knowledge and skills.

The Eighteenth-Century Literature Handbook
Edited by Gary Day and Bridge Keegan

The Medieval British Literature Handbook
Edited by Daniel T. Kline

The Modernism Handbook
Edited by Philip Tew and Alex Murray

The Post-War British Literature Handbook
Edited by Katharine Cockin and Jago Morrison

The Renaissance Literature Handbook
Edited by Susan Bruce and Rebecca Steinberger

The Shakespeare Handbook
Edited by Andrew Hiscock and Stephen Longstaffe

The Victorian Literature Handbook
Edited by Alexandra Warwick and Martin Willis

The Seventeenth-Century Literature Handbook

Edited by

Robert C. Evans

and

Eric J. Sterling

continuum

Continuum

The Tower Building
11 York Road
London SE1 7NX

80 Maiden Lane, Suite 704
New York
NY 10038

www.continuumbooks.com

British Library Cataloguing-in-Publication Data
A catalogue record for this book is available from the British Library.

ISBN: 978-0-8264-9849-6 (hardback)
       978-0-8264-9850-2 (paperback)

Library of Congress Cataloging-in-Publication Data
A catalog record for this book is available from the Library of Congress.

Typeset by RefineCatch Limited, Bungay, Suffolk
Printed and bound in Great Britain by The MPG Books Group

Contents

Contents

Detailed Table of Contents

General Editors' Introduction

The Continuum *Literature and Culture Handbooks* series aims to support both students new to an area of study and those at a more advanced stage, offering guidance with regard to the major periods, topics and authors relevant to the study of various aspects of British and American literature and culture. The series is designed with an international audience in mind, based on research into today's students in a global educational setting. Each volume is concerned with either a particular historical phase or an even more specific context, such as a major author study. All of the chosen areas represent established subject matter for literary study in schools, colleges and universities, all are both widely taught and the subject of ongoing research and scholarship. Each handbook provides a comprehensive, one-stop resource for literature students, offering essential information and guidance needed at the beginning of a course through to more advanced knowledge and skills for the student more familiar with the particular topic. These volumes reflect current academic research and scholarship, teaching methods and strategies, and also provide an outline of essential historical contexts. Written in clear language by leading internationally-acknowledged academics, each book provides the following:

- Introduction to authors, texts, historical and cultural contexts
- Guides to key critics, concepts and topics
- Introduction to critical approaches, changes in the canon and new conceptual and theoretical issues, such as gender and ethnicity
- Case studies in reading literary and theoretical and critical texts
- Annotated bibliography, timeline, and glossary of critical terms.

This student-friendly series as a whole has drawn its inspiration and structure largely from the latest principles of text book design employed in other disciplines and subjects, creating an unusual and distinctive approach for the undergraduate arts and humanities field. This structure is designed to be user-friendly and it is intended that the layout can be easily navigated, with various points of cross-reference. Such clarity and straightforward approach should help students understand the material and in so doing guide them through the increasing academic difficulty of complex critical and theoretical approaches to Literary Studies. These handbooks serve as gateways to the particular field that is explored.

All volumes make use of a 'progressive learning strategy', rather than the traditional chronological approach to the subject under discussion so that they might relate more closely to the learning process of the student. This means that the particular volume offers material that will aid the student to approach the period or topic confidently in the classroom for the very first time (for example, glossaries, historical context, key topics and critics), as well as material that helps the student develop more advanced skills (learning how to respond actively to selected primary texts and analyze and engage with modern critical arguments in relation to such texts). Each volume includes a specially commissioned new critical essay by a leading authority in the field discussing current debates and contexts. The progression in the contents mirrors the progress of the undergraduate student from beginner to a more advanced level. Each volume is aimed primarily at undergraduate students, intending to offer itself as both a guide and a reference text that will reflect the advances in academic studies in its subject matter, useful to both students and staff (the latter may find the appendix on pedagogy particularly helpful).

We realize that students in the twenty-first century are faced with numerous challenges and demands; it is our intention that the Handbook series should empower its readers to become effective and efficient in their studies.

Philip Tew and Steven Barfield

1 Introduction

Eric J. Sterling

Chapter Overview

Seventeenth-century English literature was shaped by various historical occurrences and cultural phenomena such as the death of Queen Elizabeth in 1603, the subsequent ascension to the throne by James I (James VI of Scotland), the loss of power and subsequent beheading of Charles I in 1649, the Interregnum and the Protectorate under Oliver and Richard Cromwell, the Restoration of the English royal family to the throne in 1660 under Charles II, and the Glorious Revolution of 1688. The period also saw such other important developments as the closing of the theaters in 1642 and the return of theatrical performances – ones that allowed women to perform onstage – in 1660; the fear and spread of bubonic plague early in the seventeenth century and again in 1665; the devastating Great Fire of London in 1666; the spiritual-political conflicts between and among such diverse groups as Anglicans, Catholics, Puritans, and Quakers; scientific exploration and a growing thirst for empirical knowledge; colonialism and world exploration;

and other influential cultural trends. These events – and many others – are significant because they helped to inspire the themes employed by seventeenth-century writers, and similarly, the literature by seventeenth-century authors greatly influenced historical, religious, and political occurrences and early modern cultural thought. This introduction will focus on several key cultural, historical, and literary developments during the early modern period.

The term 'early modern' is another name for 'Renaissance'; both terms refer to the literary and cultural period in England that included the sixteenth and seventeenth centuries. Although scholars still employ the term 'Renaissance', recently the term 'early modern' seems to be supplementing, if not in the process of superseding, it. This volume will include both terms because they are both still prevalent in studies of the era. Although both terms encompass the sixteenth and seventeenth centuries, this Continuum volume will focus only on the seventeenth century. It is worth noting, however, that the careers of many significant English writers (such as William Shakespeare, George Chapman, Samuel Daniel, Thomas Dekker, Michael Drayton, Thomas Campion, Richard Hakluyt, and John Marston) extended into both the centuries. The works of few English writers (such as Sir Isaac Newton and Jonathan Swift – whose *A Tale of a Tub* and *The Battle of the Books* were penned in the late 1690s but not published until 1704) encompass both the seventeenth and eighteenth centuries. Some Restoration writers such as William Congreve stopped writing when the seventeenth century terminated. Demarcations between the centuries can be too rigid and arbitrary, yet it is worth pointing out that many authors of the late sixteenth century continued writing seamlessly into the next century, yet very few writers of the late seventeenth century continued their careers into the subsequent century. It seems that the biting satires and many references to sexuality in Restoration writing did not meet the public's approbation at the beginning of the eighteenth century, as Jeremy Collier's 'A Short View of the Immorality and Profaneness of the English Stage' (1698) suggests. Collier's influence helped to curb the works of Congreve and John Vanbrugh, thus ushering in a different mode of writing in the eighteenth century. In short, this Continuum volume covers the literature of British writers that was penned or first published in the seventeenth century, during the Stuart, Caroline, Cromwellian, the Interregnum, and the Restoration periods.

The presence from 1558 to 1603 of a popular and successful female monarch undoubtedly affected how seventeenth-century citizens viewed women, for they had witnessed a female ruler lead the defeat of the Spanish Armada in 1588 and successfully govern a nation for forty-five years. English citizens realized the complexity and depth of Elizabeth's character when she delivered her heroic and patriotic 'Speech to the Troops at Tilbury' before the fight with the Armada and later saw the firmness and resolve with which she handled the Essex Rebellion of 1601. Even those Englishmen and Englishwomen who hoped that she would marry so that England would once again have a king might have recognized Elizabeth's desire for familial and political autonomy by deciding to refrain from marriage, thus avoiding the risk of losing her wealth, individual independence, and political authority to a man. English citizens mourned Elizabeth's death in 1603, and many of those people who longed for an English king probably wished that the queen was still governing rather than for the nation to fall into the hands of James I, the Protestant son of the Catholic Mary, Queen of Scots. The respect that Elizabeth attained and earned during her reign was enhanced at her death, an event that led citizens to greatly appreciate her and begin contemplating her significance in English history. Her reign as well as her death helped shape male – and even female – attitudes toward women.

Pre-Civil War Literature by and about Women

At the beginning of the seventeenth century, a transformation occurred in literature because women took a significantly more active role in writing. It is not surprising, then, that it was in the seventeenth century that a woman (Martha Moulsworth) composed what is arguably the first autobiographical poem in the English language – the first work of verse in which a woman looks within, into the heart and soul of her inner self. The poem, entitled 'The Memorandum of Martha Moulsworth, Widdowe' (1632), provides poignant insight into the life of this intriguing seventeenth-century woman. In 1656, Margaret Cavendish, Duchess of Newcastle, wrote her autobiography, 'The True Relation of My Birth, Breeding and Life'. Aemilia Lanyer wrote a collection of poems about the passion and resurrection of Jesus Christ, entitled *Salve Deus Rex Judaeorum* (1611). It is one of the first collections of poetry published by a female in England, after Anne Vaughan Locke's 'A Meditation of a Penitent Sinner' (1560) and Isabella Whitney's *Copy of a Letter, Lately Written in Meeter, by a Yonge Gentilwoman* (1567) and *A Sweet Nosgay, or Pleasant Posye: Contayning a Hundred and Ten Phylosophicall Flowers* (1573). Thomas N. Corns observes that one-third of Lanyer's publication 'is taken up with front matter in the form of dedicatory epistles, mostly in verse. Strikingly, all the dedicatory poems are addressed to women [primarily Margaret Clifford, Countess of Cumberland], which points to what is perhaps most remarkable about the volume'.[1] These panegyrics manifest how significant patronage was in early modern England. The last poem in the collection, 'The Description of Cookeham', is arguably the first country house poem in English. This country house poem is unique for its female perspective and the belief in female spirituality and sisterhood that the patron, Clifford, exhibits at Cooke-ham. Hugh Jenkins says that in the poem, Lanyer describes Cooke-ham as 'the female Eden' and that the poem suggests 'a specifically female spirituality . . .'.[2] Elaine V. Beilin claims that unlike Ben Jonson, who praised virtuous women to make a point about human nature and to call attention to himself as a poet, 'Lanyer wrote specifically to praise women, and more precisely, to redeem for them their pivotal importance as Christians'.[3] Susanne Woods points out that the virtue of the Countess, along with the contemplation and meditation enkindled by Cooke-ham, allows Lanyer to discover 'her vocation as a religious poet' and inspires her 'to produce her story of Christ's passion'.[4] It is worth mentioning that this fine collection of poems written by a female poet was ignored by scholars for centuries; even Albert C. Baugh's comprehensive *A Literary History of England* fails to mention her, yet literary scholars over the past two decades have given her poetry extensive treatment. This pattern of generally ignoring the work of seventeenth-century female writers for centuries and discovering them during the past few decades is a paradigm that fits other female authors such as Aphra Behn and Cavendish.

Women did, however, receive prominent attention in Jacobean, Caroline, and Restoration drama. Female characters seemed to have a far more significant role, as both heroines and villains, in seventeenth-century drama as opposed to sixteenth-century plays. Instead of having menial roles, as in, say, most of Christopher Marlowe's dramas of the late sixteenth century, seventeenth-century plays showed the depth and complexity of female characters, as in Thomas Middleton's *Women Beware Women* (1621) and *The Changeling* (co-authored by William Rowley) (1622), John Webster's *The Duchess of Malfi* (1614), and Philip Massinger's *The Maid of Honour* (1621), to mention just a few examples. Furthermore, Elizabeth Cary's closet drama, *The Tragedy of Mariam, Fair Queen of Jewry*, was written, as far as one can tell, in the year of the queen's death (1603) or in 1604, and published in 1613; the tragedy tells the story of Mariam, the suffering wife of Jewish King Herod the Great. The play is the first extant drama written in English by a woman. Queen Elizabeth's enormously successful forty-five year reign, which helped show the world that women could be talented leaders, also helped, to some extent, to improve English attitudes concerning the abilities of women, but this statement by no means indicates that seventeenth-century women were treated as equals or were afforded the same respect that was granted to men. In fact, Ben Jonson satirized male chauvinist attitudes toward women in his comedy *Epicoene, or the Silent Woman* (1609); one of the main characters, Morose, wants to marry but will only do so on the condition that his wife never speak so that he will never have to listen to her.

Restoration Literature by and about Women

The presence of women on the English stage, beginning in 1660, helped women to garner more respect. Most actresses had to be able to read in order to rehearse their parts, and they manifested to Restoration audiences that they were capable and talented performers who could play roles skillfully. Some actresses, however, such as Nell Gwynn, were illiterate but were still able to master their parts. Despite the effusive praise from people such as diarist Samuel Pepys for the talent of the women on the Restoration stage, some actresses were often treated as sex objects, being considered by some men to be prostitutes or mistresses (as with Nell Gwynn and Mary 'Moll' Davis, two mistresses of King Charles II), or as mere objects of desire, such as when their parts called for them to dress as men onstage (cross-dressing) in order to wear garters that exposed their legs and tight-fitting outfits that clearly delineated the shapes of their bodies, to the delight of male audiences. It should be noted that Pepys mentions several times in his diary that he lusted for actresses; his feelings were a combination of admiration for their acting talent and for their physical beauty. Great Restoration tragic actress Elizabeth Barry was known to be the lover of poet and rake John Wilmot (the second Earl of Rochester) and of playwright Sir George Etherege. Playwright and actor Colley Cibber greatly desired comic actress Anne Bracegirdle. Bracegirdle was suspected by one of her infatuated fans, Captain Richard Hill, of having an affair with actor William Mountfort; desiring Bracegirdle for himself, Hill, on December 9, 1692, enlisted the assistance of Lord Charles Mohun, and the men murdered Mountfort and attempted unsuccessfully to kidnap Bracegirdle. The reason for the abduction, perhaps, is that Hill found Bracegirdle physically desirable because he had seen her in comedies wearing breeches and thus exposing parts of her body to the audience and, because of her career, he might have suspected that she could be a loose woman. Some actresses married in order to establish a proper reputation and in hopes of not being propositioned by infatuated and lustful fans. Perhaps the best example of the disrespect afforded to actresses on the Restoration stage occurred on opening night of John Vanbrugh's comedy *The Relapse, or, Virtue in Danger* (1696); the play, a dramatic response to Colley Cibber's sentimental comedy *Love's Last Shift* (1696), included the actor Robert Powell, who played Mr. Worthy. In Vanbrugh's comedy, Worthy is supposed to attempt to seduce Amanda (played by Jane Rogers), but instead, Powell, according to Vanbrugh's preface to the published play, broke from the script and actually sexually assaulted the actress onstage in front of the audience and Vanbrugh, obviously taking the role much too far and humiliating and shocking Rogers. Vanbrugh wrote that during the opening night performance 'some indecencies had like to have happened, but it was not my fault. The fine gentleman of the play, drinking his mistresses' health in Nantes brandy from six in the morning to the time he waddled on upon the stage in the evening, had toasted himself up to such a pitch of vigour, I confess I once gave Amanda for gone'.[5]

Beginning with the Restoration, women not only appeared in plays but also began writing them for the stage. Aphra Behn, arguably the first professional woman author in England, wrote many plays for the stage as well as an important novel, *Oroonoko* (1688). Behn's most successful play was her comedy *The Rover* (1677); in fact, the play was so successful that she penned a sequel, *The Rover, Part II*, that was produced four years later. Prolific, primarily because of her love of theater and because of financial necessity, Behn penned eighteen dramas during the late seventeenth century. She was known for writing powerful roles for women, such as Hellena, Florinda, and Angellica Bianca in *The Rover*, and for portraying sexuality and female desire openly and explicitly (relative to the era, of course). In *The Rover*, although the fall of the proud and beautiful courtesan Angellica Bianca (who becomes vulnerable when infatuated with the rakish Rover, Willmore) does not seem realistic, the sympathy and pathos that her fall evokes are moving, despite her pride and temper, given the manner and speed in which she is betrayed by Willmore. Behn deftly portrays male chauvinism and misogyny in the play; Blunt, angered after being duped by Lucetta, convinces himself that all women are whores. Willmore is unwilling to treat women with respect or show commitment to one woman, going from Angellica Bianca to Hellena and back and then attempting to rape Florinda; he declares his love for Hellena and offers to marry her before even knowing her name, thereby revealing his insincerity. Behn thus manifests to her audience the inconstancy of men. In *The Rover*, the men are incessantly inconstant (Don Antonio even attempts to hire Angellica Bianca as his courtesan for a month while making plans to marry Florinda), yet the women never waver from the men they love. Willmore, Blunt, and Frederick attempt to rape the virtuous Florinda; the drama poignantly shows, from a female perspective, the dangers that women faced in society and how rape could destroy their lives. Although Behn's play is a comedy, the danger of rape as portrayed in the drama is serious and disturbing. Furthermore, the fact that Willmore, Blunt, and Frederick mistake Florinda for a whore signifies Behn's implication that men are not good judges of women and do not understand them well, often considering respectable women whores. In 'A Room of One's Own', Virginia Woolf wrote that Aphra Behn is perhaps the most influential figure for female writers, a female author who made it possible for future women writers to be taken seriously and achieve success and recognition, for which Behn had fought so tenaciously. Woolf wrote that Behn

> had to work on equal terms with men. She made, by working very hard, enough to live on. The importance of that fact outweighs anything that she actually wrote . . . for here begins the freedom of the mind, or rather the possibility that in the course of time the mind will be free to write what it likes. . . . All women together ought to let flowers fall upon the

tomb of Aphra Behn . . ., for it was she who earned them the right to speak their minds.[6]

Behn was but one of many women who began writing for the theater in late seventeenth-century England. Frances Boothby wrote *Marcelia, or, The Treacherous Friend*, perhaps the first play written by a woman that was produced on a London stage, in 1669. Elizabeth Polewheele wrote *The Faithful Virgins* in 1670 and *The Frolicks, or, The Lawyer Cheated* in 1671. In the latter play, Clarabell marries Rightwit, who tricks Clarabell's father (an attorney). Two other men are also deceived, causing them to marry masked women whom they think are Clarabell. Polewheele admitted that she was young and no scholar, but 'what I write I write by nature, not art'.[7] Catherine Trotter's first play, *Agnes de Castro*, an adaptation of Behn's novel by that name, was initially performed in 1695, and *The Fatal Friendship* in 1698. Trotter, also known as Catharine Trotter Cockburn, wrote an excellent novel entitled *Olinda's Adventures, or, The Amours of a Young Lady*. In 1696, Mary Delariviere Manley wrote both *The Lost Lover, or, The Jealous Husband* and *The Royal Mischief*. Rebecca Mertens claims that these plays by female dramatists have significant value and have been unfairly ignored because they clash with male-dominated cultural beliefs that legitimized male hegemony:

> Delariviere Manley's *The Royal Mischief* and Catherine Trotter's
> *The Fatal Friendship* reject this repressive tradition of blaming women
> for sociopolitical strife, and, instead, locate the source of tragedy
> explicitly within the contradictions and violence of patrilineal order.
> Manley's and Trotter's tragedies have long been ignored or dismissed
> by literary critics: one might argue that their absence from the canon
> and from critical studies of Restoration drama suggests the extent
> to which they threaten patriarchal notions of sociopolitical order
> and coherence.[8]

Successful dramatist Mary Pix wrote six plays, beginning with her first tragedy, *Ibrahim: The Thirteenth Emperor of the Turks* (1695). Perhaps her best play is the comedy *The Innocent Mistress* (1697). Robert Powell was so impressed with Pix's *The Deceiver Deceived* (1697) that he plagiarized it, producing his version, entitled *The Imposter Defeated* (1697). The success in theater enjoyed by Pix, Manley, and Trotter led, regrettably, to professional jealousy from male playwrights, and these three female dramatists were mocked in an anonymous satirical comedy entitled *The Female Wits* (1696). The lampoon demonstrates that some men perceived the increasing propensity of women to write and publish as a threat.

Literature and Science (Fiction)

Margaret Cavendish penned a fantasy novel, arguably the first science fiction novel written by an Englishwoman, *The Description of a New World, Called the Blazing-World*, which was published in 1666. The protagonist is abducted and then rescued; she then travels to a utopian world where she describes and analyzes a new society and becomes an empress after marrying the emperor; Cavendish's readers are encouraged to compare and contrast this new world to seventeenth-century English society. In the work, the empress and the Duchess of Newcastle (Cavendish) both seem to exist. The work manifests Cavendish's strong interest in science, politics, religion, and feminism. The emperor relinquishes control of the government to his new wife, who rules capably, demonstrating that women deserve power and can govern deftly. In a feminist vein, the empress' skills in government attest to Cavendish's readers that women have great talent and can use power admirably. This utopian society contains talented scientists who enjoy conducting scientific work. The views on science, scientific method, and natural philosophy in the text are very important to Cavendish, who even went to the trouble of inviting herself to a meeting of the Royal Society.

Cavendish might have been inspired by Sir Francis Bacon, who published his own utopian text entitled *The New Atlantis* in 1626. The utopian society contains its own learning society for people who thirst for knowledge. Bacon also published *The Advancement of Learning* (1605), which concerns different types of learning and education, and *Novum Organum* (1620), a work about logic that can be applied to the scientific method. Bacon even died when attempting to learn more about science. In *Brief Lives*, John Aubrey writes that he learned from Bacon's secretary Thomas Hobbes, later the author of *Leviathan* (1651), that Bacon was riding in a carriage in the snow. Bacon suddenly realized that snow could be used for refrigeration, to preserve meat. He left the carriage and bought a hen, had it killed, and then covered it with snow to determine whether the snow would preserve the dead animal's body. The snow, however, gave Bacon chills, and he died shortly thereafter of pneumonia. In 1646 Thomas Browne published *Pseudodoxia Epidemica*, which includes Browne's empirical thoughts on science, such as magnetic theory and static electricity. And as their prose works indicate, Bacon and Browne were both intensely curious not only about learning about science, but also learning about the world from exploration and discovery in America.

Literature and World Exploration

In seventeenth-century England there was a growing interest in other cultures and continents. The Renaissance saw the birth of England's exploration and colonization in the New World. It was an exciting time because the exploration of new places allowed the English to learn more about other cultures, to realize that there were many more lands besides England than the ones they already knew about, and to re-evaluate their own culture from a new perspective in light of what the British discoverers found and reported. Perhaps the leading force in convincing King James to establish an English settlement in the New World was explorer, translator, statesman, and non-fictional prose writer Richard Hakluyt. Hakluyt convinced James of the financial and political benefits of permanent settlements in North America and wrote legal petitions advocating the English settlement of Virginia. The name of the settlement honored the current and former monarchs, Jamestown (for the current king) and Virginia (for the recently deceased queen, often called the Virgin Queen). Naming the settlement Jamestown immortalized the king in the New World. In 1601, Hakluyt translated Portuguese author Antonio Galväo's book *The Discoveries of the World* into English, partly to increase interest in the possible New World exploration. Hakluyt also penned his monumental three volume prose tract on English exploration, *The Principal Navigations, Voiages, Traffiques and Discoueries of the English Nation* (1598–1600). This nationalistic book expresses pride in England, shows the urgent need for English exploration in the New World, and tries to persuade readers that the English need to colonize the New World before the Spanish, Portuguese, and French inhabit and control the New World for themselves. Hakluyt's *Principal Navigations* manifested that the author was truly a visionary who saw the great potential that New World settlements offered to England in regard to colonization and the trade and consumption of commodities. Hakluyt continued his support of New World exploration, Virginia in particular, when in 1609 he translated Hernando de Soto's *Virginia Richly Valued, by the Description of the Maine Land of Florida, Her Next Neighbour*. Once again Hakluyt saw fit for English readers to learn what foreign explorers such as de Soto had witnessed during explorative ventures.

Hakluyt's excitement concerning English exploration greatly influenced other seventeenth-century writers, such as poet and playwright Michael Drayton. When reading Drayton's poem 'To the Virginian Voyage', from *Poems Lyric and Pastoral* (1606), one may quickly discern the poet's nationalistic pride. The speaker begins:

> You brave heroique minds,
> Worthy your country's name,
>   That honor still pursue,
>   Go and subdue,
> Whilst loit'ring hinds
> Lurk here at home, with shame.

> Britans, you stay too long;
> Quickly aboord bestow you,
>   And with a merry gale
>   Swell your stretch'd sail,
> With vows as strong
> As the winds that blow you. . . .
>
> And cheerfully at sea
> Success you still intice,
>   To get the pearl and gold,
>   And ours to hold,
> Virginia,
> Earth's only paradise. . . .
>
> Thy voyages attend,
> Industrious Hakluyt,
>   Whose reading shall inflame
>   Men to seek fame,
> And much commend
> To after-times thy wit. (ll. 1–12, 19–24, 67–72)

The speaker considers the explorers and sailors to be great heroes who make England proud, while those who remain at home are likened to shameful cowards (unless they, like Drayton, stay home to write poetry that glorifies the expedition). Drayton's poem demonstrates the excitement that the English felt at the prospect of discovering and colonizing a new land, with such high hopes that it seemed an earthly paradise laden with pearls and gold. And Drayton credits the great prose writer Hakluyt with inspiring James and Parliament, as well as the mariners, to make the expedition become a reality.

But discovery and wealth were not the only reasons for expeditions for new lands. In the seventeenth century, Puritans sought refuge from religious persecution by leaving England. Many Puritans, such as Edward Taylor, Mary Rowlandson, and Anne Bradstreet, left England for the New World so that they could experience religious freedom; once in the New World, they wrote about their spiritual and domestic experiences. Andrew Marvell wrote about Puritans who left England for religious freedom in the Bermudas. In 'Bermudas', Marvell writes about Puritans who leave England for the place known as the Summer Isles. The sailors consider Bermudas a new Eden, just as Drayton refers to Virginia as a paradise. The Puritan rowers sing God's praise for protecting them from storms, sea monsters, and losing their way in the 'wat'ry maze' (l. 6) as they voyage to a new land with which they are unfamiliar, and they praise the Lord for providing them with safe passage to the Summer Isles, which will be 'kinder than our own' land [England] (l. 8).

Another reason for expeditions was for trade. In the poem 'The Golden Island or the Darian Song' (1698 or 1699), by the anonymous female author who called herself 'A Lady of Honour', the poet celebrates trade ventures by the Company of Scotland to the Isthmus of Darien in the fall of 1698. The anonymous author is excited about the expedition and considers Darien an earthly paradise that contains great wealth in minerals that can be exploited and returned home to Scotland. This strong desire to employ shipping and commerce to acquire wealth manifested the growth of the mercantile class.

Another poem that deals with a journey to an earthly paradise is John Milton's epic masterpiece *Paradise Lost* (1667), in which the poet 'justifies the ways of God to men'. Satan, deciding not to wage war openly against God, instead chooses to corrupt and destroy God's creation, human beings. Satan travels to the earthly paradise, Eden, in his effort to entice Adam and Eve into sin and to sever the close relationship between them and their Creator. Satan's success in enticing Adam and Eve to eat from the forbidden fruit leads to the Garden's inhabitants' knowledge of sin and ultimately death.

Literature and Death

Death was a prevalent theme in seventeenth-century poetry. In addition to enduring a high infant mortality rate, English citizens had seen the danger and destruction of the plague in England throughout the seventeenth century, until one last major outbreak of the plague was wiped out by the Great Fire of London. Death was therefore prominent in their thoughts. Manifesting the early modern preoccupation with death, Thomas Browne ponders the meaning and the inevitability of death in great detail in *Hydriotaphia, or Urn-Burial* (1658). Furthermore, several significant early modern elegies were penned in the seventeenth century, such as Ben Jonson's 'On My First Sonne' (1616), Henry King's elegy to his beloved wife in 'The Exequy' (1624), John Donne's Anniversary poems, and John Milton's 'Lycidas' (1637). Jonson writes with great sadness upon the death in 1603 of his seven-year-old son, Benjamin, whom he calls his inspiration, his 'best piece of poetry'. The poignant tone contrasts markedly with the biting satire in Jonson's drama. The conceit that God has lent Benjamin to the poet for seven years is strikingly similar to phrasing in King's 'Exequy', when the poet laments in his 120-line complaint that his recently deceased wife, Anne King, was lent to him by Heaven for a mere seven years and must now return. Like Jonson, King compares the object of the elegy to a work of literature: 'thou art the book, / The library whereon I look'. Donne's two Anniversary poems were written in honor of the deceased fifteen-year-old Elizabeth Drury, the daughter of Sir Robert Drury.

The first Anniversary poem, 'An Anatomy of the World' (1612), manifests that when Donne writes his elegy, his thoughts and verses extend beyond the death of one young woman to a contemplation of life, death, the soul, and the hereafter. Milton's pastoral elegy concerns the death of Milton's beloved Cambridge classmate Edward King, who drowned in the Irish Seas after his ship sank. The world seems to mourn; even the woods and caves are saddened (a so-called 'pathetic fallacy'), but the poet suggests that instead of mourning, people may take solace in the immortality of Lycidas (Edward King). Two other important elegies are John Dryden's 'To the Memory of Mr. Oldham' (1684) and 'To the Pious Memory of the Accomplished Young Lady Mrs. Anne Killigrew, Excellent in the Two Sister Arts of Poesy and Painting' (1686). Anne Killigrew was a talented poet who died young from smallpox.

Literature and *Carpe Diem*

Death became a significant force in seventeenth-century English poetry, yet some poets, such as Cavalier poet and Sons of Ben member Robert Herrick, wrote about cheating death by living for the present. In Herrick's 'To the Virgins, To Make Much of Time' (from *Hesperides*, 1648), the speaker advises the reader that female beauty, like roses, is fragile and mutable. Physical beauty, like flowers, must be used while in its bloom or suffer from decay:

> Gather ye rosebuds while ye may,
> Old Time is still a-flying;
> And this same flower that smiles today,
> Tomorrow will be dying.
>
> The glorious lamp of heaven, the sun,
> The higher he's a-getting,
> The sooner will his race be run,
> And nearer he's to setting.
>
> That age is best which is the first,
> When youth and blood are warmer;
> But being spent, the worse, and worst
> Times still succeed the former.
>
> Then be not coy, but use your time;
> And while ye may, go marry:
> For having lost but once your prime,
> You may for ever tarry.

Similarly, Andrew Marvell focuses on the carpe diem theme in his famous poem 'To His Coy Mistress'. The speaker warns his lover about the danger of wasting her youth and beauty by being coy when he courts her; instead, he encourages her to lose her virginity to him:

> Had we but world enough, and time,
> This coyness, Lady, were no crime.
> We would sit down, and think which way
> To walk, and pass our long love's day. . . .
>
> But at my back I always hear
> Time's wingéd chariot hurrying near;
> And yonder all before us lie
> Deserts of vast eternity.
>
> Thy beauty shall no more be found,
> Nor, in thy marble vault, shall sound
> My echoing song; then worms shall try
> That long-preserved virginity. . . .

Metaphysical Poetry

The courtly love/sexual poems by the Cavalier and Sons of Ben poets appeared in manuscript and in print during the same era as the metaphysical, or devotional, verses by poets such as John Donne, George Herbert, Francis Quarles (his so-called 'emblems', or poems accompanying illustrations), Henry Vaughan, Richard Crashaw, Edward Taylor, and Thomas Traherne. Works by Donne exemplify the coexistence of these two markedly different types of verse because he figures prominently as an author of both kinds. Donne wrote love poems, or poems with sexual themes, such as 'The Good-Morrow', 'Song', 'Woman's Constancy', 'The Sun Rising', 'The Indifferent', 'The Canonization', and 'The Flea', yet he also penned the Holy Sonnets, 'Good Friday, 1613, Riding Westward', 'A Hymn to Christ, at the Author's Last Going into Germany', 'A Hymn to God, My God, in My Sickness', and 'A Hymn to God the Father'. Religious faith was a predominant issue during the seventeenth century, with many poets penning their innermost thoughts and convictions about their relationship, including their struggles, with God. In Holy Sonnet XIV, 'Batter My Heart, Three Person'd God', for instance, John Donne wrote about his struggles with faith in light of human reason. The failings of unaided human reason were a significant theme in seventeenth-century literature as authors considered the gifts of instinct and reason, both of which seemingly were obtained from God. One question that arose was whether the faith in human reason led to the sin of pride because human beings often rely on reason alone rather than faith and consider themselves infallible and superior beings because of this gift; the possibility that God's gifts could turn people away from the Lord is one explored by George Herbert in his poem 'The Pulley'. The speaker in Donne's Holy Sonnet XIV wants to believe in God but experiences doubts because he attempts to use human reason to comprehend God. The speaker wonders how God can be one yet also three. Reason, a gift from God, ironically turns the speaker away from God and toward His enemy, either the devil or faithlessness. Therefore, the weak and passive Christian, lacking sufficient faith to come to God, begs the Lord to come aggressively to him and rape him just as soldiers would use a battering ram to rescue a hostage from a captured fort. This poem was not published in Donne's lifetime because it was not considered genteel or noble in the early seventeenth century for a gentleman to publish and receive money for his writings. In fact, Donne published very few poems, such as his Anniversary poems, in his lifetime because they were occasional works that served as tributes to Elizabeth Drury. The first Englishman who desired to make a living as a published and professional author was seventeenth-century poet and playwright Ben Jonson, who in 1616 published *The Works of Benjamin Jonson*.

Like Donne, another seventeenth-century poet who wrote metaphysical poetry that was published after his death was preacher George Herbert. Herbert wrote a collection of devotional poetry that autobiographically told the story of a Christian as he embarked on a difficult journey toward salvation. The collection of poems, taken as one unit, tells metaphorically the story of the spiritual journey of a Christian as he struggles with his faith but ultimately achieves salvation; the book perhaps served as a model to John Bunyan, who would create a similar work in prose form, *The Pilgrims Progress*, decades later. Herbert requested that his collection of poems entitled *The Temple* (1633) be published after his death if it would bring learning and comfort to Christians who, like him, had strong but imperfect relationships with God and were in the midst of a similar journey. Herbert's work entitled 'The Collar', with a pun on 'choler', demonstrates the frustration that Christians sometimes experienced in their relationship with God. The relationship could be constraining and could lead to the Christian person's anger. The sonnet 'Redemption' concerns a Christian who seeks salvation but does not fully understand Christ and thus seeks Him in the wrong places; the poem is told as a parable, which is fitting given that Christ taught by using parables. The speaker seeks a new lease, suggesting a movement toward New Testament beliefs, and is ultimately promised salvation by God, who succinctly declares, 'Your suit is granted'. Christ says few words, perhaps because the Holy Word was considered so powerful that these few words, echoing Romans

6:23, 'For the wages of sin is death; but the gift of God is eternal life through Jesus Christ our Lord', say it all and because the poet was perhaps uncomfortable with the idea of creating holy words that he would place in the mouth of Christ. 'Love (3)' concerns Herbert's view of salvation and the Last Supper, as well as man's unworthiness of salvation because of the human propensity for sin ('guilty of dust and sin'). Herbert also created shaped poems such as 'Easter Wings' and 'The Altar', in which the poems physically assume the shape of the poem's theme.

Literature and Religion

During the seventeenth century, religion and faith were tightly interwoven with politics. After the Interregnum (1649–1660), which included the Protectorates under Oliver and then Richard Cromwell, the Puritan reign was over, and Charles II returned from France and assumed the throne of England. With the 'Declaration of Indulgence for Tender Consciences' of 1672, Charles permitted religious freedom and forgave previous misdeeds, except for those responsible for the trial and execution of his father, King Charles I. Because Parliament suspected Charles II of Catholic leanings, the king was forced to repeal the declaration and then, in 1673, allow the Test Act, in which citizens had to declare their allegiance to the Church of England and deny their belief in the Catholic idea of transubstantiation in order to participate in working for the government. Antagonism between devotees of the Anglican Church and Nonconformists (including Puritans) was quite tense. John Bunyan, a deeply religious Nonconformist, published his autobiography, *Grace Abounding*, in 1666; this work tells his readers about his sins, his spiritual conversion, and his decision to become a preacher. Bunyan was arrested for preaching without a license. After three months in jail, he was allowed to leave prison if he promised not to preach again – a promise he refused to make because of his devotion to his faith. While in prison, he wrote his famous allegorical novel, *The Pilgrim's Progress from This World to That Which is to Come: Delivered under the Similitude of a Dream* (1678). This work tells the story of Christian as he sets out on a journey of faith and encounters temptations and tribulations. Christian leaves 'The City of Destruction' (his earthly home) in search of 'The Celestial City' (Heaven); his path is wayward, not direct, because of temptations from Worldly Wiseman, Wanton, and others, while his friend Faithful helps him complete his physical and spiritual journey. The work was not published for approximately seven years after he had completed it as some of his Nonconformist friends considered the work unworthy because it was not straightforward; rather, Christian's story is told indirectly, through allegory. It should be noted that Jesus himself taught his followers by using parables. The subtitle, which mentions a dream, suggests that perhaps the work is not fiction but rather is divinely inspired.

George Fox, a prominent member of the Religious Society of Friends, later known as Quakers, was also imprisoned for preaching. He earned the respect of William Penn, Oliver Cromwell, and perhaps even King Charles II. His *Journal* was published posthumously in 1694 and, like many Quaker tracts, supports religious freedom and toleration. His wife Margaret Askew Fell Fox, also a Quaker, published her prose tract 'Women's Speaking Justified' (1666) in which she writes about preaching and declares that women have the right for their voices to be heard in regard to their faith.

Religion, however, was often a subject of satire in seventeenth-century English literature. Webster's *Duchess of Malfi* (1614) and James Shirley's tragedy *The Cardinal* (1641) exposed the religious hypocrisy of the cardinals of both works. The Cardinal in Webster's play uses Bosola to execute his evil plan and then refuses to provide the servant with his promised reward. The Cardinal badly mistreats his sister, the Duchess, attempting to bully her into refraining from remarrying, abuses her during the play's dumb show, relinquishes his position in the Catholic Church when he turns soldier, and is partly responsible for the murders of his sister, his brother, and Bosola. The Cardinal, the titular character in Shirley's drama, is as sinister as Webster's Cardinal. Shirley's Cardinal is a Machiavellian plotter who easily manipulates the king. He coerces the king into forcing Duchess Rosaura to end her match to her beloved Count D'Alvarez, to whom she is betrothed, and forces her to become engaged to the Cardinal's arrogant nephew, Don Columbo. The Cardinal attempts to force Rosaura to marry his nephew rather than the man she loves in order to obtain the lady's vast fortune. The Cardinal then attempts to rape Rosaura and subsequently poisons her to death. These two works satirize the corruption of Christian clergymen, yet it is noteworthy that both villains are Catholic, so the question arises as to whether Webster, Shirley, and others were mocking Christianity, hypocritical clergymen, or only Catholics.

Religious hypocrisy, in fact, is often satirized in literature of the seventeenth century. Thus, the apparently devoutly religious Anabaptists, Ananias and Tribulation Wholesome, who appear in Jonson's satire *The Alchemist* (1610), are actually deceitful and greedy, claiming to Subtle that they prayed and then heard from God that the illegal coining of money is actually lawful. These false men of God deserve to be duped by Subtle. These are merely a few of countless works that mocked insincere religious people, but it should be noted that in most cases, such as the three above, the deceitful clergymen are not members of the Anglican Church, suggesting that perhaps the authors are not mocking Christianity but rather religious hypocrites, particularly those who are not Anglicans.

Literature, Satire, and Social Class

In *The Alchemist*, alchemy may symbolize a socioeconomic transformation. Characters such as Dapper, Drugger, Ananias, and Epicure Mammon wish to rise socially through their acquisition of the philosopher's stone. They want to rise to a higher financial level and transform their base metals to gold. In fact, characters such as Dapper and Drugger actually resemble such base metals because they come from low social classes, and, just as alchemists supposedly can transform base metals into gold, so these characters want to transform themselves quickly into wealthy people. However, the victims of Face, Subtle, and Dol Common must realize that they are unworthy of their societal ascension, of their acquisition of the philosopher's stone, because they must seek the help of a supposedly worthy and pure man (Subtle). The fact that they realize that they are unworthy of acquiring the stone themselves indicates that they do not deserve to rise socioeconomically and that they deserve to be duped because of their social pretensions and greed.

Ben Jonson, like many Renaissance dramatists, manifested his distrust of social climbing in his plays. In *Volpone, or the Fox* (1606), Mosca easily transforms himself from a parasitic servant into a nobleman merely by stealing Volpone's clothes upon his false announcement that The Fox is dead. Violating Renaissance sumptuary laws, Mosca dresses as a magnifico, and Jonson demonstrates unequivocally that people treat Mosca differently when the servant changes clothes – and consequently ascends socioeconomically. For instance, believing that Mosca has inherited Volpone's wealth, the 4th Avocatore defends Mosca when the servant is called a parasite and declares in an aside that if Volpone is dead, the servant is now '[a] proper man; and were Volpone dead / A fit match for my daughter' (V.xi). When people pretend to be wealthy, others improperly fawn over them. This last statement demonstrates Jonson's ambivalence concerning rigid demarcations in the social hierarchy because he satirizes, through the 4th Avocatore, that people treat others according to their class, not their merit. Jonson thus shows how easy it is for people of the lower classes to masquerade as members of the nobility and how such a trick can cause chaos and the disruption of the social order. However, Jonson was disturbed when wealthy people treated him disrespectfully because he was not a member of the nobility. He wanted the rich to treat worthy people of lower socioeconomic classes well, particularly himself. Jonson extols the virtue of generosity when he praises the hospitality of the Sidney family, by negation, in his poem 'To Penshurst', claiming that he is:

> not Faine to sit (as some this day,
> At great mens tables) and yet dine away.

> Here no man tells my cups; nor, standing by,
> A waiter, doth my gluttony envy:
> But gives me what I call, and lets me eate. (ll. 65–9)

Jonson's reference to a man sitting at a great man's table yet being forced to dine again elsewhere alludes to the mistreatment Jonson and architect / set designer Inigo Jones suffered at the Earl of Salisbury's house: 'Being at the end of my Lord Salisbury's table with Inigo Jones, and demanded by my Lord why he was not glad. "My Lord", said he, "You promised I should dine with you, but I do not", for he had none of his meat. He esteemed only that his meat which was of his own dish' ('Conversations', ll. 317–21). Jonson thus juxtaposes his humiliation at the Earl's table with the royal treatment he receives from the Sidneys, showing that the Sidneys should be praised for their hospitality toward their middle-class guests while the Earl of Salisbury should be embarrassed for his disrespectful treatment of guests who derive from a lower social class than his.

Late Elizabethan and Jacobean drama reflected a preoccupation with social class hierarchy and the relationship between the nobility/landed gentry and the emerging middle class. Perhaps the play that best represents the seventeenth-century focus on social class is Francis Beaumont's *Knight of the Burning Pestle* (1607). Players at the exclusive Blackfriars Theater are set to present a play about the mercantile class, *The London Merchant*. However, a proud and strong-willed grocer, called Citizen (his wife calls him George), interrupts the proposed play *The London Merchant* almost immediately to protest the drama because he is disturbed by plays that satirize the emerging middle class; he seems to take the mockery personally. The Citizen's instincts prove correct in that the play satirizes the London merchant Venturewell, who mistreats his daughter Luce, attempting to force her to marry the cowardly and rhyme doggerel-speaking fool Humphrey, when she actually wants to marry the man she loves, Jasper Merrythought. Beaumont's decision to refer consistently to the intruding grocer as Citizen provides the character with the sense of universality, as if the man represents the typical member of the mercantile class. The Citizen proposes – and demands – a new play, which he decides to call *The Grocer's Honor*, but then his title is subsequently, and subtly, changed by the actor called Prologue to *Knight of the Burning Pestle*. The grocer is too ignorant to realize that Prologue is mocking him and his guild because the pestle serves as a phallic symbol, and the fact that it is burning is a clear reference to syphilis. Beaumont mocks the unrealistic and pretentious socioeconomic aspirations of the rising middle class when the Citizen and his wife, who admits to the audience that people often call her 'damned bitch', demand that their apprentice Rafe be transformed into a grocer errant (as opposed to a knight errant) who embarks on quests and rescues damsels in distress. The quests end poorly, demonstrating that to Beaumont members of the mercantile class are not heroes, knights, or members of the nobility; the quests clearly follow those of the titular character in Miguel Cervantes' *Don Quixote*, which was first published in 1605. For instance, Rafe confuses an inn for a castle, and the Citizen therefore comes out of the audience and onto the stage to pay his apprentice's bill so that the chivalric knight will not be arrested for failing to pay his tab. Rafe's failures, as well as the absurdity of his quests, demonstrate the absurd social pretensions of the middle class that desires to be considered aristocratic. Furthermore, the Citizen and his wife's inability to distinguish between reality and theater also signifies Beaumont's mockery of the intelligence of members of the middle class.

Thomas Heywood's tragedy *A Woman Killed with Kindness* (1603) also makes a pronounced social class distinction. The play begins happily with a wedding between two members of the nobility, Master John and Anne Frankford, who clearly love each other very much, so the future looks bright for them. Unfortunately for everyone involved, Master Frankford takes a liking to Wendoll, a man who possesses little money. Frankford says to Wendoll that despite the latter's lack of money, 'Please you to use my table and my purse. / They are yours' (4.65–6). Nowhere in the play does Heywood show any reason why Wendoll deserves such a favor, suggesting that Frankford's decision to raise up someone with limited resources and allow him everything in the house and his purse is an unwise and arbitrary one, primarily because Wendoll has not earned this honor and is of a lower social class. Perhaps intoxicated with his newfound wealth and good fortune – or perhaps because of poor character, symbolized by his poor financial condition (some people in the seventeenth century considered poor fortune a sign of punishment for sin) – Wendoll mistreats the servants (demanding, for instance, that one servant put his boots on him) and, more significantly, decides to have a sexual affair with the newlywed, Anne Frankford. To a seventeenth-century audience, Wendoll's sin would have been considered more heinous considering that he not only coerces Anne to commit adultery and repays his benefactor's kindness by sleeping with the man's wife, but also because he violates the code of Christian hospitality, sinning against the very man who has invited him into his house and told him to make himself at home. In the drama, Heywood makes it clear that Wendoll is in a poorer financial situation than Frankford (4.64), and a link exists, perhaps, between Wendoll's financial straits and his unethical character. The same principle holds true for Sir Charles Mountford, whose financial prospects plummet dramatically during Heywood's play. Mountford is well regarded and popular while he is wealthy, but after he loses his fortune and home, becoming penniless, he decides to prostitute his virtuous sister, Susan, as a way of thanking Acton for releasing him from his debt and prison, believing that a nobleman would never lower his social status by marrying an impoverished woman. One could argue that his fallen social status, from nobleman to poor man, alters Mountford's character, which is why he unnecessarily attempts to force his sister to have sex with Acton, but one must remember that his great socio-economic fall is caused by his murder of two of Acton's servants. It is worth noting that a connection often exists in seventeenth-century drama between a fall in social class and a concomitant fall in virtue, unless the lack of virtue is somehow a precursor for a subsequent fall in financial fortune. (De Flores, in Middleton's play *The Changeling*, is another villain who becomes evil after losing his fortune.) Thomas Heywood further complicates his drama's stance on social class by portraying Mountford's relatives as greedy and selfish, liking Sir Charles only when he is wealthy but disowning him when he loses his inheritance, estate, and fortune. Hypocritical members of the noble class, therefore, are also treated negatively in the play. Perhaps Heywood manifests a deep suspicion of people who upset the rigid social hierarchy, parvenus such as Wendoll (whose newfound wealth actually belongs to Frankford) who do not deserve their abrupt ascension to wealth, and those who fear that they must guard their wealth rather than spending their money helping those who, through sinful actions, have fallen socially.

Thomas Dekker's comedic tribute to shoemakers and their guild, *The Shoemaker's Holiday, or The Gentle Craft* (1600), presents a unique perspective in that it portrays the shoemakers, member of the working class, in a very positive, almost glorified, light. The shoemakers are very proud of their trade and consider themselves to be gentlemen because they make shoes – hence the term 'gentle craft'. Although one could argue that Dekker satirizes the shoemakers who take such great pride in their humble profession and that Simon Eyre is a bit of a blowhard, the shoemakers are kind and decent citizens who are indeed experts in their craft. For instance, Rafe gives his wife Jane shoes as a parting gift when he goes off to war, and the shoes serve as metaphors for rings, as tokens of their love. When Rafe, upon his return from war but believed to be deceased, sees one of the shoes, he knows immediately that the shoe belongs to her, and this expertise allows him to be reunited with his wife, who is about to marry – with great reluctance – the upper-class suitor, Hammon. Thus shoes – and Rafe's expertise with them – save his marriage, and it is someone of the upper-class who wishes to break up the marriage of two members of the working class. And the fact that Rafe is severely wounded when fighting for England while Rowland Lacy shirks his martial duty by abandoning his position in the army to woo Rose manifests unquestionably that Dekker portrays the shoemaker as the good citizen and the nobleman as the coward who refuses to fight for his country – even after his uncle has purchased his commission. The strife between the guardians of

Lacy and Rose also manifests the London city comedy's ability to highlight the clash between different social classes. Lacy's proud uncle, Sir Hugh Lacy, who is the Earl of Lincoln, tells him to avoid the Lord Mayor's daughter and end their relationship:

> I would not have you cast an amorous eye
> Upon so mean a project as the love
> Of a gay, wanton, painted citizen.
> I know this churl [the Lord Mayor] even in the height of scorn
> Doth hate the mixture of his blood with thine. (i. 75–9)

In turn, Rose's father, the Lord Mayor, orders his daughter not to marry Rowland Lacy because he is wary of members of the nobility, considering them profligate and indolent. In his attempt to assure Hugh Lacy that he will not encourage the match between the aristocratic Rowland Lacy and his daughter Rose, he remarks sarcastically:

> Too mean is my poor girl for his [Rowland's] high birth.
> Poor citizens must not with courtiers wed,
> Who will in silks and gay apparel spend
> More in one year than I am worth by far.
> Therefore your honor need not doubt my girl. (i. 11–15)

Thomas Middleton's *A Trick to Catch the Old One* (1605) and Philip Massinger's *A New Way to Pay Old Debts* (1626) are two other city comedies of manners that deal significantly with class issues. Massinger's play derives markedly from Middleton's, and the connections between the plots are unmistakable. In seventeenth-century England, such similarities would perhaps be considered Massinger's way of paying homage to Middleton, but today such imitation probably would be considered plagiarism. In *A Trick to Catch the Old One*, the dramatist manifests the obsession of the upper class with wealth; rich gentlemen (gentlemen in regard to birth and money but not manners or ethics) Pecunius Lucre and Walkadine Hoard attempt to secure the fortune of a rich widow, not realizing that she is Witgood's penniless whore in disguise. Middleton suggests in the play that the rich have an insatiable thirst for wealth and are never satisfied. In order to reclaim all the property and wealth that he has mortgaged to his uncle Lucre, Witgood pretends to have excellent financial prospects – he will marry a rich widow (actually the impoverished courtesan). As Witgood remarks about Lucre when deciding to pretend to marry the rich widow, 'if his nephew be poor indeed, why, he lets God alone with him; but, if he be once rich, then he'll be the first man that helps him'. As a result of this trick to catch the old one, Lucre loses all of the property that his nephew Witgood had mortgaged to him (and the uncle also pays all of Witgood's living expenses), and Hoard demeans himself by marrying the courtesan, whom he had thought was a rich widow. Witgood is so named because he has the craftiness to outwit these two clever wealthy gentlemen who have devoted their lives to duping other people out of their money; he also outsmarts Hoard and other suitors for the hand of Hoard's wealthy niece, Joyce. Middleton shows the obsession with wealth that characterizes many of the nobility, and in the play, it is their avarice that leads to their fall.

In Massinger's reworking of the play twenty-one years later, the wealthy are still considered financially greedy. But a distinction exists between people such as Sir Giles Overreach, who has obtained wealth and land through usury and deception, and Lord Lovell, who derives from an aristocratic family. Lovell, for instance, refuses to marry Margaret Overreach primarily because he does not believe that his aristocratic family ('one part scarlet') should marry into a family that is 'the other London blue' (IV.1). This demarcation made by Lovell indicates that in the 1620s, Englishmen were clearly delineating between different facets of the upper class. They were making distinctions, for instance, between aristocrats, who had been in the noble class for generations, and financially successful members of the middle class and parvenus in London. Massinger also suggests that many members of the emerging classes (such as wealthy merchants/usurers) employ unethical means to obtain their wealth. Lovell belongs to the former group, and Overreach, to the latter. Sir Giles Overreach has destroyed the fortunes of his nephew, Frank Wellborn, who, as his name implies, is a gentleman – a gentleman who has lost his wealth in his parasitic relationship with the avaricious Overreach. Massinger, like Middleton, indicates that some members of the nobility are so greedy that they willingly cheat and destroy their own family members. Upon cheating Wellborn, Overreach even suggests that his nephew, now in debt, commit suicide because life is not worth living without money. But Wellborn instead pretends to be the prospective husband of the wealthy Mistress Allworth; believing that his nephew will marry into wealth, Overreach changes his comportment toward his nephew and even pays off his debts – hence the title. Massinger dramatizes, through Overreach's altered behavior toward his nephew – from encouraging suicide to acting like a loving uncle – how people's behavior toward others depends significantly on the financial prospects of the person in question. The belief that Massinger modeled the character of antagonist Sir Giles Overreach upon an actual person, seventeenth-century inn-licensing monopolist Sir Giles Mompesson (1584–1663), endows the play – and the social critique – with a clear sense of verisimilitude.

Restoration Political Satire

The Restoration period inspired much political and religious satire. Samuel Butler's mock-epic satire, *Hudibras* (1663), modeled loosely upon Cervantes' *Don Quixote*, was a huge sensation when it was first published. The poem is not celebrated today for its great merit, but its popularity in seventeenth-century England derived from its timeliness. The poem, which lampoons Presbyterians (Hudibras is a Presbyterian knight errant) and Dissenters, appeared shortly after the restoration of the monarchy and after Charles II claimed the throne (1660), and shortly after the end of the Interregnum and Cromwellian rule. The poem manifests Butler's support for royalism and his opposition to Dissenters and Parliament.

John Dryden's mock-heroic satire 'Mac Flecknoe' (1682) mocks the literary pretentions of rival poet Thomas Shadwell, who was a proponent of the Whig party. Dryden's attack on Shadwell is both aesthetic and political, and the rival poet/playwright attacked him in print as well. The poem, written in heroic couplets, suggests that the reign of lousy poet Richard Flecknoe is over, so a successor in regard to Dullness and Nonsense must be found; Shadwell is considered Flecknoe's counterpart as an author of inadequate poetry, and thus he becomes the incompetent poet's successor: 'The rest to some faint meaning make pretense / But Shadwell never deviates into sense'. It is noteworthy that when Dryden had to relinquish his position as Poet Laureate for refusing to swear an oath of allegiance to William and Mary, successors to James II following the Glorious Revolution, he was replaced by Shadwell.

Dryden also satirized Shadwell in 'Absalom and Achitophel'. 'Absalom and Achitophel' (1681) is a powerful political satire, perhaps written at the request of the king, about the attempted rebellion by James Stuart, Duke of Monmouth, and an illegitimate son of Charles II, against his father in an effort to seize the throne in 1681. The plot derives from the biblical story (Book of Samuel) of Absalom, the son of King David, who, with the aid of David's dishonest adviser Achitophel, rebels against his father. Although Absalom is very popular and handsome, the rebellion fails, and he dies when his beautiful, long hair becomes ensnared in the branches of an oak tree. In Dryden's poem, Absalom resembles the Duke of Monmouth, both being handsome, popular, and ambitious. David is like King Charles, an aging king who loves his son. Achitophel is like Monmouth's adviser, the Earl of Shaftesbury. Although Monmouth, unlike Absalom, survived his rebellion, the poem unwittingly foreshadows his death because Monmouth was executed in 1685 after a second rebellion, this time against his uncle James II, who had ascended to the throne upon the demise of Charles II. Monmouth and his followers were ambitious and coveted the throne, and they also wanted to prevent the Catholic James II from becoming king, particularly after the fear deriving from the alleged Popish Plot (an alleged plot to murder Charles II), with its hysteria incited by Titus Oates, from 1678–1681.

Restoration Dramatic Satire

Restoration satire also was prevalent in theater. Three great Restoration theater satirists were Sir George Etherege, William Wycherley, and William Congreve. Etherege wrote *The Comical Revenge; or, Love in a Tub* (1664), *She Wou'd if She Cou'd* (1668), and *The Man of Mode, or, Sir Fopling Flutter* (1676). Etherege, a talented playwright, excelled in writing the comedy of manners, or the comedy of wit, and satirizing various elements of London society. *The Man of Mode*, for instance, satirizes fops (Sir Fopling Flutter), rakes, the country, lustful women (such as Mrs. Loveit) who cannot govern their passions, old, lustful men (such as Old Bellair), and even orange women. William Wycherley is best known for *The Plain Dealer* (1676) and *The Country Wife* (1675). The latter, considered his masterpiece, satirizes married women who cheat on their husbands, believing that their reputation (how others perceive them), not their virtue (how they comport themselves), is what matters. The character Sparkish is a satire on those who pretend to have wit, and Pinchwife represents the excessively jealous husband.

William Congreve is known for four Restoration plays – *The Old Bachelor* (1693), *Love for Love* (1695), the tragedy *The Mourning Bride* (1697), and his masterpiece, *The Way of the World*. The latter play dramatizes the delightful repartee between Mirabell and Millamant, but the audience discerns that despite this sense of gender equality, Millamant, Mrs. Fainall, and Mrs. Wishfort ultimately require the protection and wit that Mirabell provides.

Congreve's comedies, which included sexual double entendres and sexual suggestiveness, came under attack from the moralist Jeremy Collier in his prose tract *A Short View of the Immorality and Profaneness of the English Stage* (1698). Collier's attack, and the attention and influence it engendered, clearly manifested that English society had transformed and that a backlash against satire and sexuality was occurring by the end of the seventeenth century.

The first half of the century seemed to emphasize social and religious satire, while the second half manifested a movement toward political satire. In regard to drama, many plays before the closing of the theaters manifested a growing interest in the lives of women, while Restoration theater, with its emphasis on sexuality and promiscuity, saw a consequential regression, a marginalization of women. The aforementioned statements in this paragraph are meant to be general observations, and exceptions to these statements clearly exist. But it is certain that the seventeenth century was quite eventful in regard to literature and literary history.

Uses of this Handbook

Readers of this comprehensive handbook will find many uses for it. Deborah Solomon's useful timeline will help scholars and students quickly find the names and dates for seventeenth-century writers as well as significant historical and cultural facts that relate to literary history. Richard Harp focuses on historical contexts, employing various aspects of culture, such as politics, religion, the arts, economics, and science, to manifest how these cultural themes relate to the English Civil War, the Interregnum, and the Restoration, as well as to the canonical literature of the century. The contribution by Brian Blackley and Lara M. Crowley provides helpful biographical and literary information about seventeenth-century writers and also covers different genres and literary movements. Matthew Steggle's chapter on reading literary texts focuses on close reading and relates it to performance criticism, studying for exams, and critical perspectives, using John Donne's 'The Flea', John Webster's *The Duchess of Malfi*, John Milton's *Paradise Lost*, and William Wycherley's *The Country Wife*; the work by Steggle, who teaches at Sheffield Hallam University, is useful not only to scholars but also to instructors and students. James Hirsh covers the scholarship of four major critics – Stanley Fish, Barbara Lewalski, Jonathan Dollimore, and Leah Marcus. Hirsh not only discusses the scholarship but also critiques and engages it; his analysis of their criticism provides valuable insights into many of the literary works addressed by these prominent scholars. The chapter by Nancy Mohrlock Bunker and James S. Baumlin will unquestionably prove valuable to students and teachers of seventeenth-century literature; the chapter provides helpful definitions of many key literary themes and periods, applying these definitions to canonical literary works; it differs from Schechter's chapter in that Bunker and Baumlin cover aspects of the early modern period such as Jacobean Drama while Schechter focuses on literary terms. In Chapter 8, Robert C. Evans discusses current approaches to literature, manifesting how scholars, teachers, and students can apply various facets of literary theory to seventeenth-century literature. Evans covers fourteen literary approaches, such as Historical, New Historical, Marxist, Structuralist, Psychoanalytic, Feminist, Deconstructive, and Multicultural theory; this chapter serves as an excellent introduction to literary theory. Bruce Boehrer focuses on changes in the seventeenth-century literary canon; he discusses neglected works by prominent Renaissance authors as well as works by little-known writers of the early modern period. Using thoughts from renowned critic Terry Eagleton, Boehrer also investigates non-literary genres as they are relevant to the period. The chapter by Robert C. Evans and Eric J. Sterling covers sexuality, gender, and ethnicity in seventeenth-century texts such as Ben Jonson's 'The Masque of Blackness'; the chapter focuses on homoerotic literature, texts dealing with race and blackness, and recent trends in these areas in literary scholarship. In Chapter 11, the late Albert C. Labriola focuses in great depth on four types of literary criticism – New Historicism, Feminist Criticism, Gay and Lesbian Criticism, and Ecocriticism. He deftly analyzes the most significant critical studies in all four literary theories. Whereas Evans uses fourteen theories to analyze one canonical work, Labriola focuses on the seminal statements of the theories his chapter discusses. Finally, Jonathan Wright's bibliography, divided by subjects (such as politics, aspects of culture, genre, and gender, among others) and by author, provides readers with easy access to valuable scholarship covering the century. Julie Sutherland, who teaches at the University of British Columbia in Canada, writes about teaching core topics, curriculum, and learning. She provides the readers of this Continuum volume with ideas about which books and articles instructors should read to learn more about teaching early modern literature, and she also demonstrates how to use the Internet and film as teaching tools. Finally, Laura Schechter contributes a glossary of critical and theoretical terms, such as 'allegory', 'epigram', and 'metaphysical'. This chapter will prove quite useful to students, and the book as a whole will greatly benefit Renaissance scholars, college professors and high school teachers, and college students.

2 The Seventeenth-Century Timeline

Deborah Cosier Solomon

The following timeline is indebted to a number of highly useful sources.[1] Whenever possible, dates of plays are those of the first performance. Persons whose birth dates and death dates are listed are generally writers (unless otherwise noted). Published works that are interesting more for their cultural impact rather than for their 'literary' relevance are listed in the third column.

Year	Literary	Historical	Cultural
1603	Samuel Daniel, *A Defence of Rhyme* Michael Drayton, *The Barons' Wars* John Florio, translation of *Essays of Montaigne* Thomas Heywood's *A Woman Killed with Kindness* acted Ben Jonson's *Sejanus* acted	**March** Death of Queen Elizabeth I; accession of King James VI & I **Summer** Plague in London kills more than one-fifth of the population	Lord Chamberlain's Men (Shakespeare's company of actors) become The King's Men when the new king becomes their patron; Orlando Gibbons, organist and composer, joins the royal court
1604	George Chapman's *Bussy D'Ambois* acted John Marston's *The Malcontent* acted William Shakespeare's *Othello* acted Thomas Middleton, *Father Hubbard's Tales* and *The Black Book*	**January** Hampton Court Conference on religious disputes **March** Parliament opens; union with Scotland formally proposed **August** War with Spain ends	King James, *Counterblast to Tobacco*; Publication of composer John Dowland's *Lachrimae, or Seven Teares*
1605	Michael Drayton, *Poems* *Eastward Ho* (by George Chapman, Ben Jonson, and John Marston) acted Ben Jonson, *Masque of Blackness* performed Thomas Middleton's *A Trick to Catch the Old One* acted William Shakespeare's *King Lear* and *Macbeth* acted	**February** Campaign against non-conforming Catholics begins **November** Discovery of Gunpowder Plot (Catholic conspiracy to blow up the government); some Puritan clergymen expelled from the Church of England	Sir Francis Bacon, *Advancement of Learning*; English exploration of New England coast; composer William Byrd's *Gradualia* (Book I) published

Year	Literary	Historical	Cultural
1606	Ben Jonson's *Volpone* acted Thomas Middleton's *A Mad World, My Masters* acted Thomas Middleton's *The Revenger's Tragedy* acted	**April** Union flag ordered flown on ships **June** Charter issued for Virginia colony	Music by Alfonso Ferrabosco the younger is featured in the court masque *Hymenaei* (written by Ben Jonson); Red Bull theatre built
1607	Francis Beaumont's *Knight of the Burning Pestle* acted Shakespeare's *Antony and Cleopatra* acted	**May** Revolts in Midlands against enclosures; Jamestown colony in Virginia founded	*Lord Hay's Masque* at court features music by Thomas Campion and other composers
1608	Thomas Dekker and Thomas Middleton, *The Roaring Girl* acted Ben Jonson, *The Masque of Beauty* performed	**May 1608** Robert Cecil becomes lord treasurer **Summer** English Protestant separatists arrive in Amsterdam, Holland	Joseph Hall, *Characters of Virtues and Vices*; John Smith, *True Relation of Virginia*; fourth (and last) volume of madrigals by composer Thomas Weelkes published
1609	Francis Beaumont's and John Fletcher's *Philaster* acted Samuel Daniel, *The Civil Wars* Thomas Dekker, *Gull's Hornbook* William Shakespeare, *Sonnets* published	**May** James promises not to sell or give away royal land English formulate plans to 'plant' settlers in Ireland ('Ulster plantation')	Gerard Winstanley (1609–1676) Francis Bacon, *De Sapientia Veterum*; composer and musicologist Thomas Ravenscroft publishes two significant collections
1610	Ben Jonson, *The Alchemist* acted George Chapman, *Revenge of Bussy* acted Samuel Daniel's *Tethys' Festival* performed Giles Fletcher, *Christ's Victory and Triumph* Thomas Heywood, *The Golden Age* William Camden, *Britain*	**February** Parliament begins debating 'The Great Contract', a proposal to guarantee James' finances in exchange for concessions. Eventually the proposal fails **May** King Henri IV of France is stabbed to death by a Catholic fanatic	William Camden, *Britannia*; John Donne, *Pseudo-Martyr*; Douai (Roman Catholic) translation of the Old Testament The Stationers' Company in London, which supervises publishing, agrees to donate a copy of each newly registered book to the Bodleian Library at Oxford University

Year	Literary	Historical	Cultural
1611	George Chapman's translation of Homer's *Iliad* Aemilia Lanyer, *Salve Deus Rex Judaeorum* 'King James' translation of the Bible Thomas Middleton's *A Chaste Maid in Cheapside* acted	**March** Robert Carr, King James' current favorite, is made Viscount Rochester **May** Rank of baronet created; baronetcies sold to raise money	John Donne, *Ignatius His Conclave*; James Harrington (1611–1677); John Speed, *History of Great Britain*; court masques written by Ben Jonson, with music by Alfonso Ferrabosco the younger and by Robert Johnson, are performed
1612	John Donne, First and Second *Anniversaries* Michael Drayton, *Poly-Olbion* Thomas Heywood, *Apology for Actors* John Webster's *The White Devil* acted	**May** Death of Robert Cecil, the king's chief advisor **November** Death of Prince Henry, heir to the throne	Samuel Butler (1612–1680) Francis Bacon, *Essays* (second edition); Thomas Heywood, *Apology for Actors*; Pendle witch trials
1613	William Browne, *Britannia's Pastorals* Thomas Campion, *Two Bookes of Ayres* George Chapman's *The Memorable Masque* performed Clement Cotton, *The Mirror of Martyrs* Samuel Daniel, *History of England* George Wither, *Abuses Stript and Whipt*	**February** Princess Elizabeth is married to Frederick, Elector Palatine **September** Sir Thomas Overbury, an opponent of marriage by Robert Carr (the king's favorite) to Lady Frances Howard, dies in the Tower of London **December** Robert Carr, now the Earl of Somerset, marries Lady Frances Howard	John Cleveland (1613–1658); Richard Crashaw born (dies 1649); *Purchas His Pilgrimage* (travel literature); Globe Theatre burns down during a staging of Shakespeare's *Henry VIII*; man-made 'New River' is finished to deliver water to London; King James issues a proclamation against dueling
1614	George Chapman's translation of Homer's *Odyssey* Samiel Daniel's *Hymen's Triumph* performed Ben Jonson's *Bartholomew Fair* acted John Webster's *The Duchess of Malfi* acted	**July** The Earl of Somerset, the king's favorite, is appointed Lord Chancellor **August** King James is introduced to the handsome young George Villiers in an effort to diminish Somerset's influence	Sir Thomas Overbury, *Characters*; Sir Walter Ralegh, *History of the World*; in Virginia, the Englishman John Rolfe marries the Indian woman Pocahontas; composer Thomas Ravenscroft publishes *A Brief Discourse . . . on music*; Globe Theatre rebuilt
1615	John Harington, *Epigrams* Ben Jonson's *The Golden Age Restor'd* performed Joseph Swetnam, *The Arraignment of . . . Women*	**October** Earl and Countess of Somerset arrested on suspicion of murdering Sir Thomas Overbury [see 1613]	King James sends an ambassador to India; Edward Wright (1561–1615), mathematician and map-maker

Year	Literary	Historical	Cultural
1616	George Chapman, *The Whole Works of Homer* Ben Jonson's folio *Works* King James' folio *Works* Dorothy Leigh, *The Mother's Blessing*	**July** Earl and Countess of Somerset tried and convicted of murder of Sir Thomas Overbury [see 1615] **August** George Villiers, the king's new favorite, made a viscount and important officer at court	William Shakespeare (1564–1616), Francis Beaumont (c. 1584–1616); British ambassador begins duties in India; Sir Walter Ralegh is released from prison; controversy in the Catholic Church regarding Copernicus' theory of the solar system
1617	Thomas Campion, *Third and Fourth Booke of Ayres* Ester Sowernam, *Ester hath hang'd Haman* Rachel Speght, *A Muzzle for Melastomus*	**January** George Villiers, the king's new favorite, is appointed Earl of Buckingham **May–August** James makes his only visit to Scotland since becoming king	Court masques written by Ben Jonson, designed by Inigo Jones, and with music by Nicholas Lanier, are performed; John Napier publishes *Rabdologiae*, a major mathematical work
1618	Robert Burton, *Philosophaster* Ben Jonson's *Pleasure Reconciled to Virtue* performed Thomas Gainford, *The Glory of England*	**January** Sir Francis Bacon appointed Lord Chancellor; George Villiers appointed a marquis **August** Thirty Years War (religious conflict) begins in Europe **October** Execution of Sir Walter Ralegh	King James' 'Declaration of Sports' authorizes recreations on Sundays for those who have first attended church; Abraham Cowley (1618–1667); William Harvey discovers circulation of blood
1619	Michael Drayton, *Collected Poems* Sir Francis Bacon, *Wisdom of the Ancients* John Mayor, *A Pattern for Women* Thomas Middleton's *Inner Temple Masque* performed	**March** Queen Anne dies **Late summer** First African slaves in North America brought to Virginia **September** Frederick, son-in-law of King James, agrees to become King of Bohemia	Construction begins on the Banqueting House, designed by Inigo Jones in the Palladian style, as part of the royal palace at Whitehall; death of Nicholas Hilliard, great painter of miniature portraits; William Jaggard prints the so-called 'False Folio' including both Shakespearean and non-Shakespearean plays
1620	Anonymous, *Swetnam the Women Hater, Arraigned by Women* Ben Jonson's *News from the New World* and *Pan's Anniversary* performed	**October** King Frederick expelled from his kingdom by forces of the Holy Roman Empire [see 1619] **December** Pilgrims arrive in America	Sir Francis Bacon, *Novum Organum*; Thomas Campion (1567–1620); John Evelyn (1620–1706)

Year	Literary	Historical	Cultural
1621	John Barclay, *Argenis* Robert Burton, *Anatomy of Melancholy* Rachel Speght, *Mortality's Memorandum* Mary Wroth, *Urania* (part I)	**January** First Parliament since 1614; it impeaches Sir Francis Bacon **June** Opposition leaders arrested	Roger Boyle, first Earl of Orrery (1621–1679); John Donne appointed Dean of St. Paul's Cathedral, London; first news books in London
1622	Elizabeth Clinton, *The Countess of Lincoln's Nursery* Thomas Middleton's and William Rowley's *The Changeling* acted Henry Peacham, *The Compleat Gentleman*	**March** Indians massacre Jamestown colonists **August** King James restricts preaching on controversial political topics	Henry Vaughan (1622–1695); Whitehall Banqueting House (designed by Inigo Jones in Palladian style) completed
1623	Samuel Daniel, *The Whole Works* William Drummond, *The Cypress Grove* William Shakespeare, first folio edition George Wither, *Hymnes and Songs of the Church*	**March** Prince Charles and Buckingham, the king's favorite, journey to Spain to negotiate a marriage for the prince **May** Buckingham receives the extraordinary title of Duke **October** Prince Charles and Buckingham are immensely popular when their negotiations for Charles' marriage to a Catholic Spanish princess collapse	Francis Bacon, *De Augmentis*; Margaret Cavendish, Duchess of Newcastle (1623–1673); Giles Fletcher (1588–1623)
1624	Thomas Heywood's *The Captives* licensed Thomas Heywood, *Gunaikeion: or Nine Books of Various History concerning Women* Thomas Middleton's *A Game at Chess* acted	**February** Parliament meets; many Protestants favor war with Spain **November** A treaty with the French provides for Prince Charles' marriage to Princess Henrietta-Maria	John Donne, *Devotions Upon Emergent Occasions*; George Fox (1624–1691)

Year	Literary	Historical	Cultural
1625	Francis Bacon, *Essays* (final edition) Thomas Dekker, *A Rod for Run-Awayes* James Shirley's *Love Tricks* licensed	**March** Death of King James; accession of his son as Charles I **May–June** Marriage and first meeting of Charles and Henrietta Maria **Summer–Fall** Buckingham, Charles' favorite, increasingly unpopular	Nicholas Ferrar retires to Little Gidding: John Fletcher (1579–1625); John Florio (1553–1625)
1626	Lady Eleanor Douglas, *A Warning to the Dragon* Ben Jonson's *The Staple of News* acted Philip Massinger's *The Roman Actor* acted	**February** Religious conference reflects growing tension between Calvinists and Arminians **September** A 'forced loan' to the government provokes controversy and legal dissent	Lancelot Andrewes (1555–1626); John Aubrey (1626–1697); Francis Bacon (1561–1626); Robert Howard (1626–1698); William Rowley (c. 1585–1626); George Sandys' translation of Ovid's *Metamorphoses*; Cyril Tourneur (c. 1580–1626)
1627	John Cosin, *A Collection of Private Devotions* Michael Drayton, *Battle of Agincourt* Thomas May's translation of Lucan's *Pharsalia*	**October** In war with France, Buckingham suffers stunning loss **November** Increasing legal controversy over the forced loan	Francis Bacon, *New Atlantis*: Robert Boyle (1627–1691); Thomas Middleton (1580–1627)
1628	John Earle, *Microcosmographie* John Ford's *The Lover's Melancholy* acted	**July** William Laud appointed Bishop of London **August** Assassination of the Duke of Buckingham	Sir Edward Coke, *Institutes*; John Earle, *Microcosmography*; Fulke Greville (1554–1628); William Temple (1628–1699); George Villiers, second Duke of Buckingham (1628–1687)
1629	John Ford's *The Broken Heart* acted Ben Jonson's *The New Inn* acted John Milton, 'On the Morning of Christ's Nativity'	**March** King Charles dissolves parliament in the midst of much controversy; eleven years of 'personal rule' begin	Katherine Austen (1629–c. 1683), diarist and poet; Thomas Goffe (1591–1629); Thomas James (c. 1573–1629), librarian

Year	Literary	Historical	Cultural
1630	Diana Primrose, *A Chaine of Pearle* Francis Quarles, *Divine Poems* John Milton, *Arcades* and 'On Shakespeare' Thomas Randolph, *Amyntas* John Taylor, *Works*	**May** Birth of future King Charles II **Summer** Plague **November** Peace with Spain	Charles Cotton (1630–1687); Gabriel Harvey (c. 1545–1630); John Heminges (1556–1630), actor and co-compiler of Shakespeare's first folio; William Herbert, third Earl of Pembroke (1580–1630); Samuel Rowlands (c. 1573–1630)
1631	Philip Massinger's *Believe as You List* acted John Selden, *Titles of Honor* George Wither, *Psalms of David*	**January** Latest 'Book of Orders' issued (often seen as effort by central government to impose greater control on localities)	John Donne (1572–1631); Michael Drayton (1565–1631); John Dryden (1631–1700)
1632	John Donne, *Death's Duel* Philip Massinger's *The City Madam* acted Francis Quarles, *Divine Fancies* William Shakespeare, second folio edition	**November** Sir John Eliot, parliamentarian and steadfast opponent of the King, dies after years of imprisonment	Thomas Dekker (c. 1572–c. 1632); John Locke (1632–1704); Martha Moulsworth composes autobiographical poem; Anthony Van Dyck, royal portrait-painter, settles in London and is knighted by King Charles
1633	Abraham Cowley, *Poetical Blossoms* John Donne, *Poems* Fulke Greville, *Works* George Herbert, *The Temple* Alice Sutcliffe, *Meditations of Man's Mortality*	**August** William Laud – distrusted by Puritans – becomes Archbishop of Canterbury **October** Birth of Prince James (eventually King James II)	George Herbert (1593–1633); Samuel Pepys (1633–1703); William Prynne, *Histriomastix*; George Savile, Marquess of Halifax (1633–1695)
1634	George Wither, *Emblems* John Milton, *Comus*	**October** Controversial 'ship money' collections begin in coastal areas	George Chapman (c. 1560–1634); John Marston (1576–1634); John Webster (c. 1580–1634)
1635	Richard Brome's *The Sparagus Garden* acted Francis Quarles, *Emblems*	**June** 'Ship money' collections imposed on the country at large	Thomas Bateson (c. 1570–1630), composer; Thomas Randolph (1605–1635)
1636	James Shirley's *The Duke's Mistress* acted at court	Continued legal controversy over required payment of 'ship money'	George Etherege (1636–1692)

Year	Literary	Historical	Cultural
1637	Court performance of William Cartwright's *The Royal Slave* Thomas Heywood, *Pleasant Dialogues and Dramas* Shakespeare's *Hamlet* is performed at court Five plays by James Shirley published in single-play editions	**June** Critics of bishops are punished by being branded and having their ears cut off **July** Riots in Scotland against imposition of English Church's Prayer Book	Robert Fludd (1574–1637), physician, astrologer; Philemon Holland (1552–1637); Ben Jonson (1572–1637); Gervase Markham (c. 1568–1637); Theatres reopen in October after having been closed because of plague
1638	John Milton, 'Lycidas' published Thomas Randolph, *Poems* John Suckling, *Aglaura*	**November** War breaks out with Scotland when Scots reject bishops	Francis Pilkington (c. 1565–1638), composer
1639	John Taylor, *A Juniper Lecture*	**June** King Charles fails in his efforts to use force to impose his will on the Scots	Henry Adamson (1581–1639); Elizabeth Cary (1585–1639); Charles Sedley (1639–1701)
1640	Thomas Carew, *Poems* William Davenant's *Salmacida Spolia* performed James Howell, *Dodona's Grove* Francis Quarles, *Enchiridion* Mary Tattlewell and Joan Hit-Him-Home, *The Women's Sharp Revenge* Ben Jonson's second folio *Works*	**October** English lose in second war with Scots over bishops **November** 'Long parliament' begins meeting; it objects to ship money and monopolies and impeaches Archbishop Laud and the Earl of Strafford, one of the king's chief advisors	Aphra Behn (1640–1689); Robert Burton (1577–1640); John Crowne (c. 1640–1712); John Ford (1586–c. 1640); Philip Massinger (1583–1640); Izaak Walton, *Life of Donne*; George Thomason, London printer and bookseller, begins collecting published tracts
1641	Katherine Chidley, *The Justification of the Independent Churches of Christ* James Shirley's *The Cardinal* licensed for performance Thomas Urquhart, *Epigrams Divine and Moral* John Wilkins, *Mercury* George Wither, *Halleluiah*	**March–May** Earl of Strafford tried for treason and eventually executed **May** Proposal presented in parliament to eliminate bishops **July** Parliament votes to abolish 'ship money' **October** Rebellion breaks out in Ireland **December** 13 bishops impeached in parliament	John Everard (c. 1584–1641), nonconformist preacher; Thomas Heywood (c. 1574–1641); Jeremiah Horrocks (1618–1641), astronomer; John Milton, *Of Reformation* and *The Reason of Church Government*; Thomas Mun (1571–1641), writer on economics; Thomas Shadwell (1641/42–92); John Suckling (1608–1641); William Wycherley (1641–1715)

Year	Literary	Historical	Cultural
1642	Thomas Browne, *Religio Medici* Edward Coke, *Second Part of the Institutes of the Laws of England* John Denham, *Cooper's Hill* Thomas Fuller, *The Holy States* Thomas Hobbes, *De Cive*	**February** Act to exclude bishops from parliament passes **August** Civil War begins **September** Parliament closes the theatres	John Suckling (1609–1642); Henry Peacham, *The Art of Living in London*
1643	Richard Baker, *A Chronicle of the Kings of England* Thomas Browne, *Religio Medici* (authorized edition) George Wither, *Campo-Musae, or the Field-Musings*	**April** Efforts to negotiate a peace treaty break down **Spring–Summer** The king's armies score victories **August** Parliament allies with the Scots	John Bainbridge (1582–1643), astronomer; William Browne (1591–1643); William Cartwright (1611–1643); Lucius Cary (1610–1643), statesman, soldier, author
1644	Translation into English of two works by Jacob Boehme John Cotton, *The Keyes of the Kingdom of Heaven; The Way of the Churches of Christ in New England*	**January** Scottish army enters England **Summer** Battles won by both sides **Fall** Tensions within Parliamentary forces	John Milton, *Of Divorce, Areopagitica, Of Education*; Henry Robinson, *Liberty of Conscience*; Roger Williams, *The Bloody Tenent of Persecution*; Francis Quarles (1592–1644)
1645	James Howell, *Epistolae Ho-Elianae* John Milton, *Poems* Edmund Waller, *Poems*	**January** Execution of Archbishop Laud **Summer–Fall** Victories by Parliamentary forces	Katherine Chidley, *Good Counsel, to the Petitioners for Presbyterian Government*; Aemilia Lanyer (c. 1570–1645); John Lilburne, *England's Birthright Justified*
1646	Richard Crashaw, *Steps to the Temple* James Shirley, *Poems* Sir John Suckling, *Fragmentam Aurea* Henry Vaughan, *Poems*	**Spring–Summer** Surrenders of royalist armies; war ends in June **October** Parliament votes to abolish bishops	Thomas Browne, *Pseudodoxia Epidemica*; Alexander Henderson (1583–1646); John Row (1568–1646)

Year	Literary	Historical	Cultural
1647	John Cleveland, *Several Select Poems* John Fletcher and Francis Beaumont, first folio edition Henry More, *Philosophical Poems* Thomas Stanley, *Poems and Translations*	**Winter–Summer** Increasing friction between Parliament and the New Model Army, which seizes the king in June and occupies London in August **December** Charles allies with the Scots against Parliament	Mary Cary, *A Word in Season*; Thomas Farnaby (c. 1575–1647); Thomas May, *The History of the Parliament of England*; Francis Meres (1565–1647); Nicholas Stone (1586–1647); Jeremy Taylor, . . . *A Discourse of the Liberty of Prophesying*
1648	Richard Corbett, *Poetica Stromata* Mildmay Fane, *Otia Sacra* Robert Herrick, *Hesperides* and *Noble Numbers*	**August** Oliver Cromwell's forces defeat the Scots in Second Civil War **December** New Model Army occupies London again; Parliament is 'purged'	Edward Herbert (1583–1648); Elizabeth Poole, *A Vision: The Disease and Cure of the Kingdom*; Elkanah Settle (1648–1724)
1649	Richard Lovelace, *Lucasta: Epodes*	**January** Trial and execution of Charles I **May** Republic declared **September–October** Cromwell brutally suppresses revolt in Ireland	Richard Crashaw (1613–1649) William Drummond (1585–1649) John Gauden, *Eikon Basilike* John Milton becomes Latin secretary of the Republic (1649–1659) John Milton, *Eikonoklastes*
1650	William Davenant, *Gondibert* Henry Vaughan, *Silex Scintillans*	**January** All adult males ordered to swear allegiance to the Republic **September** Cromwell victorious over Scottish royalists	Richard Baxter, *The Saints Everlasting Rest*; Phineas Fletcher (1582–1650); Marchmont Nedham, *The Case of the Commonwealth of England Stated*
1651	John Cleveland, *Poems* William Davenant, *Gondibert* Henry Vaughan, *Olor Iscanus*	**September** Cromwell defeats Charles II, who goes into exile	Thomas Hobbes, *Leviathan*; John Milton, *Defensio pro Populo Anglicano*
1652	Richard Crashaw, *Carmen Deo Nostro* Anonymous, *Eliza's Babes*	**May** War with the Dutch begins	Richard Brome (c. 1590–1652); Thomas Otway (1652–1685); Nahum Tate (1652–1715)

Year	Literary	Historical	Cultural
1653	Margaret Cavendish, *Poems and Fancies; Philosophical Fancies* An Collins, *Divine Songs and Meditacions*	**April** Cromwell dissolves 'Rump Parliament' **July** 'Barebones Parliament' begins meeting **December** Cromwell becomes Lord Protector	Thomas D'Urfey (1653–1723); Robert Filmer (1588–1653); John Playford, *Select Musicall Ayres*; Izaak Walton, *The Compleat Angler*
1654	R.C., ed., *The Harmony of the Muses* Thomas Washbourne, *Divine Poems*	**September** First parliament of the Protectorate begins meeting	John Milton, *Defensio Secunda*; Anna Trapnel, various prophetic works published
1655	Margaret Cavendish, *World's Olio* John Denham, *Cooper's Hill* (revised) Henry Vaughan, *Silex Scintillans* (second edition)	**January** Cromwell dissolves parliament **March** Royalist uprising defeated	Margaret Cavendish, *Philosophical and Physical Opinions*; Thomas Hobbes, *De Corpore Politico*
1656	Margaret Cavendish, *Nature's Pictures Drawn by Fancy's Pencil to the Life* Abraham Cowley, *Poems*	**September** Second parliament of the Protectorate begins meeting, but only after its membership is purged	Opera *The Siege of Rhodes* performed; John Gamble, *Ayres and Dialogues* (Book I)
1657	Henry King, *Poems*	**May** Cromwell refuses offer of kingship	William Harvey (1578–1657)
1658	John Dryden, *Stanzas on the Death of Cromwell*	**September** Oliver Cromwell dies; his son, Richard, succeeds him as Lord Protector	Thomas Browne, *Urn Burial* and *Garden of Cyprus*; John Cleveland (1613–1658)
1659	Richard Lovelace, *Lucasta: Posthume Poems* John Suckling, *Last Remains*	**May** Richard Cromwell forced to resign; Protectorate ends **August** Royalist uprising defeated	Richard Baxter, *A Holy Commonwealth*; Thomas Southerne (1659–1746)
1660	John Dryden, *Astraea Redux*	**May** Restoration of the monarchy under King Charles II, who returns from exile	Jane Barker (1660–1723); Anne Killigrew (1660–1685); Royal Society founded; Samuel Pepys begins his *Diary*

Year	Literary	Historical	Cultural
1661	Abraham Cowley's *Cutter of Coleman Street* acted	**January** Bodies of Oliver Cromwell and other republicans exhumed and hanged **May–July** 'Cavalier' Parliament reverses many policies of the Interregnum	John Bunyan, *Profitable Meditations*; Joseph Glanvill, *The Vanity of Dogmatising*; Hannah Wolley, *The Ladies' Directory*
1662	Alexander Brome, *Rump* Margaret Cavendish, *Plays* Robert Howard's *The Committee* and *The Surprisal* acted	**April–May** King Charles II marries Catherine of Braganza in multiple ceremonies **August** Act of Uniformity, to strengthen conformity to Anglican Church, introduced	Thomas Fuller, *The History of the Worthies of England*; Michael Wigglesworth, *Day of Doom*
1663	Samuel Butler, *Hudibras* (Part I) John Dryden's *Wild Gallant* acted	**January** Royal African Company (designed to engage in slave trade) chartered **April** Under parliamentary pressure, King Charles withdraws his Declaration of Indulgence (designed to protect religious freedom)	Theophilus Bird (1608–1663), actor; Elizabeth Egerton (1626–1663); Balthazar Gerbier (1592–1663), diplomat and painter; Drury Lane Theatre (or Theatre Royal) built
1664	Samuel Butler, *Hudibras* (second edition) George Etherege's *The Comical Revenge* acted Edmund Waller, *Poems*	**May** Parliament passes act against religious nonconformists **August** England annexes what is now New York	Margaret Cavendish, *Philosophical Letters*; *CCXI Sociable Letters*; Katherine Philips (1632–1664); John Vanbrugh (1664–1726)
1665	Roger Boyle's *Mustapha* acted John Dryden's *Indian Emperor* acted Robert Howard's *Vestal Virgin* acted	**February–March** Second Anglo-Dutch war begins **April** The Great Plague descends on London **October** Parliament again legislates against religious nonconformists	Eliabeth Bourchier (1598–1665), wife of Oliver Cromwell; John Bunyan, *One Thing is Needful*; John Goodwin (1594–1665), preacher; Thomas Simon (c. 1623–1665), engraver

Year	Literary	Historical	Cultural
1666	Margaret Cavendish, *Description of a New World, Called the Blazing-World*	**Summer** Major naval battles in second Anglo-Dutch war **September** The Great Fire destroys much of London	Mary Astell (1666–1731); John Bunyan, *Grace Abounding*; Margaret Fell, *Women's Speaking Justified*; James Shirley (1596–1666)
1667	Robert Boyle's *The Black Prince* acted John Dryden, *Annus Mirabilis* John Dryden's *Secret Love* acted John Milton, *Paradise Lost* Katherine Philips, *Poems*	**June** Dutch fleet inflicts major damage on England **July** Second Anglo-Dutch war ends	Abraham Cowley (1618–1667); George Wither (1588–1667); Thomas Sprat, *History of the Royal Society*; theatres close in July
1668	Abraham Cowley, *Davideis* John Denham, *Poems and Translations* John Dryden's *Evening's Love* acted	**February** Parliament criticizes conduct of Dutch war and also criticizes the king's tolerant religious policies	William Davenant (1606–1668); John Dryden, *Essay of Dramatic Poesy*
1669	John Dryden's *Tyrannick Love* acted	**October** Scottish Church brought under English control	John Denham (1615–1669); Henry King (1591–1669); theatres close because of death of the Queen; Samuel Pepys ends his diary
1670	Aphra Behn's *The Forced Marriage* acted John Dryden's *Conquest of Granada* (part I) acted	**February** Parliament makes major increase in monetary allotment to royal government **May** England signs secret treaty with its traditional enemy, France; treaty signed in public in December	William Congreve (1670–1729) John Dryden appointed Poet Laureate
1671	John Milton, *Paradise Regained* and *Samson Agonistes* John Dryden's *Conquest of Granada* (part II) acted	**September** Direct royal control of customs resumes	Nell Gwyn retires as an actress Jane Sharp, *The Midwives Book*
1672	John Dryden's *Marriage à la Mode* and *The Assignation* acted William Wycherley's *The Gentleman Dancing Master* acted	**March** Charles II again grants new freedoms to religious nonconformists; third war with the Dutch begins	Abiezer Coppe (1619–1672); Richard Steele (1672–1729); John Wilkins (1614–1672); Bridges Street theatre burns

Year	Literary	Historical	Cultural
1673	Aphra Behn's *The Dutch Lover* acted	**February** Criticism in parliament of king's indulgences to religious nonconformists, which are cancelled in March **Spring–Summer** Parliamentary acts against Catholics affect James, the king's brother and heir apparent	Richard Braithwaite (1588–1673); Matthew Locke, *Melothesia* (on music theory); Henry Herbert (1595–1673), Master of the Revels
1674	Duke of Newcastle's *The Triumphant Widow* acted	**February** Third Anglo-Dutch war ends	Robert Herrick (1591–1674); Edward Hyde, first Earl of Clarendon (1609–1674); John Milton (1608–1674); Thomas Traherne (1636–1674)
1675	John Dryden's *Aureng-Zebe* acted William Wycherley's *The Country Wife* acted	**Spring** Parliament refuses to vote funds for king and is suspended	Construction of Royal Observatory begins; Matthew Locke composes music for Thomas Shadwell's *Psyche*
1676	Aphra Behn's *The Town Fop* acted George Etherege's *The Man of Mode* acted William Wycherley's *The Plain Dealer* acted	**May** Major fire in southern London suburb **Fall** Major influenza epidemic	William Cavendish, first Duke of Newcastle (1592–1676); Matthew Hale (1609–1676); Henry Purcell composes music for various plays; Gerard Winstanley (1609–1676)
1677	Aphra Behn's *The Rover* acted John Dryden's *All for Love* and *The State of Innocence* acted Nathaniel Lee's *The Rival Queens* acted Charles Sedley's *Antony and Cleopatra* acted	**February** House of Lords disciplines dissident peers **November** William of Orange (of the Netherlands) marries Princess Mary, daughter of Prince James, the heir apparent	Isaac Barrow (1630–1677), mathematician; Matthew Locke (1621–1677), composer; James Harrington (1611–1677), political theorist

Year	Literary	Historical	Cultural
1678	John Bunyan, *Pilgrim's Progress* (Part I) Samuel Butler, *Hudibras* (third edition) John Dryden's *Oedipus* acted Thomas Otway's *Friendship in Fashion* acted Thomas Shadwell's *Timon* and *The True Widow* acted Henry Vaughan, *Thalia Rediviva*	**Winter** Growing tensions between Parliament and the royal court **Late Summer / Early Fall** Titus Oates alleges Catholic conspiracy to kill the king **Fall** Numerous anti-Catholic measures taken	John Jenkins (1592–1678), composer; Andrew Marvell (1621–1678); Thomas Rymer, *The Tragedies of the Last Age*
1679	Nathaniel Lee's *Caesar Borgia* acted Thomas Shadwell's *The Woman-Captain* acted Nahum Tate's *The Loyal General* acted	**Winter–Spring** Parliamentary efforts to exclude James, the heir apparent, from the right to succeed as king because of his Catholicism **August** King Charles seriously ill	Thomas Hobbes, *Behemoth* Thomas Hobbes (1588–1679)
1680	John Dryden's *The Spanish Friar* acted Nathaniel Lee's *Lucius Junius Brutus* and *Theodosius* acted John Wilmot, second Earl of Rochester, *Poems*	**Fall** Further controversy in Parliament over efforts to exclude James, King Charles' Catholic brother, as heir to the throne	Samuel Butler (1612–1680); John Wilmot, Earl of Rochester (1647–1680); John Bunyan, *The Life and Death of Mr. Badman*; Robert Filmer, *Patriarcha*
1681	John Dryden, *Absalom and Achitophel* Andrew Marvell, *Miscellaneous Poems*	**Spring** Further debates about efforts to exclude James from the throne	Richard Allestree (1619–1681), Royalist churchman; Richard Alleine (1611–1681), Puritan clergyman; William Walwyn (1600–1681)
1682	Aphra Behn's *The City Heiress* acted John Dryden, *Mac Flecknoe, The Medall, Religio Laici*	**November** Earl of Shaftesbury flees to Holland after being accused of plotting against King Charles	Thomas Browne (1605–1682); John Bunyan, *The Holy War*
1683	Nathaniel Lee's *Constantine* acted John Oldham, *Poems and Translations*	**Summer** Alleged 'Rye House Plot' to assassinate Charles and James discovered	Thomas Killigrew (1612–1683); John Oldham (1653–1683); Izaak Walton (1593–1683)
1684	John Bunyan, *Pilgrim's Progress* (second edition)	Public sympathy for James allows King Charles to re-appoint him to the Privy Council	Roger Williams (1603–1684), theologian and colonist

Year	Literary	Historical	Cultural
1685	John Dryden's *Albion and Albanius* acted Edmund Waller, *Divine Poems*	**February** Charles II dies; his brother becomes King James II **Summer** The Duke of Monmouth, illegitimate son of King Charles II, declares himself king; his forces are defeated in July and he is executed shortly thereafter	Margaret Hughes (1630–1685), actress; Lady Alice Lyle executed for harboring rebels; Thomas Otway (1652–1685); John Pell (1610–1685), mathematician
1686	Aphra Behn's *The Lucky Chance* acted Thomas Jevon's *The Devil of a Wife* acted Thomas Killigrew, *Poems*	**Spring** Controversy about King James' efforts to suppress anti-Catholic sermons **Fall** Efforts by King James to impose greater control over the Church	William Dugdale (1605–1686), antiquarian; John Fell (1625–1686), churchman; John Pearson (1612–1686), theologian; John Playford (1623–1686), musical publisher
1687	Aphra Behn's *The Emperor of the Moon* acted John Cleveland, *Works* John Dryden, *The Hind and the Panther*	**Spring–Fall** King James' growing support for Catholics and nonconformists causes controversy	Charles Cotton (1630–1687); Isaac Newton, *Principia Mathematica*; Edmund Waller (1606–1687)
1688	Aphra Behn, *Oroonoko* Thomas Shadwell's *The Squire of Alsatia* acted	**Spring–Summer** Growing controversy over James' pro-Catholic policies; birth of a Catholic heir in June alarms Protestants **November** William of Orange, James' Protestant son-in-law, invades England **December** James flees to France	John Bunyan (1628–1688); Winston Churchill (1620–1688), soldier, historian, and politician; Elisha Coles (1608–1688), lexicographer; Ralph Cudworth (1617–1688), philosopher; Thomas Flatman (1637–1688), poet and painter; Thomas Jevon (1652–1688)
1689	Aphra Behn's *The Widow Ranter* acted John Dryden's *Don Sebastian* acted	**February** William of Orange crowned as William III; his wife, Mary (Protestant daughter of overthrown King James II), becomes Mary II	Aphra Behn (1640–1689); Bishop Seth Ward (1617–1689), mathematician and astronomer; Thomas Sydenham (1624–1689), physician

3 Historical Contexts

Richard Harp

Chapter Overview

Introduction

The watershed national event of the seventeenth century in England was the Civil War fought between the years 1642–1649. Among its consequences was the legal trial and execution of the King of England by some of his own countrymen and the firm establishment of Parliament as the most important governing body in the country. The reasons for this conflict were numerous and they had their origins at least as far back as the sixteenth century. Contributing factors included the religious quarrel between Protestants and Catholics and the rise of the gentry and the middle class as economically powerful elements in society. In addition, by the seventeenth century English social life was no longer limited to the three traditional divisions of nobility, clergy, and commoners. As a result, the monarch had great difficulty holding the country's various political factions together.

The Sixteenth-Century Background to the Civil War

The Protestant Reformation began in England when Parliament, in 1534, declared King Henry VIII, not the Roman Catholic Pope, the supreme head of the Church in the country. Henry desired this authority not out of any fundamental theological disagreement with Rome but because he wished to have his marriage to Catherine of Aragon annulled, as he had not been able to father with her a male heir to the throne of England. When Pope Clement VII refused to do this (the Pope had previously given Henry a papal dispensation to marry Catherine because she had first been married to the King's late brother Arthur), the King severed the English church's obedience to Rome. It was a dramatic break, as only thirteen years before Clement's predecessor Pope Leo X had declared Henry 'defender of the faith' for his treatise defending the validity of Church's seven sacraments against Martin Luther's attacks. After his break with Rome, Henry proceeded to dissolve the monastic communities which were so prominent a feature of the country (in 1500 there had been 900 such communities). He gave a portion of the vast wealth with which the monasteries were endowed to the nobles who supported him. This helped to solidify his own rule, but in the long run it increased and enriched an aristocracy which in the next century would find that its interests no longer coincided with those of the monarch.

It was Henry's daughter Elizabeth, though, who solidified the Protestant reformation in England. Coming to power in 1558, after an abortive attempt by her sister Mary to restore Catholicism to the country, she managed during a reign of forty-five years to defeat threats to the nation's security from abroad and from rival claimants to the throne from within. The former was typified by the defeat of the Spanish Armada, the latter by the execution of Mary, Queen of Scots. The Armada was a great naval invasion in 1588 in which 130 ships sailed toward Britain with nearly 20,000 soldiers aboard. Winds and other unfavorable elements spelled the doom of this expedition. Its defeat was a signal moment in the coalescence of the British national identity.

Mary Stuart, the Queen of Scotland, held the next best claim to the throne of England after Elizabeth. She was popular and Elizabeth was always wary of her, keeping her in prison in England for nearly nineteen years. During this time Elizabeth was alarmed about reports of Mary's conspiring to overthrow her and as a result had her executed in 1587.

The Road to Civil War: Philosophy and Political Thought

Theology and political thought were to be closely entwined throughout the seventeenth century. But the grounds upon which the Civil War was fought were brought into particular focus as early as the final decades of the sixteenth century. Queen Elizabeth was an intellectual ruler but her political philosophy was pragmatic. No doubt her enemies would have called her a 'Machiavel', a derogatory term deriving from the famous Italian philosopher Niccoló Machiavelli who wrote the sixteenth-century primer on power politics, *The Prince* (published in 1532), but Elizabeth knew it was her first duty to remain on the throne, a goal not easily accomplished in the cauldron of religious/ political strife of the times.

In religion she had tried to steer a middle ground. For the accouterments of Catholicism such as its pictorial imagery and ecclesiastical vestments she had some sympathy and, in addition, many of the prayers in the Anglican *Book of Common Prayer* of 1559, the year after she became Queen, were taken from the Roman Catholic missal, or prayer book, and translated into sonorous English by the Archbishop of Canterbury, Thomas Cranmer. She also of course enjoyed the drama and the arts, not in favor with Puritans, who were the country's extreme Protestant reformers. Indeed, she saw them as much of a threat to her compromise method of organizing the church – the retention of bishops as church governors but with no allegiance to the Pope in Rome – as the Catholics. The Puritan challenge to her government was dramatized during the Marprelate controversy of 1588–1589. A series of pamphlets written by Puritans under the pseudonym of Martin Marprelate attacked bishops and the episcopacy (a preview of the controversies of the 1630s); the government responded by persecuting its presumed authors and printers. Freedom of the press – or religion – was hardly known in early modern England.

Intellectual good did come from this difficult time, though, in that one of Elizabeth's defenders was the Anglican clergyman Richard Hooker, who absented himself from the vitriol of the controversies to write one of the masterpieces of English prose, *Of the Laws of Ecclesiastical Polity* (1594, 1597). This unprepossessing title described a church and society based on natural law (an idea inherited from the Middle Ages) and decorous Episcopal rule but was presented in such graceful and non-contentious prose that some Catholics (including Pope Clement VIII) and Puritans as well as Anglicans could admire it.

Elizabeth's successor to the throne, King James I (who reigned from 1603 to 1625), was greatly interested in both political philosophy and theology. He had specific views about his own powers as monarch and was one of the most famous champions of the early modern philosophy of the 'Divine Right of Kings', a view that clashed with Parliament's increasing insistence on their prerogatives. Conflicts between church and state indeed extended all the way back to medieval times and resulted in one of the most famous martyrs in English history, St. Thomas Becket, giving his life in 1170 attempting to establish the Church's independence of King Henry II. In early modern times there was still disagreement about the degree to which the Church had authority over civil political officials. The Pope argued that kings derived power from the people, whereas his own spiritual power, coming from God, was superior to the temporal power of a monarch; therefore, the reasoning went, he might depose a monarch. Pope Pius V had essentially tried to do this in 1570 when he excommunicated Elizabeth from the Catholic Church, saying her subjects no longer had to obey her. Into this climate came the political doctrine of James I and his exposition of the 'divine right of kings'. In 1598 he published two works which promoted the right of the monarch to rule the Church. *The True Law of Free Monarchies*, for example, argued that 'A good king will frame all his actions to be according to the law, yet he is not bound thereto but of his good will and for good-example giving to his subjects'. He held that kings too derived their power from God, independently of religious officials. This did not necessarily mean that kings could act capriciously and arbitrarily – Parliament had rights also extending back to the Middle Ages – but James was perfectly clear about who had the supreme authority in the state: 'For albeit the king make daily statutes and ordinances, enjoining such pains thereto as he thinks meet, without any advice of Parliament or estates, yet it lies in the power of no Parliament to make any kind of law or statute without his scepter be to it, for giving it the force of a law'.[1]

Later developments of the century's political thought had great influence not just in England but in the new world. Thomas Hobbes' *Leviathan* (1651) strongly depreciated individual rights in favor of those of an absolute monarch – man in the hypothetical 'state of nature', Hobbes argued, was too savage to be trusted and therefore needed the restrictions of a strong state to live peaceably. This view was compatible both with the strong centralized authority desired by both James I and by Oliver Cromwell during his post-revolutionary Protectorate in the 1650s. Hobbes was inclined to materialism in philosophy. Much more moderately, the empiricist John Locke published in 1690 his *Two Treatises of Government*, which outlined that man in his natural state had rights of life, liberty and property, and that citizens formed their government to protect these rights. Such a view underlay the American 'Declaration of Independence' eighty-four years in the future. Locke was much more sympathetic than Hobbes to the increasing power that Parliament held during the century as a representative body of the people.

The Road to Civil War: Church and State in the Reign of James I

Although Mary Stuart did not get the throne to which she and many English people thought she was entitled, her descendants were in the political spotlight throughout most of the seventeenth century. When her son succeeded Elizabeth in 1603 as King of England, he had already reigned in Scotland as King James VI since 1567 (when he was still an infant). His Catholic mother had very little part in his upbringing. As a result the future English king was raised as a Protestant in a decidedly Protestant Scotland. James did have his troubles with the Scottish protestant church (or 'Kirk'), though, before he ever came to England. He had fought vigorously in Scotland for freedom to appoint bishops to the feisty and independent-minded Kirk there. Among the notable members of the Scottish Kirk was Andrew Melville, who plainly told James that he was 'God's silly vassal', and that there were 'two kings and two kingdoms in Scotland: there is king James, the head of the common-wealth; and there is Christ Jesus, the king of the Church, whose subject King James VI is, and of whose kingdom [he] is not a king, nor a lord, nor a head, but a member'.[2]

Nonetheless James had many difficulties in imposing his will on the country, especially in religious matters. He had initially some hopes of allowing members of the established Church, the Anglican (later called Episcopalian in America), Puritans (who desired to 'purify' Anglicanism of its Catholic ritual and doctrinal remnants) and Catholics to live in tolerant peace. But this dream did not last long. Puritan and Anglican leaders met with the King at a conference at Hampton Court in 1604, but the Puritans, who did not favor bishops in the church and who were aware of James' partiality for them from his years in Scotland, thought that the King was not fairly disposed towards them. He required that all ministers follow Anglican worship, which meant the use of an authorized manual of worship, the Book of Common Prayer. The major lasting achievement of the conference, as it turned out, was to begin the process which resulted in 1611 in a landmark work in English prose, the King James Bible, the only great book, it has often been said, ever written by a committee.

Catholics had long been denied the right in England to practice their religion and were not represented at the Hampton Court conference. Through various 'Penal Laws', such as prohibiting persons from attending Catholic Mass and requiring attendance instead at the Anglican service, and even more extremely, at times enforcing laws of capital punishment against priests, Queen Elizabeth's administration had sought to suppress the old religion, claiming that Jesuits and others conspired against her rule. The resulting executions undoubtedly killed more innocent persons than guilty ones (as had the executions in the 1550s of Protestants by Elizabeth's Catholic half-sister Mary Tudor), but in 1605 a genuine Catholic plot against the reigning monarch ended whatever sympathy James I harbored toward the adherents of his mother's religion. The notorious 'Gunpowder Plot' was an attempt by Catholics disaffected from their government (as in fact many, perhaps most, Catholics were not) to blow up a sitting Parliament on November 5. The plot was discovered, the malefactors executed and strict enforcement of the penal laws began again.

The Road to Civil War: Church and State in the Reign of Charles I

James liked to think of himself as Britain's King Solomon, the biblical king who kept his country out of war abroad and managed prosperity at home. The reign of his son Charles I (1625–1649), unfortunately, produced increasing economic hardship in the country and a war not fought abroad but in England itself.

Charles was in many ways a sincere and dedicated ruler but one who lacked to a disastrous degree political instinct and who had no appreciation that the landed gentry and the increasingly prosperous middle class of bankers and shopkeepers had greater power in the country through Parliament than did he and the old nobility allied with him. He insisted on unwise taxes, some of which he had no right to collect, going beyond, for example, Parliament's one-year only authorization to collect import and export duties on goods, or demanding 'ship money' from the entire country, rather than from just coastal cities and ports for their protection in time of war, as had been the custom. 'Ship money' was to all intents and purposes a new tax he imposed in 1634 when there was no Parliament to oppose him, it having been dissolved in 1629, not to meet again until 1640. This was all done within the context of an important petition that Parliament had demanded the King agree to, the 'Petition of Right' of 1628. This petition, which the King had reluctantly accepted, declared 'that no man hereafter be compelled to make or yield any loan, gift, benevolence, tax, or such like charge, without common consent by act of Parliament'.[3] Although the King surely did not realize it, this document was a milestone in the achievement by the legislature (Parliament) of dominance over the executive (monarch) during the course of the seventeenth century.

Those who opposed the King in Parliament, and those whom they represented – an ever-expanding middle class with wealth derived from business and land – also opposed the King in religious matters. These issues were important to a degree hard to imagine in the twenty-first century, and they were discussed and debated by all levels of society. Differences in belief even within a common Christian framework resulted by the 1640s in dozens and dozens of distinctive religious communities, some with colorful names such as 'Levellers' and 'Ranters'. Charles had no doubt which Christian body he preferred, though; his firm conviction was that the Anglican Church should be the nation's anchor in matters of worship. During his reign Puritan ideas continued to gain strength in the country. Puritan demands included: no bishops to oversee individual congregations, a stripped down ritualism diminishing the importance of the altar, the abandonment of the cross as a religious symbol, the de-emphasizing of holidays because of their Catholic origins (including Christmas because of its association with the word 'mass'), less emphasis on sacraments, and a highlighting of lengthy sermons. Charles responded with a renewed emphasis on ceremony and ritual. He did not have his father's ability to compromise when compromise was necessary. His appointment of William Laud as Archbishop of Canterbury in 1633 made this all too clear.

Laud was one of the Anglican Church's very highest of 'high churchmen', that is, those who wished to maintain the same kind of ritualism and many of the doctrines of their Catholic ancestors, without ceding authority for the Church's governance to the Pope. Puritans considered Laud to have likenesses to the Anti-Christ, the biblical figure who would oppose Christianity at the end of time, and confronted him therefore with all appropriate vigor. Laud knew perhaps even less about compromise than his king. The severity with which he punished his opponents was no more (and frequently less) than others in power had used throughout the sixteenth and seventeenth centuries in the conflicts over religion, but he used them in a country where now such measures had little support. Far-sighted leaders in the seventeenth century would eventually at least attempt policies of toleration in religion but Laud was not in this category. He was executed during the approaching English Civil War in 1645 at the age of 72.

The Road to Civil War: Arts and Popular Culture

The Court's encouragement of the arts also provoked antipathy from Puritans, and in miniature this issue revealed the tensions in the country. Drama, which had flourished under Elizabeth and James, continued into the 1630s, although with fewer acknowledged masterpieces. So did the expensive court masques, in which noble persons danced to the accompaniment of very basic plots drawn from mythology. Puritans attacked the low social morality they thought the theater fostered and found a daring spokesman in the lawyer William Prynne, who published a 1000-page tome attacking all aspects of the theater from ancient times to his own day. While this was undoubtedly an extreme view, so was the response of the King and his 'Star Chamber'. This body, his cabinet or Privy Council acting in a judicial capacity with very little concern for modern rules of legal procedure, meted out extremely harsh punishment. Prynne was stripped of his profession, given an inordinately large fine, and punished with a term of life imprisonment. He was also put into a pillory and had his ears cut off. Censorship of the press had been rigorously enforced since the days of Elizabeth, but given the King's other troubles these punishments were particularly noted. Parliament was able to free Prynne in 1640 (and shut down the theaters for fourteen years in 1642) and his career had a happy end when he was rewarded by Charles II in 1660 with a government position as a record keeper after he had written a treatise defending monarchy.

Popular culture provided a recreational outlet for the poorer classes of society. Literacy expanded in the reigns of James I and Charles I, with perhaps thirty per cent of the population able to sign their names. James approved of popular outdoor country activities, publishing in 1618 a *Book of Sports* (reissued in 1633) which gave royal sanction to Sunday amusements. But even here politics played a role. James wanted to keep his nobility occupied with country activities and away from the political hothouse of London. Puritans objected to any recreational activities on Sundays and opposed customs such as maypoles and of course Christmas celebrations as idolatrous. During the Interregnum (1649–1660, the period between the reigns of Charles I and II) Puritans were indeed able to suppress many such activities but at the Restoration they were revived by the 'Merry Monarch', Charles II. He notoriously carried his own merriment to extremes not practiced by his father or grandfather, as seen, for example, by the large number of mistresses that he maintained, and Puritans were no longer able to enforce rigorous morality upon the country. In this, there were both losses and gains. Eliminating popular pastimes that promoted sexual indulgence might reduce the number of illegitimate children a village would have to care for, but carrying such programs too far would go against a common description of human nature at the time, that of *homo ludens*, or, 'man the player'.

The Civil War

For all the troubles in England, it was Scotland that precipitated the opening of hostilities against the King. Presbyterianism – a much looser system of church government than Anglicanism – was the dominant religion of the Scots, and Charles' marriage to a French Catholic woman, Queen Henrietta Maria, along with his support of the high-church Anglicanism of Bishop Laud, made him deeply suspicious to his northern neighbors. Charles attempted to support the bishops in Scotland by making himself the authority in all church issues; Presbyterian clergymen and laity thought this was too close to repealing the Reformation and prepared for battle with the King by passing in 1638 a 'National Covenant' affirming their brand of Protestantism as the religion of Scotland and, shortly thereafter, repudiating any church governance by bishops. One battle was fought between the King's armies and the Scots, which the latter won in August 1640. They remained on English soil in the vicinity of Newcastle in northern England, an ally of Charles' other enemies, the members of his own English Parliament.

Charles had no option but again to summon Parliament to meet in order to raise money to fight his enemies. He had convened them earlier in 1640 but had failed to persuade them to support him against the Scots; he abruptly dissolved the body after only a few weeks (thus justifying its nickname of 'Short Parliament'). But after his defeat in August he was forced to convene them again, and what was to be known to history as the 'Long Parliament' gathered in London on November 3, 1640. The future leader of the country, Oliver Cromwell, was present at both these assemblies, representing Cambridge.

Parliament did not initially take the most extreme actions available to it, rejecting an early petition, for example, to abolish all bishops in the church. But by February 5, 1642, bishops could no longer be members of Parliament, this being but one of a series of actions which brought armed conflict nearer. Such conflict began on October 23, 1642, at Edgehill in Warwickshire in the middle of the country; the battle was fought without a clear victor, which was not to be the case with the war as whole.

In the early months of the war, though, Parliamentary armies suffered reverses, so that they were required to make an alliance with Scotland in the autumn of 1643. The Scots were to provide an army for the rebels in exchange for financial considerations and an agreement that the form of church government in England and Ireland (also of course ruled by Britain) would be Presbyterian – that is, that there would be no supervision of congregations by bishops. The Westminster Confession passed in England in 1648 formally set forth the theological basis for this new church, which included Calvinistic predestination: 'By the decree of God, for the manifestation of His glory, some men and angels are predestined unto everlasting life, and others foreordained to everlasting death' (Chapter III).[4] Toleration of other forms of Christianity was not part of this new church order.

The Era of Oliver Cromwell

Cromwell was the towering figure of mid-century England, perhaps of the whole century. He was a devoutly conservative Protestant. Given the charge of re-energizing Parliament's armies, though, he was tolerant to a limited degree in welcoming men of any persuasion into his forces – as long as they were neither Catholic nor Anglican. His character and devotion to biblical religion made him an effective molder of his troops, who were highly disciplined and were called the 'New Model Army'. His cavalry achieved an important victory in 1645 at Naseby, after which the King's fortunes declined to such a degree that he surrendered himself to the Scots on May 5, 1646, ending the first phase of the Civil War. Charles hoped that the Scots would be sympathetic to him, but instead they demanded that he accept the Presbyterian form of church government, which he refused to do. As a result, the Scots turned him over to Parliament in January 1647 as a prisoner, where he was housed in Northamptonshire. This began a confusing time in the war, when Cromwell's 'Independents', Puritans who wanted less church government than even the Presbyterians proposed, became disenchanted with parliamentary leadership. 'New Presbyter is but Old Priest writ large', said the poet John Milton in a 1646 sonnet, 'On the New Forcers of Conscience', addressing the subject from an Independent point of view and making a play on a famous aphorism of Plato, 'The state is the soul writ large'. There was pressure in Parliament to invite the King to resume his throne; the Army, dominated by Independents, brought the King to London and basically took control of Parliament. Cromwell resisted the proposals of the more radical Independents, who proposed abolishing government altogether. This caused difficulty for him, but when the King escaped from the army and engaged the Scottish army to fight on his side, Cromwell managed to rally his troops and defeat the Scots and Cavaliers (as the king's warriors were called) on August 17, 1648, thus effectively ending the brief, so-called 'Second Civil War'. The Army purged Parliament of Presbyterian and Royalist members to insure that they would be able to have their way with the King's fate. Charles showed courage in rejecting the military's offer to spare his life if he would sell land belonging to the bishops and give up his authority over measures passed by Parliament. Parliament, now reduced by nearly nine-tenths of its original membership when it was convened in 1640 and hence called a 'Rump Parliament', appointed commissioners to try the King for his life. He was charged with violating the newly passed law that it was treason for the monarch to wage war against Parliament. Amidst a fair amount of agitation in London in favor of the king, not least because of his stately deportment during his trial ('He nothing common did or mean / Upon that memorable scene', wrote the Puritan poet Andrew Marvell), the king was beheaded on January 30, 1649.

The next eleven years in which there was no king in England were dominated by Cromwell. Even his enemies – of which there were many – were compelled to testify to his virtues as well as to criticize his vices. 'No (mere) man was better and worse spoken of than he', said the respected Presbyterian minister Richard Baxter, and Cromwell's loyalist opponent Edward Hyde thought Cromwell an extreme in both virtue and vice: 'he will be looked upon by posterity, as a brave, bad man'.[5] The country was dominated after the king's death by the group known as 'Independents', puritans who showed little toleration for either their former Presbyterian allies or their Royalist enemies. Cromwell was increasingly excoriated, with some justification, by both as an absolutist who wanted to be himself a king. Maintaining public order became a greater and greater challenge. Radical groups on the left such as the Levellers advocated a state in which goods would be held in common – a position of no interest to Cromwell – while adherents of the King could look to his son Charles and armies in both Ireland, where Catholics joined the Royalist cause, and Scotland, which favored Presbyterianism rather than Cromwell's more independent, congregational form of church government, to restore monarchy. Cromwell again proved his military mettle in disposing of both of these armed threats, although many have charged that his army's victories were tarnished by showing particular cruelty against Irish civilians in battles such as that at Drogheda (1643). Cromwell took the title in 1653 of Lord Protector, a term used in earlier centuries when a member of the nobility would stand in for a monarch who had not yet come of age. He held power until his death in 1658; Cromwell nominated his son Richard to succeed him in office but Richard had no taste for power and resigned his position in 1659.

Church and State, 1660–1888

The English people rejoiced at the return of Charles II from his nine-year exile in France to restore the monarchy in 1660. Despite his popular reputation as merely a party-loving ruler and the image of his Court as populated by rakes pursuing illicit amours, he nonetheless found time and energy to pursue worthwhile governmental measures. For example, in 1672 he announced a 'Declaration of Indulgence for Tender Consciences' which revoked religious penal laws against Catholics and other Nonconformists, that is, those who did not attend the Church of England. This was clearly a wise and forward-thinking measure, but it ran into hard political reality the very next year when, in order to get the support of Parliament to fight against England's commercial rivals, the Dutch (whom the English had opposed militarily, off and on, for a number of years), he had to annul it. What made many English suspicious of Charles as an advocate of toleration were his clear sympathies towards Catholicism. His wife, like the wives of his father and grandfather, was a Catholic; his brother James, whom he hoped to see on the English throne as his successor, was also Catholic; and he concluded diplomatic man-euvers, some of them clandestine (such as the 1670 Treaty of Dover) with the French Catholic king Louis XIV that had both political and religious implications. Politics and religion were constantly getting mixed up in the seventeenth century, when countries which shared the same faith, such as France and Spain, were bitter enemies, and a country of an officially different faith, such as England, found it expedient to ally itself at various times with one or the other of its two continental rivals. Politics and religion became a bit less confused for England in 1674 with a peace treaty that concluded the Dutch wars; the Dutch alliance helped counterbalance the possibility of a Catholic king (James II) eventually on the English throne, who would try to unite the island kingdom alongside the French and Spanish against the Protestant Dutch. Such were the shifting calculations made about politics and religion throughout the seventeenth century by European nations.

The two houses of Parliament also passed in 1673 a so-called 'Test Act', by which all those engaged in civil or military administration in England were forced to renounce belief in the Catholic doctrine of transubstantiation (i.e., that the communion wafer and wine become the literal body and blood of Christ) and to take the Church of England's sacrament, in which there was a great deal more latitude in belief about the manner in which Christ was present in the bread and wine. What was in general, though, a quiet period in English inter-religious strife was broken by the 'Popish Plot', a plot denounced by a former Catholic seminarian named Titus Oates, who told the King in 1678 that Jesuits, in league with the Pope and King Louis XIV of France, planned to assassinate Charles and destroy the city of London by fire. Despite the fact that Oates lied and condemned innocent men to death by his testimony, an anti-Catholic hysteria was whipped up in England that lasted for four years. The plot's existence was more in Oates' mind than anywhere else, but Charles II's undeniable sympathies toward English Catholics and his desire that his brother James should succeed him made many Englishmen anxious that something be done to secure a Protestant succession to the English throne. The issue came to a head in 1685 when Charles died, having become a Roman Catholic upon his deathbed with his wife in attendance.

The succession of Charles' brother James II provoked the quick end of the Stuart dynasty. James had virtues, such as bravery and industriousness, but his ultimate lack of respect for religious toleration and for the century's steady increase in the authority of Parliament, along with a vengeful nature, all spelled a quick end for his reign. The Duke of Buckingham knew both brothers and compared them this way: Charles 'could see things if he would', while James 'would see things if he could'.[6] James did attempt for a time a policy of broad religious toleration but did not achieve the support of the Anglicans and Protestant dissenters, such as the Puritans and Quakers, necessary to make such a policy work. His obvious haste to remake an unwilling country into one with substantial Catholic leadership and royal advisers failed, so his Protestant daughter Mary and her husband William of Orange crossed the English Channel and assumed the throne of England in 1689. James fled the country to try to rally an army for his cause in Ireland. The conflict was settled at the famous 'Battle of the Boyne' in Ireland in 1690; on this occasion James hardly distinguished himself in battle, fleeing the scene of the conflict when he saw his troops were not putting up a good fight.

The success of this so-called 'Glorious Revolution' had tremendous consequences for the subsequent history of England. It affirmed and solidified, among other things, Parliament's independence of the monarch and also ushered in an era of religious toleration for all except Unitarians and Catholics. It also assured the political and economic ascendancy of the land-owning gentry and the commercial middle classes.

London

In the sixteenth and seventeenth centuries, London grew to be one of the greatest cities in Europe, with a concentration of its country's wealth and power unequalled by any other European city. In the year 1600 London had a population of 200,000, having grown by 150,000 people in just over one hundred years. This was in a country that had a total population of only four million persons, so that the capital contained five percent of its total population. In the next one hundred years, though, the city more than doubled its share of the country's inhabitants, growing to a metropolis of 600,000 persons, while England, growing slowly, had just over five million in population. In 1700 London rivaled Paris as the largest city in Europe but demographically, at least, had a much greater influence on its country, as France's total population was many times larger. London's influence was also increased by its being both the political and the economic capital of the country. In the city young men became apprenticed to a trade, as did the future playwright Ben Jonson to bricklaying, or attended law school at the Inns of Court as did the poet John Donne, or came from the country to make a living in the burgeoning theatrical arts, as did William Shakespeare, or simply came to benefit from the capital's assistance programs for the poor. There was good access for international trade, as the River Thames provided entry to the sea, and the city was also advantageously situated for domestic trade. In addition, Parliament met not far from the city walls in Westminster.

The country's population numbers were held down by the mortality rates. There were numerous outbreaks of plague and relatively few times during the century when it was not a threat to the capital. There were major outbreaks in 1603 (33,000 dead), in 1625 (41,000 dead), and, worst of all, 1665 (perhaps 110,000 dead out of a total population of 470,000). Only another disaster, the Great Fire of 1666, put an end to this last outbreak. The Fire began in a bakery and destroyed the city, which until this time had physically retained its medieval character. Its wood construction contributed greatly to the fire's destructiveness, in which over 13,000 houses and about ninety churches were burned. The reconstruction effort required brick and stone materials for building; the architect Christopher Wren designed a number of modern London's famous buildings during this effort, including St. Paul's Cathedral. The old medieval cathedral was one of the churches which had been destroyed.

London as Trade Center

London was the center of the country's trade enterprises. Regulated trading companies gave merchants the security of practicing trade as part of a much larger body. In the seventeenth century the Merchant Adventurers was the oldest of these companies, having been established in the fourteenth century and also having been granted by the Crown a monopoly in the woolen trade, England's most important export. There were also joint-stock companies where individuals who were not merchants could buy stock in a company to share in its profits. The East India Company was established in 1599 to compete with the Dutch in trade in the Far East. Other companies were established that opened trade missions to Russia, Africa, and Virginia, and as a result English overseas trade developed rapidly, along with the navy required for cargo and protection.

In the middle part of the century, as noted above, London had been a center of radicalism in politics that went farther than Cromwell and his Presbyterian allies were prepared to go. This radicalism was moderated by Charles II after the Restoration, but economic inequality was prevalent by the end of the century, when perhaps five per cent of the country was dependent upon government relief. Workhouses were built to give the deserving poor some wages, and laws against vagabonds required that they be sent overseas. By 1700, England was a leader among European nations in the comprehensiveness of its poverty legislation.

Science

The turmoil in politics and religion by no means prevented the sixteenth and seventeenth centuries from being the first great age of science. Many of the great names in the period, it is true, were not English: Galileo (1564–1642), who first used the telescope to explore the heavens, was Italian, while Copernicus (1473–1543), who showed that the earth revolved around the sun, was Polish. But there were still significant scientific advances by Englishmen early in the seventeenth century. William Gilbert, for example, contributed greatly to the study of magnetism in a 1600 treatise, and in one of the century's most important works, William Harvey analyzed the circulation of the blood in *An Anatomical Exercise on the Motion of the Heart and Blood in Animals*, published in 1628.

Science had not become so separated from literature that poets and dramatists could not make some of these discoveries important to their own work. Ben Jonson, for example, wrote a play entitled *The Magnetic Lady* (1632) and John Milton discussed at some length in *Paradise Lost* (1667) the comparative merits of the new Copernican astronomy and the older system of Ptolemy which made the earth the center of the universe. Francis Bacon combined scientific investigation and holding high political office with essay writing. He promoted inductive investigation into nature (as had Aristotle) by means of experimentation as basic to scientific research, which became the cornerstone of further scientific and technological progress. It also was a keynote to subsequent developments in English philosophy, such as the empiricism of John Locke all the way to the nineteenth-century utilitarianism of John Stuart Mill and beyond. One of the curious features of scientific advances in the century was their co-existence, to a degree, with the magical arts. Both 'seemed' to achieve startling results from carefully elaborated methods. And both Bacon and Isaac Newton, for example, believed in alchemy, from which modern chemistry had not yet distinguished itself, and Newton also spent a good part of his life studying astrology.

To mention Newton's name, though, is to name the greatest man of science of the century, who also wrote one of the greatest books of the modern world, the *Principia Mathematica* (1687), which proposed a theory that gravitation affected all parts of the universe: the force that caused an apple to fall to earth from a tree was the same as that which kept the planets in their particular orbits. Poets could appreciate the great man's accomplishments. After Newton died in 1727, Alexander Pope provided this epitaph: 'Nature and Nature's laws lay hid in night; / God said, Let Newton be! And all was light'.

One of the great organizers and disseminators of scientific research in the century in England was the Royal Society, whose history was already being written by Thomas Sprat in 1667. Not only did the Society help bring mathematical and experimental methods to the study of nature; its members also advocated a prose style that was much less ornamental and 'adorned', seeking a less metaphorical, more plain style in literature. But poets such as John Dryden and Edmund Waller did belong to the Society.

The seventeenth century was an age of transition. Until the mid-century Civil War, society, literature, and philosophy retained many of their medieval features. Kings and natural law philosophers such as Richard Hooker as well as churchmen still derived their authority from God. But the second half of the century was more modern in character than medieval, as philosophers looked to nature rather than to the supernatural for the origins of government, and a mechanistic, scientific world view replaced the older cosmos that was full of angels and demons. Sir William Temple did publish an influential book in 1690 entitled *Of Ancient and Modern Learning* which held that if modern persons knew more than those in classical Greece and Rome, it was only because they were dwarves standing on the shoulders of giants. But regardless of their relative heights, modern persons in 1700 were no longer looking at nature and history in the same ways nor from the same perspectives as their illustrious ancestors.

4 Literary and Cultural Contexts

Brian Blackley and Lara M. Crowley

Chapter Overview

Figures

Sir Francis Bacon (1561–1626)

Major Works: *Essays* (1597, 1612, 1625), *The Advancement of Learning* (1605), *Cogitata et Visa* (1607), *De Sapientia Veterum* (1609), *Novum Organum* (1620), *History of Henry VII* (1622), *Historia Naturalis et Experimentalis* (1622), *De Dignitate et Augmentis Scientarum* (1623), *New Atlantis* (1627).

See also: *Thomas Hobbes, John Locke, Masques.*

Sir Francis Bacon, Viscount St. Alban, was born the son of Sir Nicholas Bacon and a heir to power and privilege. He was noted in his time as a prominent voice in Parliament and a prosecutor of the Earl of Essex, but his lasting influence was conceived while he was still a student at Trinity College, Cambridge. Only 14 years old but already thoroughly trained in Latin and Greek, he rejected Aristotelian philosophy and ultimately revolutionized the thought of his age. He wanted to replace the Aristotelian idea of science as the contemplation and organization of eternal truths with a concept of science as a discovery of the unknown. Through his ideas of 'natural philosophy' he initiated the movement toward modern, active scientific study.

In 1592 he wrote to his uncle Sir William Cecil (Lord Burghley), 'I have taken all knowledge to be my province. . . . I hope I should bring in industrious observations, grounded conclusions, and profitable inventions and discoveries'. In 1597 he published his first work, a volume of ten *Essays*, which remains his most widely read text. It represented a shift from the elaborate, 'euphuistic' prose typical of the era. His curt, Senecan writing was no less remarkable than his opinions regarding the need for precise scientific observation.

When James ascended to the throne in 1603, Bacon arranged through his uncle's influence to be knighted at the coronation ceremony; thereafter he found more access to position and preferment. He became solicitor general in 1613 and by 1617 was named Lord Keeper of the Great Seal, the office once held by his father. The enormous influence he possessed by the position was his ruin, however, as he was prosecuted for accepting bribes scarcely three years later. Convicted and fined 40,000 pounds, he was also sentenced to a prison term in the Tower that was remitted. He devoted his last years to scholarship.

Brian Blackley

Aphra Behn (1640–1689)

Major works: *The Rover* (1677), *Poems upon Several Occasions* (1684), *Love-Letters between a Noble-Man and His Sister* (1684), *Oroonoko* (1688).

See also: *John Dryden, John Wilmot, Second Earl of Rochester, Restoration Comedy.*

Though Virginia Woolf famously enjoined women to honor Behn, 'who earned them the right to speak their minds',[1] only during the last two decades has scholarly attention surged regarding the first woman to earn her living by her pen. Behn's extensive canon has been clarified, although her biography has not. She was likely born in Canterbury to Bartholomew and Elizabeth Johnson, though some scholars claim that she was Catholic and/or born outside of England, based on the scarcity of records of her life combined with autobiographical comments in her texts, such as her concern in a dramatic dedication that others might label her 'an *American*'. Scholarly consensus is that she did travel outside of England to Surinam in 1663–1664, as evidenced by the attention to detail in her most famous work *Oroonoko*, a novel about an African man of royal parentage forced into slavery and his tragic love affair. Behn's own romantic life has fueled much speculation, including queries about whether she actually ever married 'Mr. Behn', whom she supposedly wed in 1664 (though, if so, he must have died soon after), as well as speculation (lacking convincing evidence) that she maintained lovers such as the Duke of Buckingham and the Earl of Rochester. Scholars also debate when Behn's early career as a spy for King Charles II began. It seems to have ended with a trip to debtor's prison due to wages left unpaid by the king, contributing to her decision to write for the theater.

After the success of her first play *The Forc'd Marriage* (1670), Behn began to make her living as a playwright, and most famous among her many acclaimed plays was *The Rover*, in which actress and royal mistress Nell Gwyn performed the leading part – a whore, Angellica Bianca. Contemporaries criticized the increasingly explicit sexual content of Behn's plays, labeling her a libertine, and later readers vilified her supposed lewdness. But the popular, successful playwright generally eschewed entry into the fray of verse lampoons that many wrote in response to their critics, choosing instead to praise those she admired, such as James II (in line with her consistent Tory politics). In addition to writing short novels and multiple plays, Behn translated various works, particularly from French. She also edited and contributed to verse miscellanies and composed other poems, and she wrote *Love-Letters between a Noble-Man and His Sister* (1684), a *roman à clef* that helped usher in the epistolary novel in Britain. Behn was a controversial and influential professional author 'forced to write for Bread and not ashamed to owne it' ('To the Reader', *Sir Patient Fancy*, 1678, sig. A1v).

Lara M. Crowley

Margaret Cavendish (1623–1673)

Major works: *Poems and Fancies* (1653), *Philosophical and Physical Opinions* (1655), *Nature's Pictures* (1656), *The Blazing World* (1666), *The Life of William Cavendish* (1667).

See also: *Civil War and the Interregnum, The Royal Society.*

In writing and publishing poems, plays, short fiction, essays, autobiography and biography, utopian romance, and even science fiction, Margaret (Lucas) Cavendish, Duchess of Newcastle, broke the seeming boundaries that limited female literary production in England. Prior to the Civil War, a number of English women composed literary works, but only some disseminated their writings via scribal publication or print. The number of printed items written by women, as well as the variety of their subjects, expanded during the 1640s and 1650s. Cavendish became England's first prominent female author in print, discussing subjects ranging from her upbringing and opinions about marriage to her theories regarding natural philosophy.

Born the eighth child in a wealthy family, Margaret Lucas was chosen as a maid of honor to Queen Henrietta Maria in 1643 and accompanied her the following year into exile in Paris, where Margaret met and married royalist widower William Cavendish. William encouraged his wife's writing, instructed her in science and philosophy, and later published his own compositions alongside hers. After fifteen years in exile, they returned to England, and their fortunes were restored, allowing them to publish at their own expense many of Margaret's works in ornate editions. Some contemporary readers criticized her style, her grammar, even her spelling; meanwhile, her eccentric dress and her invitation to attend the Royal Society (although she could not join) drew additional public notice. Yet, Margaret celebrated her singularity and continued to lambaste the patriarchal system that discouraged female education. She acknowledged frankly her yearning for fame: 'there is little difference between man and beast, but what ambition and glory makes' ('To the Two Universities', *Philosophical and Physical Opinions*, sig. B3r). With authorship, she claimed, comes authority: unlike Alexander and Caesar, women cannot conquer and rule terrestrial lands, but they can create and rule imaginary domains. Although critical reception of her works has been mixed, her reputation as an innovator is solid. Cavendish declares appropriately in the prologue to the prose romance *The Blazing World*, 'though I cannot be

Henry the Fifth, or Charles the Second, yet I endeavour to be Margaret the First' (sig. b*2r).

Lara M. Crowley

King Charles II (1630–1685)
See also: *John Dryden, John Milton, Civil War and the Interregnum, Thomas Hobbes.*

After the execution of his father in 1649, Charles was proclaimed King by the Scots, who supported his intentions to re-take the English throne largely due to his Protestant faith. But after Oliver Cromwell defeated the Scots in 1650 and Charles' invasion resulted in defeat at Worcester in 1651, he escaped to safety in France. There, outmaneuvered by Cromwell diplomatically, he could not mount effective opposition among European princes. After Cromwell died in 1658, his son Richard Cromwell failed to establish control, and the Protectorate was abolished. Public sympathies had shifted to favor returning to the stability of a legitimate monarchy. As the country fell into political turmoil, one of Cromwell's former generals, George Monck, used force to restore Charles in 1660. Charles issued the Declaration of Breda, a statement favoring general pardon for his enemies, liberty of conscience, and settlement of all land and debt disputes. Specific terms were to be set by a free Parliament, whereupon Charles was proclaimed King of Great Britain and Ireland in May 1660.

Charles was remarkably fortunate, as his survival and success in troubled times attest, but he was also unmistakably charming. He was noted for his almost constant good humor and for meeting even dire challenges with a smile or a jest. He was nicknamed the 'Merrie Monarch' as much for this reason as for his acknowledged 14 illegitimate children (his marriage however was childless). He was also active, almost hyperactive, as a monarch, participating in all the pastimes of the ruling class and unusually adept at dancing, horseback riding, and sailing. Accusations of his laziness stem from his dislike of paperwork – it was said that any letter of more than 500 words was too long for Charles and that he never read correspondence if there were someone available to read it to him. Another trait, however, was his great physical courage, shown as he led a cavalry charge uphill against a fortified position in the battle at Worcester, but that boldness was tempered in later years as he learned caution in his political decision-making. He was, in the words of John Evelyn, 'a prince of many virtues and many great imperfections'.

Brian Blackley

John Donne (1572–1631)
Major Works: *Pseudo-Martyr* (1610), *Ignatius His Conclave* (1610), *An Anatomy of the World: The First Anniversary* (1611), *Of the Progress of the Soule: The Second*

Anniversary (1612), *Devotions upon Emergent Occasions* (1624), *Poems by J.D.* (1633), *Six Sermons on Several Occasions* (1634), *LXXX Sermons, with the Life and Death of Dr. Donne, by Izaak Walton* (1640), *Biathanatos* (1646), *Fifty Sermons* (1649), *Essays in Divinity* (1651), *XXVI Sermons* (1660).

See also: *George Herbert, Ben Jonson, Manuscript and Print Culture, Andrew Marvell, Metaphysical Poetry, John Milton.*

John Donne was perhaps the most innovative and sometimes outrageous poet of the era. His father was a prosperous London tradesman, while his mother was a descendant of Sir Thomas More, the great Catholic martyr. Donne's own early Jesuit training and the deaths of members of his immediate family under religious persecution left indelible marks on his life and art, but he eventually chose not to follow his family's religious heritage. Compelled, however, by his early Catholicism to leave Oxford University before earning a degree, he then studied law at Lincoln's Inn in London while also reading widely in many areas, especially theology. His life at Lincoln's Inn was not all study, however. He was socially active in a circle that included other gifted youth of the day, and during this period he composed some of the most passionate and suggestive love poems in the language. Not desiring publication for his verse, he circulated these works in manuscript; these poems grew famous among the intellectual elite for their sometimes audacious wit, testing limits of poetic tradition and public reception.

Even Donne, in personal letters, admitted that he had cause for some 'fear' and 'shame' over some of his poems. Two representative and widely read lyrics, 'The Canonization' and 'The Flea', illustrate some key traits of his verse. The first poem offers serious and witty variations on the image of lovers as saints who 'die' because of their devotion to one another; it suggests that their bodies are necessary sacrifices in their martyrdom to love. In the second poem, a flea-bite is compared to sex, and the speaker characteristically uses religious language to advance an erotic argument. The blasphemous humor and seductive wittiness of such speakers boldly separated Donne from the more conventional writers of his time. Even his Holy Sonnets have provoked readers, as in 'Batter my heart', in which the speaker asserts in the final lines that his only means to salvation is to have God 'ravish' him. Donne's collected poetry, *Poems by J.D.*, appeared posthumously in 1633 to great popularity, going through many subsequent printings and editions, but his literary influence had begun years earlier thanks to manuscript circulation of many of his poems.

Donne adventured in the world as he did in books, traveling to Italy and Spain and participating in two naval expeditions (1596 and 1597). By 1598 he had become secretary to the Lord Keeper, Sir Thomas Egerton, a position of considerable promise, and he had stood as a Member of Parliament, but he ruined his fortunes by eloping with Lady Egerton's niece, Anne More, in December 1601. He was fired by his employer and imprisoned by Anne's father, Sir George More, for the deed. Later forgiven by More but not reinstated by Egerton, he entered an extended period of study, writing, and travel that ended with his ordination as deacon and priest in 1615. His studies included writing *Biathanatos* (1607–1608), an apparent mock-argument that 'selfe homicide is not so naturally sinne, that it may never be otherwise', and *Pseudo-Martyr*, an argument that Catholics could take the oath of allegiance to the Protestant King James with clear consciences, and that those who did not were not martyrs. He also wrote *Ignatius His Conclave*, primarily a satire against Jesuits, while his *Essayes in Divinity* were written about 1614 but not published until 1651. Between his marriage to Anne in 1601 and his divine orders, his family grew rapidly, but she died of complications attending her twelfth childbirth in 1617. He celebrated her life in a magnificent sermon and poetry.

In 1621 he was made Dean of St. Paul's Cathedral, and he became known as one of the greatest preachers in a period famed for its pulpit oratory. The man famous today for his irreverent verse was famous in his own time for his sermons. In 1623, while quite ill, he wrote *Devotions upon Emergent Occasions*, a collection of religious meditations on his disease, which included in Meditation 17 his most frequently quoted lines, 'No Man is an Island' and 'never send to know for whom the bell tolls; It tolls for *thee*', arguing for the unity of all Church members as the body of Christ. In Lent, 1631, he preached the harrowing 'Death's Duell' sermon before Charles I. When Donne realized that he himself was dying, he had himself drawn in his burial shroud. A sculpted monument based on that drawing can be seen in St. Paul's today.

Brian Blackley

John Dryden (1631–1700)

Major Works: *Heroic Stanzas* (1659), *Astraea Redux* (1660), *Annus Mirabilis* (1667), *An Essay of Dramatic Poesy* (1668), *A Defence of an An Essay of Dramatic Poesy* (1668), *Almanzor and Almahide* (1670), *All for Love* (1678), *Absalom and Achitophel* (1681), *The Medall* (1682), *Mac Flecknoe* (1682), *Religio Laici* (1682), *The Hind and the Panther* (1687), *Alexander's Feast* (1697), *Fables Ancient and Modern* (1700).

See also: *Aphra Behn, The Civil War and Interregnum, John Milton, Restoration Comedy*.

John Dryden seems more like a Roman orator in his writings than the first English man of letters, due to his self-conscious neo-classicism. Esteemed a genius for finding the exact expression to capture his ideas, he produced writing distinguished by control, balance, and precision. It was precisely these features in his heroic couplets that helped make that form so influential in English literature.

He was born in Aldwinckle, Northamptonshire to Puritan parents who allied with Parliament during the Civil War. He joined the poets of his day in honoring Oliver Cromwell in *Heroic Stanzas* but shifted politically to welcome the Restoration of Charles II in 1660 and remain a Royalist and Tory thereafter. He entered Westminster School as a King's Scholar in 1646 and was elected to Trinity College, Cambridge in 1650, taking his degree in 1654. He obtained no fellowship in college, showing no great promise; he later said his varied readings and vast curiosity provided him with the general knowledge essential for a poet.

His political shift was not scorned since so many in the country also changed with the Restoration, but his conversion to Catholicism in 1685, the same year in which the Catholic James became King, was more questioned. However, the fact that he did not revert after James was deposed, though Dryden lost his long-standing court offices as Poet Laureate and Historiographer Royal, implies the principles behind his choices. Many of his early works were for the stage, though they are not as esteemed as his poetry. Perhaps most noted is his seventeenth-century version of Shakespeare's *Antony and Cleopatra*, titled *All for Love*.

Given Dryden's biographical background, it is not surprising that so many of his poems are politically charged or deeply implicated in religious controversy. *Absalom and Achitophel* was prompted by an attempt by the Whigs, led by the Earl of Shaftesbury, to exclude King Charles II's brother James, the Duke of York, from the succession (Charles had no legitimate heir). Whigs wanted the King's illegitimate son, the Duke of Monmouth, to be next in line. Shaftesbury was awaiting his trial on charges of high treason when Dryden started his satire, which supported the King and his brother in the conflict.

When a London grand jury refused to indict Shaftesbury for treason, the Whigs voted him a medal. In response Dryden wrote *The Medall*, a work full of invective against the Whigs. In the same year, anonymously and without Dryden's permission, there appeared in print his famous extended lampoon *Mac Flecknoe*, written some four years previously. What prompted this attack on the Whig playwright Thomas Shadwell has never been fully explained, but in *Mac Flecknoe*, Shadwell's abilities as a literary artist are ridiculed with such clever contempt that his reputation has suffered ever since. The satire, which represents Shadwell as a literary dunce, resulted from the disagreement between him and Dryden over the quality of Ben Jonson's wit. The poem, the first mock-heroic poem in English, would become the model for Pope's

Dunciad. Given the poem's savage attacks on Shadwell, it was especially ironic that Shadwell succeeded Dryden as Poet Laureate in 1688.

Brian Blackley

George Herbert (1593–1633)

Major Works: *Parentalia* (1627), *The Temple: Sacred Poems and Private Ejaculations* (1633), *A Priest to the Temple, or The Country Parson, His Character and Rule of Holy Life* (1652).

See also: *John Donne, Ben Jonson, Metaphysical Poetry, John Milton.*

Herbert is a major 'Metaphysical' poet notable for his direct language and especially apt use of meter and metaphor. He wrote in virtually every known form of verse, even composing poems such as 'The Altar' and 'Easter Wings' that are 'pattern' poems, the lines forming the shape of the subject suggested by the title. But it is conversational language and religious fervor that distinguish his works.

He enjoyed a brilliant and promising early career. Educated at Westminster School and Trinity College, Cambridge, he was named orator of the university in 1620, a position that generally went to its brightest student and involved making public speeches in Latin on behalf of the university at public functions. It was a stepping stone to greatness, and his two immediate predecessors in the office had risen to important government roles. But by 1625 Herbert's political ambitions waned, and he was ordained a priest, becoming rector at the rural parish of Bemerton and dedicating himself to reconstructing the modest church and serving its members.

He wrote *A Priest to the Temple* (published in 1652), as a 'how to' guide for country parsons, and the text exemplifies the intelligence and devotion of his service to his parishioners. Later in his life, Herbert was long in ill health. On his deathbed, he sent the manuscript of his collection of lyrics titled *The Temple*, which he regarded as 'a picture of the many spiritual conflicts that have passed between God and my soul', to his friend, deacon Nicholas Ferrar, asking him to publish the poems only if he thought they might do good to 'any dejected poor soul'. The book achieved remarkable popular acclaim, going through 13 print editions by 1680.

Brian Blackley

Thomas Hobbes (1588–1679)

Principal Works: *De Cive* (*The Citizen*), 1642; *Human Nature*, 1650; *Leviathan*, 1651; *Questions Concerning Liberty, Necessity, and Chance*, 1656; *Behemoth*, 1679.

See also: *Sir Francis Bacon, The Civil War and Interregnum, John Locke.*

In his own day, so many responded so strongly to Hobbes' skeptical and relativist ideas that he assumed Promethean status in the struggle between Christianity and atheism. His advocacy for a secular monarchy, his intellect and sense of individuality, and his stubborn persistence in following his premises to their ultimate conclusions all made him an irresistible target of the champions of theological orthodoxy. At times the materialistic foundation of his philosophy – his reduction of all events, even thought, to the motion of physical particles – was so controversial as to put his life in danger, but his works permanently changed the course of modern thought in political theory.

He took his B.A. at Oxford in 1608 and spent much of the next twenty years employed primarily as a tutor to William Cavendish, second Earl of Devonshire, and then later to his son, the third Earl. With both young men he took extended European tours, visiting France and Italy, becoming acquainted with the work of Montaigne and Kepler, and actually meeting Descartes and Galileo. His first publication was a translation of Thucydides' history of the Peloponnesian War in 1629. He later wrote in his autobiography that Thucydides 'taught me how stupid democracy is and by how much one man is wiser than an assembly'. However, he did not begin publishing his philosophical ideas until after age 40. In 1640, fearing reprisals for his manuscript *The Elements of Law*, he fled to Paris, where he lived for the next decade.

In his masterpiece *Leviathan*, he sets out the human needs for peace and security and then offers a prescription for creating the ideal state to meet those needs. His utilitarian ideas are essentially based on a human right to self-preservation. Without peace and protection by a sovereign, people live in an inevitable state of war. His famous aphorism that assessed such life characterized it as 'continual fear, and danger of violent death; and the life of man, solitary, poor, nasty, brutish, and short'.

Brian Blackley

King James VI & I (1566–1625)
Major works: *Essayes of a Prentise* (1584), *The Trew Law of Free Monarchies* (1598), *Basilicon Doron* (1599), *Workes* (1616), *A Meditation on Matthew* (1616), *The Book of Sports* (1618).

See also: *Francis Bacon, John Donne, Ben Jonson, William Shakespeare, Civil War and the Interregnum, Manuscript and Print Culture, Masques.*

More than any monarch before or after him, James VI (of Scotland) & I (of England) was an author. By the time he ascended the English throne in 1603, he had published poems and a treatise on poetry, theoretical and practical guides to kingship, and works attacking witchcraft and tobacco, among various other writings. He commented frequently on scripture, and, an adamant believer in the divine right of kings, he fashioned himself another David via verse translations of the Psalms, which he originally intended to include in the new 'Authorized' English translation of the Bible (1611) that he commissioned and patronized. Though no longer patron and leader of his band of court poets in Scotland – where he had ruled since his mother Mary, Queen of Scots, was forced to abdicate when he was thirteen months old – James supported a court writing culture in England. In addition to writings produced by the King and his courtiers, works circulated in manuscript and print that celebrated or satirized them. Some lampooned his English favorites Robert Carr (Earl of Somerset) and George Villiers (Duke of Buckingham); though his sexual proclivity for males was widely acknowledged, James apparently maintained a sound relationship with his wife, Anne, and with their children, Henry (who died in 1612), Elizabeth, and Charles.

Both King and Queen were enthusiasts for court entertainments. James offered support and protection to actors, especially the Lord Chamberlain's Men (Shakespeare's company), who became the King's Men. Ben Jonson also found favor, and Queen Anne and her ladies-in-waiting performed in Jonsonian masques. The King appreciated fine sermons as well and encouraged John Donne and others to publish those that seemed to celebrate royal policies, utilizing various formats to disseminate his own ideas to his subjects. Such writers participated frequently in domestic and international religious and political debates on the King's behalf, but James also was an effective advocate of his own policies, vying through the press to promote peace with Catholic neighbors and to discourage radical English factions, be they Puritans, Papists, or others. Speeches to Parliament, correspondence, and other prose and poetry from his later years reveal an increasingly sentimental and anxious monarch, frustrated by his waning popularity – a problem Charles would inherit and exacerbate. Yet, James, the 'cradle king', produced a vast corpus of writings and patronized some of the greatest literary talents ever known.

Lara M. Crowley

Ben Jonson (1572–1637)
Major Works: *Every Man in His Humour* (1598), *Cynthia's Revels* (1600), *Poetaster* (1601), *Sejanus* (1603), *The Masque of Queens* (1609), *Volpone* (1605), *Masque of Beauty* (1608), *Epicoene, or the Silent Woman* (1609), *The Alchemist* (1610), *Catiline* (1611), *Bartholomew Fair* (1614), *Epigrams* (1616), *The Forrest* (1616), *Works* (1616), *Pleasure Reconciled to Virtue* (1618), *Under-wood* (1640), second volume of *Works* (1640–1641).

See also: *Cavalier Poetry, John Donne, George Herbert, King James VI & I, Manuscript and Print Culture, Andrew Marvell, John Milton, John Dryden.*

Arguably the most dynamic man of the early seventeenth-century stage, Jonson was the journeyman son of a bricklayer, a successful actor and playwright, a soldier in Flanders (where according to William Drummond he defeated an enemy soldier in single combat), and a literary figure whose ideas and followers greatly influenced the literature of the Jacobean and Caroline periods.

His breakout play *Every Man in His Humour*, which featured Shakespeare in the cast, was performed by the Lord Chamberlain's company in 1598. Jonson was close friends with Shakespeare, whom he claimed he loved 'on this side idolatry'. Their careers and lives were intertwined. *Every Man Out of His Humour* appeared at the Globe in 1599, and his first extant tragedy *Sejanus* was given at the Globe by Shakespeare's company. In total, Shakespeare's company produced nine of Jonson's plays. But unlike Shakespeare, Jonson did not write exclusively for one acting company, and he disapproved of mixing the conventions of tragedy and comedy. A strict classicist, he generally adhered to Aristotelian principles of drama. In any other age, Jonson would have been the standout dramatist of the day; as it is, he is still remembered as a fine playwright and author of court masques in Shakespeare's time.

His dramatic career peaked between 1603 and 1614, when he produced two historical tragedies, *Sejanus* (1603) and *Catiline* (1611), and the four city comedies that established his reputation as a playwright: *Volpone* (1606), *Epicoene, or the Silent Woman* (1609), *The Alchemist* (1610), and *Bartholomew Fair* (1614). During the reign of James I, Jonson's literary presence was formidable. He presided over groups of authors who met regularly at various taverns, and he wrote masques for the court. His masques displayed his classical knowledge and wit and contained some of his finest lyric verse. Popular masques such as *The Masque of Beauty* (1608) and *Masque of Queens* (1609) were created in collaboration with Inigo Jones, whose elaborately designed, Italianate costumes and sets were unrivalled. Jonson's many non-theatrical pieces, including epigrams, sonnets, and an array of lyrical verse, are collected in *The Forest* (1616) and *Under-wood* (1640–1641).

His life was renowned for controversy as well. Jonson and two others were jailed for their parts in writing *The Isle of Dogs* (1597), now lost, a satiric work reported to have been 'seditious'; imprisoned again in 1605, he was threatened with having his nose and ears slit for his share in *Eastward Ho*. He gave testimony to the Privy Council regarding the Gunpowder Plot, and in 1606 he was again in court to explain his lack of participation in the Anglican Church. His most serious arrest was in 1598 when he narrowly escaped execution after killing fellow actor Gabriel Spencer in a duel. Jonson escaped by pleading benefit of clergy because he could read Latin, but he was literally branded on his thumb so he could not make a second such escape. Jonson was rugged, fearless, but also warm-hearted, and his reputation was well captured in the inscription his tombstone bears in Westminster Abbey: 'O rare Ben Jonson'.

Brian Blackley

John Locke (1632–1704)

Principal Works: *Epistola de Tolerantia* (Letters on Toleration) (1689), *Two Treatises of Government* (1690), *An Essay Concerning Human Understanding* (1690), *Some Thoughts Concerning Education* (1693), *The Reasonableness of Christianity as Delivered in the Scriptures* (1695).

See also: *Sir Francis Bacon, Thomas Hobbes*.

Arguably the thinker who influenced the US Declaration of Independence and Constitution more than any other, Locke is most celebrated for his *Essay Concerning Human Understanding*, which provided a basis for the deistic or rationalistic theology of the eighteenth century as well as the theoretical groundwork that gave rise to the scientific method. The *Essay* is noted for its thorough expression of empiricism, its disdain for religious fervor as 'contemptible', and its assertion that science 'deserves our respect' but that its scope is limited and therefore unlikely to achieve conclusive success. His central political principle is that private rights in property are the basis of human freedom and that government exists foremost to protect those rights and maintain public order.

Despite taking a master's degree from Oxford in 1658 and holding positions at the university for the next six years, he was denied tenure because of his refusal to take holy orders. By that time he had taken a stand against state religion, a position articulated in detail in his *Letters on Toleration*. He left Oxford rather than conform. Nevertheless, his brilliance in chemistry and medicine won him the respect of colleagues and a fellowship in the Royal Society in 1668. He also won the favor of Anthony Ashley Cooper, the first Earl of Shaftesbury, and became his household physician and personal secretary. When Shaftesbury rose to the chancellorship in 1672, Locke rose also and was ultimately appointed the president of the Board of Trade.

After Shaftesbury fell from power, Locke lost his lucrative posts and took refuge in Holland from extradition attempts until the accession of William of Orange in 1688. Restored to office as Commissioner of Appeals, Locke lived out his life mostly in the household of Sir Francis Masham, free to continue his work.

Brian Blackley

Andrew Marvell (1621–1678)

Major Works: *Last Instructions to a Painter* (1667), *The Rehearsal Transpros'd* (1672), *Miscellaneous Poems* (1681), *Poems on Affairs of State* (1689).

See also: *The Civil War and the Interregnum, Metaphysical Poetry, John Milton*.

Marvell's greatest gift to English poetry, 'To His Coy Mistress', offers some of the most memorable lines in the language, including, 'But at my back I always hear / Time's wingéd chariot hurrying near. . . .' But he nearly missed recognition as a Metaphysical poet of the seventeenth century. If not for his housekeeper Mary Palmer, who found his poetry after his death, the world might never have known his subtle and enigmatic verse. Even after his volume titled *Miscellaneous Poems* was published in 1681, the work was not highly regarded. Only after the publication of H.J.C. Grierson's *Metaphysical Lyrics* (1921) did Marvell's verse begin to enjoy the high reputation it holds today.

During his lifetime, Andrew Marvell was regarded mostly as a politician, patriot, and satirist. During the English Civil War, Marvell favored Cromwell, though he was not a Puritan himself. From 1650 to 1652 he was a tutor to Mary Fairfax, daughter of one of Cromwell's generals, at Nun Appleton House in Yorkshire. Several of his best-known poems were apparently written but not published during this period, including 'Upon Appleton House', 'The Garden', and the Mower poems. In 1557, he was appointed Latin Secretary to the Council of State (a position previously occupied by his friend John Milton, who was by then blind). In 1659 he was elected to Parliament for Hull, a post he held until his death. He continued writing while occupied with political business. *Last Instructions to a Painter* (1667), perhaps his finest political satire, attacked the financial corruption and immoral conduct he witnessed at Court. His satires were so strident that they were passed from hand to hand secretly or published anonymously. Only in works addressing religious oppression did Marvell acknowledge publication, as he did for the two parts of *The Rehearsal Transpros'd*.

Brian Blackley

John Milton (1608–1674)
Major works: *Poems of Mr. John Milton* (1645), *Paradise Lost* (1667, 1674), *Paradise Regained* (1671), *Samson Agonistes* (1671).

See also: *Andrew Marvell, Civil War and the Interregnum, Manuscript and Print Culture, Masques*.

In attempting to 'assert th' Eternal Providence, / And justifie the wayes of God to men', *Paradise Lost* bears little resemblance to the English epic on Arthurian legends that Milton imagined writing in his youth (1667, sig. A1v). As an adult, Milton had witnessed the military triumph of his republican compatriots in the 1640s lead not to a glorious, ideal commonwealth but to a sort of Caesaric English Protectorate under former Roundhead General Oliver

Cromwell. Soon after Cromwell's death in 1658, that form of English government crumbled altogether, culminating in the Restoration of the monarchy in 1660. With the freedoms of religion and speech that Milton adamantly championed via printed pamphlets during the Civil War and Interregnum beginning to falter under Charles II, Milton – who had lost two wives and two children, as well as his sight – apparently was less interested in martial prowess than in the heroic virtues of patience, fortitude, and self-sacrifice celebrated in his epic poem on the fall of mankind.

Milton's faith had played a significant role in his allegiances and choices since childhood, when he attended Christ College, Cambridge, with the intention to join the clergy. Son of a scrivener (and musician) with Puritan leanings, Milton became disillusioned with the ceremonialism of the Anglican Church headed by Archbishop Laud and increasingly devoted himself to poetry as his vocation. Although Milton composed some early verse in Latin (one of his eight languages), his first published poem was in English: an anonymous tribute to Shakespeare appearing in the Second Folio (1632). Milton also triumphed in the early English poem 'On the Morning of Christ's Nativity' in melding the pagan classics of Greece and Rome with the Christian aspirations of the English poets. Upon graduation, he continued composing verse during six years of extensive reading and study (sponsored by his father) and his period of travel on the continent, where he met prominent intellectuals such as Galileo. Other works from those periods include celebrated poems such as the impressions of mirth and melancholy in 'L'Allegro' and 'Il Penseroso' and the pastoral elegy 'Lycidas', as well as *Comus*, a masque that defied its genre in championing rural life, not the court.

Milton continued to compose poems in the 1640s and 1650s, including innovative sonnets on such topics as political controversies and personal anxieties. Yet, as he became embroiled in the English 'revolution', prose pamphlets became his dominant medium for disseminating ideas. In support of Presbyterian reform efforts, he composed five 'antiprelatical tracts' denouncing bishops, and during the Civil War he wrote impassioned arguments supporting Puritan and republican positions, culminating in his defense of the revolution in *The Tenure of Kings and Magistrates* (1649). As the Commonwealth's Latin secretary, he defended the new government in his correspondence with other European heads of state. Yet, not all of Milton's prose writings were sanctioned. Upon marrying the much younger Mary Powell in 1642, only to see her return to her royalist family within months of the union (though husband and wife reunited in 1645), Milton composed the 'divorce tracts', which call for one's right not only to divorce but to remarry if necessary for establishing domestic joy and a true spiritual bond. When his companionate marriage treatises were not licensed and were vilified by Parliament and preachers alike, Milton composed *Areopagitica*, a defense of free speech and free press that (perhaps appropriately) was also not licensed. *Areopagitica* denigrates obedience gained through ignorance; only through encountering various perspectives, Milton argues, can people recognize and choose truth.

Milton's outspoken commitment to republican ideals put him in danger of execution upon publication of *The Ready and Easy Way to Establish a Free Commonwealth* just weeks before the Restoration. But, with help from friends such as the poet Andrew Marvell, Milton was released from prison with heavy fines to live in quiet retirement under the care of his third wife Elizabeth Minshull. Fully blind since 1652, Milton spent his final decade dictating to professional scribes and friends his great epic *Paradise Lost*, as well as the shorter epic *Paradise Regained* on Christ's temptation in the wilderness, and *Samson Agonistes*, a closet drama with a seemingly autobiographical protagonist. In 1674, probably in part as tribute to his primary literary models Virgil and Spenser, Milton published a second edition of *Paradise Lost* in twelve volumes instead of ten. In an introduction, he rallies yet again for freedom from tyranny, this time in his choice of blank verse as liberation 'from the troublesom and modern bondage of Rimeing' (sig. A4v). Thus, Milton is remembered not only for his inventive and intellectually vigorous literary productions but for his commitment to (and delineation of) concepts now viewed as staples of Western thought, such as freedom from censorship, religious tolerance, companionate marriage, and republicanism.

Lara M. Crowley

John Wilmot, second Earl of Rochester (1647–1680)

Major works: *Alexander Bendo's Brochure* (1676), *Poems on Several Occasions* (1680), *Lucina's Rape* (1685).

See also: *Aphra Behn, John Dryden, Manuscript and Print Culture, Restoration Comedy*.

John Wilmot's most explicit verses exemplify his belief that 'Expressions must descend to the nature of things expressed'.[4] Nearly all of the salacious erotic poems, scathing lampoons of contemporary politics (and poets such as Dryden), and other works composed by Wilmot, Earl of Rochester, were intended for circulation in manuscript among fellow courtiers, though a collection of Rochester's verse was printed within months of his death. An earl since his royalist father's death in 1658, Rochester was intimately familiar with Charles II and his court. In spite of Rochester's frequent missteps such as quarreling with courtiers and satirizing the King, which caused the Earl's frequent banishments from court during his brief life, it seems that Charles II could never part company with him for long. The King encouraged Rochester's affections for the wealthy beauty Elizabeth Malet; when she refused to marry him, Rochester seized her coach and kidnapped her with the intention of forcing her to acquiesce, earning him a temporary stint in the Tower. But his charms eventually prevailed on Malet, who married him in 1667. A lover of the theater, Rochester also charmed actresses such as Sarah Cooke and Elizabeth Barry, who became his mistresses, and he adapted John Fletcher's play *Valentine* as *Lucina's Rape*, performed after the Earl's death. Though his station barred him from performing on stage, Rochester took opportunities to perform in private for his friends, and he famously appeared on a mountebank stage as 'physician' Alexander Bembo, a lampoon of the quack Hans Buling. Rochester also surfaced as a character in various productions by Aphra Behn, George Etherege, and others, and his life and writings continue to inspire responses such as Stephen Jeffreys' play and film *The Libertine*. Just prior to the Earl's death, the seeming atheist supposedly experienced a religious conversion, abandoning his former licentious lifestyle and commanding that his writings be burned. Yet, numerous extant copies of his candid, audacious works in manuscripts and early printed editions attest to their early popularity. Though dismissed by many contemporary and subsequent readers as a producer of pornography, Rochester is lauded by most modern readers for his innovative neo-classical verse satires and his exemplary courtly-cynical love lyrics.

Lara M. Crowley

William Shakespeare (1564–1616)

Major works: *Venus and Adonis* (1593), *Rape of Lucrece* (1594), *Sonnets* (1609), *First Folio* (1623).

See also: *Francis Bacon, King James VI & I, Ben Jonson, Manuscript and Print Culture*.

The life of the most recognized author to compose in the English language, or perhaps any language, continues to fuel controversy. We know that Shakespeare was born to Mary Arden and John Shakespeare in Stratford-upon-Avon, where his education at the free Stratford grammar school would have included training in Latin and (most likely) performances in Latin plays. In 1582, he married Anne Hathaway, already pregnant with their first child, Susanna. After twins Judith and Hamnet were born in 1585, Shakespeare probably moved to London to work as a playwright and/or player, though we cannot be sure of his whereabouts until the early 1590s. By 1592, he was an established London playwright and actor, already successful enough to be resented by some university-educated wits: *Greenes Groats-Worth of Witte* (1592) labels him 'an vpstart Crow, beautified with our feathers', with a 'Tygers hart wrapt in a Players hyde' (sig. F1v).

In 1593, with theaters closed due to plague, Shakespeare published *Venus and Adonis*, the first of two narrative poems he dedicated to Henry Wriothesley, Earl of Southampton. *The Rape of Lucrece* (1594) contained such an affectionate dedication that many scholars believe Southampton to be the fair youth of the sonnets and perhaps 'Mr. W.H.' (initials reversed), mysterious dedicatee of that 1609 printed collection; others argue for William Herbert, Earl of Pembroke, though the young man and the so-called Dark Lady might not have living counterparts. Shakespeare composed some if not most of his 154 sonnets in the 1590s, for, in *Palladis Tamia* (1598), Francis Meres refers to circulation of Shakespeare's 'sugred Sonnets / among his priuate friends' (sigs. Oo1v-Oo2r) and two sonnets were printed in the 1599 verse miscellany *The Passionate Pilgrim*.

When London theaters reopened in 1594, Shakespeare joined the newly formed Lord Chamberlain's Men (later the King's Men, under the patronage of James I). From that time onward, he wrote plays solely for actor Richard Burbage and his fellows, unlike most playwrights, who composed entertainments for various companies and collaborated frequently. Shakespeare became a ten-percent shareholder in the company and eventually a gentleman, purchasing New Place in Stratford, where he lived upon retirement. Early in his career, he primarily composed comedies and histories. His interests turned in the early seventeenth century toward tragedies and more darkly woven comedies, or 'problem plays'. In his final years as a playwright, Shakespeare's focus shifted yet again to comedies later termed 'romances', stories infused with magic and revenge as well as redemption and forgiveness. Like the writings of his contemporaries, his plots often echo Raphael Holinshed's *Chronicles*, Ovid's *Metamorphoses*, and Virgil's *Aeneid*, among numerous sources recognizable to contemporary audiences, allowing Shakespeare to tap into shared experiences for recognition and, at times, for surprise. In *King Lear*, for instance, he did not offer his audience the Lear they expected – a champion who defeated his rebellious daughters and took back his throne until, upon his death, his daughter Cordelia succeeded him – but rather a Lear who, howling in madness and cradling his dead daughter in his arms, died to the certain shock of the audience.

References in *Palladis Tamia* to *Richard III*, *Romeo and Juliet*, *A Midsummer Night's Dream*, and other plays provide a means to date them, a task that with Shakespeare's plays often proves challenging, even impossible. It seems that the playwright played little or no part in the publication during his lifetime of many plays in inexpensive quarto editions. Seven years after his death, fellow actors John Heminges and Henry Condell compiled a collection of thirty-six plays as a folio volume. Numerous textual variants between First Folio versions and (sometimes multiple) quarto versions, as well as the lack of authorial involvement, complicate editorial practices and energize debates regarding Shakespeare's texts and canon. Though some readers challenge authorship of all plays attributed to Shakespeare – offering candidates such as Christopher Marlowe, Francis Bacon, and Edward de Vere, seventeenth Earl of Oxford – the scholarly community generally accepts Shakespeare's singular authorship of thirty-seven plays (those in the First Folio and *Pericles*) and co-authorship with John Fletcher of *Two Noble Kinsmen*, and many believe that he contributed three pages to the extant manuscript copy of the collaboratively composed play *Sir Thomas More*.[2]

Shakespeare's works continue to be celebrated, though they have garnered criticism as well. Samuel Johnson faulted Shakespeare for what he considered to be loose plots, application of the same manners to all times and places, overdone diction, overused puns, and lax morality. On the other hand, in response to *The Tempest*, probably Shakespeare's last singularly authored play, Samuel Taylor Coleridge rejoiced in terms that elucidate Shakespeare's enduring popularity: 'Merciful, wonder-making Heaven! what a man was this Shakespeare! Myriad-minded, indeed, he was'.[3]

Lara M. Crowley

Genres, Movements, and Contexts

Cavalier Poetry

See also: *Margaret Cavendish, John Donne, George Herbert, Ben Jonson, Civil War and the Interregnum, Metaphysical Poetry.*

As well as indicating those who favored the Royalist cause, the category 'Cavalier poets' seems to have arisen as an alternative to 'Metaphysical poets'. Instead of employing intellectual conceits, Cavalier poets generally employ frank, colloquial diction in amatory, celebratory, and occasional poems, while, according to critical traditions, they supposedly 'attempt no plumbing of the depths of the soul. They treat life cavalierly, indeed, and sometimes they treat poetic convention cavalierly too'.[5] Certainly Robert Herrick's 'To the Virgins to Make Much of Time' and 'Corinna's Going A-Maying' seem to champion a simple *carpe diem* imperative, inviting women to 'seize the day' while they still possess their youth. Yet, time was passing in other ways as well, for Herrick, Thomas Carew, John Denham, Mildmay Fane, Edward Herbert, Richard Lovelace, James Shirley, John Suckling, Henry Vaughan, and Edmund Waller were witnessing the crumbling of English monarchical and Anglican traditions and the rise of Puritan republicanism. Thus, the apparently 'simple' command to overcome apathy, to delight in every moment since one cannot predict what is ahead, and to participate in the nation's rural celebrations (such as May Day) acquires new resonance in light of the fledging republic's efforts to eliminate such rituals, while perhaps calling the reader to take arms in defense of the continuity and stability of English society. Cavalier poets generally praise tradition, loyalty, hospitality, and the good life. They also admire the elegance and the imitation of classical poetic models evident in Jonson's lyrics; in fact, many poets now labeled 'Cavalier' once labeled themselves the 'sons' or 'tribe' of Ben and held regular meetings with Jonson at various taverns.

Yet, like some Jonson lyrics, many Cavalier poems such as Carew's 'A Rapture' suggest familiarity with and appreciation for Donne's elaborate metaphors, while others are exalted religious lyrics reflecting a Donnean preoccupation with the nature of God's relationship with man. Vaughan's passionate spiritual verse collection *Silex Scintillans*, inspired by Herbert's *The Temple*, has encouraged scholars to place him, among various others, in both the Cavalier and the Metaphysical camps – categories established prior to the recovery of many texts by women such as Margaret Cavendish, whose verse might also be called 'Cavalier'. While 'Cavalier' has been a useful descriptor for poets with some common preoccupations and tendencies, Cavalier poets' verses often prove genuinely subversive, even earnest – far from cavalier.

Lara M. Crowley

The Civil War and the Interregnum
See also: *Cavalier Poetry, King James VI and I, Manuscript and Print Culture, Andrew Marvell, John Milton.*

On January 30, 1649, Charles I stepped out of the Whitehall Palace Banqueting House that was commissioned by his father and onto a scaffold. Wearing two cotton shirts for warmth, lest the large crowd of his former subjects mistake shivers for fear, he was beheaded. Scholarly debate continues regarding the primary causes for the English Civil War (1642–1646 and 1648–1649), which resulted in the king's trial, conviction, and execution for treason, followed by the subsequent eleven-year period of an English Commonwealth and Protectorate, known comprehensively as the Interregnum. But certain contributing factors seem clear. Parliament grew frustrated with King Charles' inclination, like that of his father King James, toward autocratic rule. After dissolving Parliament three times during his first four years of rule (1625–1629) due to it being unproductive (and in his view insubordinate), Charles stopped summoning it altogether for over a decade. Thanks to his Catholic queen, Henrietta Maria of France, and his own inclination toward ceremonialism, Charles was accused of 'popish' tendencies by many discontented Puritans, who resented efforts by William Laud, Archbishop of Canterbury, to align Anglican services (as well as the interiors of English churches themselves) with Catholic traditions. When forced to summon Parliament in 1640 in order to levy taxes, Charles encountered a resentful group poised to challenge monarchical policies in what came to be known as the Long Parliament – whose members became the heart of the republican (or 'roundhead') armies that would oppose and ultimately defeat the royalist forces.

Writers on both sides of the political controversy took advantage of the printing press to disseminate their arguments. Many composed polemical prose pamphlets, such as Milton's *Tenure of Kings and Magistrates* (1649), a defense of the regicide that championed the new government for readers at home and abroad. Prose works flourished generally, as both men and women produced scientific and philosophical treatises, informal essays, and autobiographical and biographical writings, such as Lucy Hutchinson's memoirs for her husband, a republican colonel. While plays suffered with the closing of the theaters (1642–1660), poetry flourished. Cavalier poets praised the good life of an idyllic monarchical past in verses commemorating loyalty, hospitality, and rural traditions no longer celebrated, such as May Day. Republican poets, on the other hand, praised the newly austere society, which they believed afforded limited distractions to righteous living. They celebrated in verse and prose the burgeoning Puritanical government and its administration, particularly General Oliver Cromwell, who in 1653 became Lord Protector of England, Scotland, and Ireland. Milton and other writers also championed free speech and free press in a period that witnessed a proliferation of 'radical' ideas and the reprinting of older literary works that resonated in new ways in this new political climate.

Many works from the 1650s criticized the somewhat unstable government and its leader, whom many deemed dictatorial. Marvell's 'An Horatian Ode', for instance, reveals subtle critique amidst praise for Cromwell. Upon Cromwell's death in 1658, no system was in place for a successor, although his son Richard briefly took his place before the regime became a Commonwealth yet again in 1659. The lack of structure for a proper republican system quickly led to Parliament's decision to restore monarchical rule. In 1660, the English invited the late king's eldest son, an exile in France, to return to England as King Charles II, initiating the period known as the Restoration. However, many writings of this brief revolutionary period – works that celebrate freedom of religion, uncensored expression, and a society's right to self-government – greatly influenced later generations, particularly the eighteenth-century colonists in America who would challenge the authority of another English king.

Lara M. Crowley

Manuscript and Print Culture
See also: *John Donne, Ben Jonson, John Milton, William Shakespeare, John Wilmot, second Earl of Rochester, Cavalier Poetry, Metaphysical Poetry.*

The recent focus on early modern literary manuscripts, along with an increasing scholarly emphasis on book history, has heightened interest in early printed and manuscript versions of texts. Though printed books proliferated dramatically in seventeenth-century England, the production, dissemination, and collection of manuscript texts continued. Many writers attempted to limit circulation of their works to manuscript copies for reasons such as print censorship, fear of persecution, concern for privacy, and lack of interest in a commercial medium available to an increasingly literate public. Instead, they issued copies primarily to friends and potential patrons; yet, both autograph and non-autograph copies frequently circulated beyond immediate circles long before they appeared in print, if they were printed at all. Manuscript versions can differ significantly from each other and from printed versions, challenging editors not only to present appropriate texts but to establish a work's likely author. For example, countless poems are misattributed to Donne, the period's most popular manuscript poet. Although over 5,000 separate transcriptions of his verses are extant (only one of them in his hand), Donne eschewed the printing of the vast majority of his poems.[6] However, they were collected and printed posthumously in 1633. Though Jonson was among a relatively small group of contemporary authors who took an active interest and role in seeing their own texts through the press, the Civil War and Interregnum witnessed an explosion of printed works, as writers such as Milton disseminated their writings in printed books and pamphlets. Various factions took advantage of the seeming collapse in censorship and the availability of printing presses to publish impassioned and often inflammatory prose in cheap and popular news books in order to inform (and sway) public opinion. The 1662 Licensing Act implemented under Charles II curbed publication of unlicensed works, muffling some such radical and sometimes slanderous voices. Yet, this Act also paved the way for the establishment of copyright law early in the eighteenth century, empowering British authors in what had become by then a predominantly print culture.

Lara M. Crowley

Masques
See also: *Francis Bacon, John Milton, William Shakespeare, King James VI and I, Ben Jonson.*

Although Francis Bacon labeled English masques 'toys', he contributed to the genre, as did writers and musical composers such as Francis Beaumont, Thomas Campion, John Milton, and even William Shakespeare (within *The Tempest*), though none more than Jonson and his partner, the set designer Inigo Jones. The English masque combined a dramatic framework with songs, dances, and (often grand) spectacle. A form with Italian roots, the masque first

appeared in England at the court of Henry VIII and developed via such entertainments as Philip Sidney's *Lady of May* into the phenomenon of the late
Elizabethan, Jacobean, and Caroline periods. Masques marked occasions
such as Christmas revels, betrothals, and weddings, and their primary venue
(and subject) was the court, though they were also performed at places such
as the Inns of Court (which provided lodgings to law students and lawyers)
and aristocratic homes. Actors took the speaking roles, but court members –
including women, even queens – participated frequently in the choreo-
graphed dances, wearing extravagant costumes and disguises. Queen Anne
and her ladies-in-waiting shocked spectators by appearing in Jonson's *Masque
of Blackness* (1605) in blackface, as Ethiopians seeking 'Britannia'. Soon
afterward, Jonson's *Masque of Queens* (1609) introduced through its dance
of witches the anti-masque, which was generally a humorous (and perhaps
subversive) performance of disorder that would inevitably be 'resolved' by
the establishment of order in the masque proper.

Feuds between Jonson and Jones and the cessation of their joint ventures
signaled the end of the English masque's heyday, and the final nail in the
coffin came when Parliament closed the theaters in 1642. Some critics dismiss
masques as excessively luxurious displays of classical learning and as
encomia for the monarchy, designed to win patronage. But recent scholarship
emphasizes masques as vehicles for monarchical counsel and social critique.
From this perspective, masques often performed polemic originating from
competing court factions, both reflecting and determining cultural politics in
Stuart England.

Lara M. Crowley

Metaphysical Poetry
See also: *John Donne, John Dryden, George Herbert, Ben Jonson, Andrew Marvell,
Cavalier Poetry, Civil War and the Interregnum.*

Establishing which poets composed 'Metaphysical' verse proves nearly as
complicated as defining the anachronistic term itself. In 1693, Dryden com-
plained that Donne 'affects the Metaphysicks' in 'perplex[ing] the Minds of
the Fair Sex with nice Speculations of Philosophy, when he shou'd ingage
their hearts'.[7] Building upon this criticism, the renowned eighteenth-century
scholar Samuel Johnson labeled Donne and certain seventeenth-century poets
influenced by Donne's writings 'Metaphysical poets', for, in order 'to shew
their learning', these poets develop elaborate conceits (extended metaphors)
in which 'the most heterogeneous ideas are yoked by violence together'.[8]
While a reader may be surprised indeed to find two parted lovers compared
to the 'stiff twin' legs of a mathematical compass (in Donne's poem 'A
Valediction: Forbidding Mourning'), such unusual, memorable comparisons

point to the poet's willingness to employ all available tools in his struggle to comprehend and to verbalize the nature of secular and sacred love. This 'Metaphysical' wit, ingenuity, and rigor pervade the poems of such writers as John Cleveland, Abraham Cowley, Richard Crashaw, George Herbert, and Thomas Traherne – poets traditionally labeled 'Metaphysical' – and appear in the verses of Andrew Marvell, certain women writers such as Aemilia Lanyer and Katherine Philips, and even some writers also categorized as 'Cavalier' poets, such as Thomas Carew, Edward Herbert, Richard Lovelace, John Suckling, and particularly Henry Vaughan. These poets cannot be called a school of Donne, for their poems vary as much as their backgrounds, pursuits, and political and religious perspectives. Nevertheless, common themes and techniques can be traced. For example, the charged relationship between man and God expressed in the graceful scriptural metaphors of poems in Protestant minister George Herbert's *Temple* is comparable to the same relationship described in the vigorous, tortured baroque verses in expatriate and Catholic convert Crashaw's *Steps to the Temple*. And Royalist poet Philips seems influenced by Donne's parted lovers in the 'Valediction: Forbidding Mourning' when she writes of the 'twin souls' of Orinda and Rosania to idealize intimate female friendship ('To Mrs. M.A. at Parting'). Only in the early twentieth century, with the publication of H.J.C. Grierson's critical editions and with the praise of the influential poet and literary critic T.S. Eliot, did Metaphysical poetry ascend to academic prominence. However, some modern scholars seem disinclined to pigeonhole these poets by assigning them to traditional categories that, though useful, involve limitations as well.

Lara M. Crowley

Restoration Comedy

See also: *Aphra Behn, Margaret Cavendish, John Dryden, William Shakespeare, John Wilmot, second Earl of Rochester.*

With the Restoration of the English monarchy in 1660 came the restoration of English drama as theaters were opened for the first time since the new government closed them in 1642. Charles II, greatly influenced by his years in France, was an admirer and patron of theater. He offered Royal patents to Caroline playwrights William Davenant and Thomas Killigrew to manage two acting companies, the Duke's Company and the King's Company, respectively. Christopher Wren designed grand theaters for the competing companies, allowing them to employ elaborate scenery and machinery. Lacking contemporary English plays, Davenant, Dryden, and others began adapting Renaissance plays, particularly those of Shakespeare, for Restoration tastes, which initially changed from week to week as the two companies vied for audience approval. Although adapted and original tragedies were staged, Restoration comedies proved especially influential.

Audiences of the 1660s and 1670s, increasingly diverse in station, appreciated energetic comedic plots containing sexual exploits that mirrored those of court members, who were represented (and frequently lampooned) in aristocratic comedies. English playwrights borrowed freely from classical and contemporary continental sources. Although influenced by French fashions in particular, English writers preferred structurally multi-faceted, seemingly frantic plots to the simple schemes of Molière. Swift variations in tone – from sophisticated wit to mocking cynicism to bawdy obscenity – were common as playwrights held characters' moral and social behavior up for ridicule in self-consciously artificial productions. Particularly popular was the 'comedy of manners', in which stock characters such as the fop are satirized while a hero seeking amorous glory chases a beautiful, free-spirited woman, his equal in wit and grace. Successful comedies of this period include Dryden's *Marriage a-la-Mode* (1672), William Wycherley's *The Country Wife* (1675), and George Etherege's *The Man of Mode* (1676), the latter a celebration of the rakish Earl of Rochester in the character of Dorimant, originated by the stage's first celebrity actor, Thomas Betterton.

Early Restoration audiences were far more interested in which actors graced the stage than which playwrights constructed the plays, and they especially appreciated the novelty (and titillation) of witnessing professional actresses, not young boys, playing female parts. Frequently, women displaced males as cross-dressers, taking on 'breeches roles' in which female characters pretended to be men. Other female roles became increasingly suggestive, stretching the limits of decorum and affording actresses both celebrity status and public gossip. Nell Gwyn famously became mistress to Charles II, and other working actresses, subverting traditional gender roles by earning professional livings, were associated with whores, often with little or no cause. The age also saw England's first female professional playwright in Aphra Behn, whose extensive canon includes *The Rover* (1677).

The quality (and quantity) of comedies began to suffer in 1682 when the Duke's Company subsumed the struggling King's Company, forming the United Company, and their primary interest turned to tragedies. Disgruntled with management, many actors (led by Betterton) left the company in 1695 to form their own cooperative company. Plays such as John Vanbrugh's *The Provoked Wife* (1697), William Congreve's *Love for Love* (1695), and Congreve's *The Way of the World* (1700) briefly reinvigorated comedies. Yet, attacks such as Jeremy Collier's *Short View of the Immorality and Profaneness of the English Stage* (1698) signaled a shift in public taste away from 'indecorous' comedies toward consummate morality, as demonstrated in the sentimental comedies of the early eighteenth century. Eighteenth- and nineteenth-century companies rarely performed Restoration comedies without significant censorship and alteration, but modern companies often stage (and celebrate) these witty, fast-paced, and salacious entertainments.

Lara M. Crowley

The Royal Society
See also: *Francis Bacon, Margaret Cavendish, Thomas Hobbes.*

Nullius in verba – the Royal Society's motto, adopted from Horace's *Epistles* – roughly translates as 'Take nobody's word for it' and points to the Society's early commitment to empiricism, as opposed to the deductive reasoning associated with Scholasticism. As the voyages of explorers and the studies of mathematicians and astronomers, such as Galileo Galilei and Johannes Kepler, challenged traditional assumptions regarding the Earth's laws and its relationship to the universe, intellectuals in seventeenth-century England grew increasingly interested in 'natural philosophy' (later called 'natural science'). In the 1640s, members of an 'invisible college' met weekly to discuss Francis Bacon's scientific writings, and in 1660 the 'Colledge for the Promoting of Physico-Mathematicall Experimentall Learning' formed at Gresham College. This 'Colledge', called the Royal Society in the 1662 charter granted by Charles II, planned to view experiments and to discuss issues related to the 'new' philosophy. Though provided a Coat of Arms in a second charter (1663), the Royal Society maintained autonomy from the Crown in order to promote independent, unfettered experimentation and analysis.

Founding Society members included William, Viscount Brouncker, its first president; astronomer and architect Christopher Wren; and Robert Boyle, who developed important laws about gases. Other influential early members included Robert Hooke, 'father of microscopy' and developer of 'Hooke's Law' of elasticity, and John Aubrey, perhaps best remembered for his somewhat empirical approach to the *Brief Lives* of contemporaries. Among early Society presidents were Samuel Pepys, best known for an unrelated literary contribution (a diary that offers illuminating accounts of Restoration England), and Isaac Newton, whose manifold scientific contributions include his three laws of motion and his law of universal gravitation.

Similarly fundamental principles of modern science trace back to various Royal Society members and publications, particularly to articles in *Philosophical Transactions of the Royal Society*, first published in 1665 and currently the world's oldest continuously published scientific journal. Some critics labeled early Royal Society writings as heresies, but most early members maintained Puritanical leanings and challenged the notion that Christianity and science prove mutually exclusive. Their writings initiated a dramatic shift away from an interest in mysterious, secretive alchemical processes toward modern scientific methods: experiments became repeatable and testable thanks to carefully recorded objective details. This characteristic 'realism' translated into narrative styles of many Royal Society authors, influencing literary movements as well.

Lara M. Crowley

5 Case Studies in Reading Literary Texts

Matthew Steggle

Close Reading

'Close reading' is a term which covers a range of subtly different activities. At one extreme, 'close reading' can be meant almost literally as a technique of reading: going back and forth over a difficult text in slow and painstaking detail, to work out what it means. At the other, it is the term applied to a highly formalized, structured piece of required writing which students produce in examinations. In between, various other shades of meaning are possible. The following four examples of close reading take four representative texts of seventeenth-century literature – a lyric poem; a tragedy; an epic poem; and a comedy – but they also pursue four different sorts of close reading. Section 1 looks at methods of reading that help to establish the sense of a passage; Section 2 looks at two representative analytical techniques one can use, once the sense is sorted out; Section 3 considers the essay as an examination-based literary form; and Section 4 considers close reading as a springboard to making a wider critical argument about a text.

Reading Closely to Establish Meaning

 ### John Donne, 'The Flea' (printed 1633)

The seventeenth century contains much which is, by the standards of the twenty-first century, intellectually unfamiliar: much which depends on mastering another set of beliefs, or at least on getting sufficiently familiar with those beliefs to recognize them when they come up. How does one get to grips with, and look for things to appreciate in, literature written in such alien conditions?

The poems of John Donne – witty, intellectually difficult, and passionate – exemplify the dilemmas that arise from this problem. Donne is often considered as the representative specimen of the 'Metaphysical poets', a literary group which also includes George Herbert, Henry Vaughan, and Andrew Marvell. However, these writers could hardly have regarded themselves as a team – Marvell, for instance, was only twelve when Donne died – and the term 'metaphysical poet' was not coined until long after their deaths, so that even Donne would not have called himself a metaphysical poet. And even if some poetry of the era could be considered as possessing a distinctive, metaphysical style, Donne's poems are not the ones that one would choose as being entirely typical of the poetry of his contemporaries: they are too fast-moving, too supple in their representations of a speaker in the act of thinking.

In one respect, though, Donne's poetry is entirely typical of the work of his contemporaries: reading it brings us face to face with a mental world that is unfamiliar and sometimes unpalatable, and making sense of it requires patience and puzzle-solving skills. In particular, reading a metaphysical poem is usually a matter of breaking the poem up into sections and worrying away at factual details in each section until they are solved. Consider, for instance, perhaps Donne's second most famous poem, 'The Flea', and for the moment we will restrict ourselves to the first stanza.

The Flea

Mark but this flea, and mark in this,
How little that which thou deniest me is;
It sucked me first, and now sucks thee,
And in this flea, our two bloods mingled be.
Thou know'st that this cannot be said
A sin, nor shame, nor loss of maidenhead,
Yet this enjoys before it woo,
And pampered swells with one blood made of two,
And this, alas, is more than we would do.[1]

A first port of call might be a dictionary, and for university-level work, this almost certainly means the mighty *Oxford English Dictionary* or *OED*, either in its multi-volume paper form or in its online incarnation (http://www.oed.com, subscription required). The *OED* informs one, as many smaller dictionaries will, that 'maidenhead' means 'virginity'. Smaller dictionaries might not, however, give you the interesting extra information that 'pampered' at this date implies specifically 'stuffed with food', rather than the more modern meaning, 'spoiled and fussed over' (and the *OED* includes various examples of the word in use in this sense, from which you can gain a precise sense of the range of ideas it usually conveys).

With the unfamiliar words glossed, a next step is to visualize what is being described, as if proposing to make a video of the poem. For instance, the opening lines make it clear that this is a scene at which three characters are present: an 'I', a 'thou', and 'this flea'. The flea, seemingly, is in the process of biting the second person. One could go on guessing from first principles about the nature of the relationship between 'I' and 'thou' (and the second stanza will provide more information on that relationship), but a welcome shortcut is provided by the notes to the *Norton Anthology* edition, which inform us that 'the narrator here addresses a woman who has scorned his advances'. There is no shame in using such a shortcut: indeed, it is far easier to work on Donne from a decent print edition, rather than from one of the many texts lacking notes that can be downloaded for free. Donne's poem, then, features one of the standard situations of classical and Renaissance love poetry: a lover addressing a beloved, and specifically a beloved who is refusing to have sex with him.

The *Norton* furnishes us with an even more useful subsequent note, supplying the obscure fact that Renaissance medical theory held that during sexual intercourse the blood of the man and the woman mingled, and that this was how children were conceived. This fact enables us to paraphrase the rest of the first stanza, with its audacious comparison between sexual intercourse and a fleabite: 'You know that a fleabite is not a matter for shame to you. But this flea is even cheekier than I am: it hasn't even asked permission to enjoy your body first. And it is swelling, with our mixed blood in it: that's even worse than what I have in mind, since I only want to sleep with you, not make you pregnant'.

The first thing that strikes one, when making a summary of the stanza in this way, is just how shockingly and calculatedly tasteless it is, even to a twenty-first century audience who generally pride themselves on a lack of squeamishness, especially around sexual matters. In the course of a single stanza, the speaker has managed to travel from an opening which sounds almost schoolmasterly in its pedantry – 'Mark but this flea' – to a complaint that it is entirely unreasonable of the woman not to have sex with him.

The situation develops further in the second stanza:

> Oh stay, three lives in one flea spare,
> Where we almost, yea, more than married are.
> This flea is you and I, and this
> Our marriage bed, and marriage temple is;
> Though parents grudge, and you, w'are met,
> And cloistered in these living walls of jet.
> Though use make you apt to kill me,
> Let not to that, self murder added be,
> And sacrilege, three sins in killing three.

Again, it is helpful to try and imagine a video of what action the poem is describing. Evidently, the woman, having seen the flea to which the speaker drew attention in the previous paragraph, makes a move to squash the flea, to which this speech – this stanza – is a response. The speaker defends the small black insect within which their bloods are mingled, seeing it as a 'temple' to their relationship. In his brilliant study of Donne, an enormous help to any serious student of the poet, John Carey observes that a recurring feature in Donne's poems is an obsession with the enormous magnification of the very small: this image of the flea as a temple, and its sides as 'living walls', can certainly be collected as a manifestation of that tendency. And the religious imagery implicit in words like 'temple' and 'cloistered' offers other interesting possibilities to the reader: how might one relate those to the career of a man who started off as a Catholic but ended up as a Protestant priest?

'Though use make you apt to kill me' is a difficult line, until one has read several other Renaissance love poems and realized that in them the lover is always complaining that he is on the verge of dying from the effects of the mistress' cruelty. (Donne, in particular, enjoys ringing changes on this joke in others of his poems, such as 'The Damp'.) With this piece of information in place, one can work toward a paraphrase of those dense lines at the end of the second stanza: 'you're practised at killing me by being cruel to me, so it's appropriate that you kill that bit of me that's in the flea: but it'd be sacrilege to kill the flea (because it's like a temple), and suicide to kill a bit of yourself (in the form of your blood that is in the flea)'. Like most jokes, it loses some of its force once paraphrased and explained: but at least one can now return to the original and read it there, and at least one is now prepared for the next Renaissance poem one encounters that makes jokes about a lady killing her lover by her disdain.

Things are wrapped up in a third stanza:

> Cruel and sudden, hast thou since
> Purpled thy nail, in blood of innocence?
> Wherein could this flea guilty be,
> Except in that drop which it sucked from thee?
> Yet thou triumph'st, and say'st that thou
> Find'st not thy self, nor me the weaker now;
> 'Tis true; then learn how false, fears be;
> Just so much honor, when thou yield'st to me,
> Will waste, as this flea's death took life from thee.

'Cruel and sudden' – and it is worth noting the elegant mimesis, the way in which these words themselves break suddenly and unexpectedly upon the reader – the lady kills the flea. Again, in a very visual way, the poem homes in to an extreme close-up on the fingernail, stained with the 'blood of innocence' (a phrase which, again, seems to have Christian overtones: many readers, for instance, may be reminded of Herod's 'Massacre of the Innocents'). In this one decisive action, and in her indirectly reported speech in lines five and six of the last stanza, the woman appears to have won the debate. But undeterred by the crushing turn of events, the speaker goes on to ring a dazzling series of changes on the relationship between 'me', 'thee', and 'the flea', arguing (with a logic that does not, perhaps, stand up to close reflection) that the fact she can kill the flea so easily means that therefore she should sleep with him after all.

One response to this poem – shared both by new undergraduates today and by established scholars up until about a hundred years ago – is to take it at face value as lyric, and to go on to extrapolate about John Donne's personality and lifestyle on the basis of it. But in the 1920s Pierre Legouis proposed a useful alternative terminology in which the poems of Donne should be thought of not so much as pure lyric giving insight into Donne's personal emotional states, but as dramatic monologues which create a character – generally a witty and rather vainglorious lover – and put him in a situation where he does not have everything his own way. 'The Flea' is a particularly good test case for this, with its preposterous set-up; the action progressing through the speaker's speech; and so on. From a literary-critical standpoint this is most useful, because it enables one to think about the poem as a story, not merely a description of Donne's personality.

Having examined the whole poem in this close reading fashion, a reader can then go on to think about the shape of it as a whole. The three stanzas, like the three acts of a play, tell an entire story, progressing from stanza to stanza and reaching a climax at the end with the speaker's triumphant assertion that he has now won: almost like the punch-line of a joke. Another way of thinking about the shape is in what might be called numerological terms: for a poem about three characters, 'me', 'thee', and 'the flea', it is obviously appropriate to be patterned in threes (three stanzas of nine lines, each stanza ending with a triplet of lines rhyming with one another). Donne's games on the idea of three-in-one-ness, one might further reflect, are delicately blasphemous in their overtones, flirting with the Christian idea of God as a Trinity of beings. One might say that the journey into the seventeenth-century mindset has taken us from the most trivial of conventions to the very heart of a system of Christian belief.

Reading Closely with Computer Assistance and for Performance Criticism

 John Webster, *The Duchess of Malfi* (1613, 1623)

In the first scene of Webster's tragedy *The Duchess of Malfi*, the unnamed Duchess of the play's title reverses social convention by making, rather than receiving, a proposal of marriage. The man to whom she is proposing is her servant, Antonio:

> ANTONIO: O, my unworthiness.
> DUCHESS: You were ill to sell yourself:
> This darkening of your worth is not like that
> Which tradesmen use i'th' city; their false lights
> Are to rid bad wares off; and I must tell you,
> If you will know where breathes a complete man,
> (I speak it without flattery) turn your eyes,
> And progress through yourself.

ANTONIO: Were there nor heaven nor hell,
I should be honest, I have long served virtue,
And ne'er ta'en wages of her.
DUCHESS: Now she pays it.
The misery of us that are born great!
We are forced to woo, because none dare woo us;
And as a tyrant doubles with his words,
And fearfully equivocates, so we
Are forced to express our violent passions
In riddles, and in dreams, and leave the path
Of simple virtue, which was never made
To seem the thing it is not. Go, go brag
You have left me heartless: mine is in your bosom,
I hope 'twill multiply love there. You do tremble:
Make not your heart so dead a piece of flesh,
To fear, more than to love me. Sir, be confident:
What is't distracts you? This is flesh and blood, sir;
'Tis not the figure cut in alabaster
Kneels at my husband's tomb. Awake, awake, man.
I do here put off all vain ceremony,
And only do appear to you a young widow
That claims you for her husband, and like a widow
I use but half a blush in't.[2]

In what follows, I contrast two possible techniques, each a set of intellectual and practical tools, for close analysis of this passage: computer-aided textual analysis, and performance criticism.

To begin with, though, one should clear up two particular details of meaning. Firstly, the Duchess compares herself to a tyrant, reduced to 'equivocating' – that is, speaking with deliberate ambiguity, so as to reveal her wishes but also maintain deniability – rather than simply being able to say what she means. The reason that she can't simply come out and say it is that it's not the accepted gender convention to do so: the general assumption of patriarchal societies is that the male should be the sexually aggressive and dominant partner, and women should be, in the famous formula, 'Chaste, silent, and obedient'. In herself proposing marriage, she's doing something unacceptable by the usual standards of patriarchy, and therefore (claims!) she cannot say it out loud. Of course, there is a particular sense in which calling herself a 'tyrant' draws attention to her power: she is able to act like this toward Antonio precisely because she has power over him (since he is her servant, her employee, and her social inferior). The image of the tyrant is one that draws attention to the power relations of the scene, and invites the audience to think about how power could be used and abused even in this, the most intimate of relationships.

Secondly, the Duchess goes on to deny that she is defined by her recently dead husband: she is not merely the 'figure cut in alabaster' (a white stone) that kneels at her husband's tomb, but a living woman. As such, it is her right to remarry. In doing so, of course, she defies her two brothers, Ferdinand and the Cardinal, whose reluctance that she should remarry is presented as almost morbidly intense (particularly in the case of Ferdinand, whose feelings for her seem to verge upon the incestuous), and as we have noted above, she defies the usual expectations of patriarchy as a whole. And yet the interesting thing is that, as Jennifer Panek has recently demonstrated, in Webster's England, at least, the specific case of a widow wanting to remarry was generally looked upon with great sympathy.[3] In Jacobean London, widows frequently remarried, often taking as husbands younger and less established men. A young widow had much to offer a young suitor: above all, her late husband's money, with which the new husband could be made a man. In addition, such remarrying young widows were proverbially lusty and sensuous, so that the Duchess' closing line, 'I use but half a blush in't', reflects not merely her own personality, but also a contemporary stereotype of the Merry Widow. The Duchess' denial that a young widow is a mere tomb-monument would have struck a chord with many in the first audiences of *The Duchess of Malfi*.

Each of these two details seems a promising line for further enquiry, and one might start by looking for other occurrences in the play of the words 'tomb', and 'tyrant', to see whether their use here fits into a larger pattern of imagery within the play. In the past, such systematic searches were very labor-intensive, particularly if one was searching a large body of text. For Shakespeare, the Bible, and a handful of the best-known authors of the period, it was possible to use a 'concordance' – a book which consisted of an alphabetical list of all the words used by a particular author, together with cross-references to the line numbers where they were used. The preparation of a concordance was a work of many years' labor, and for most authors, no such book existed in the first place. Now, however, it is quick and easy to use computer searches to do the job that a print concordance previously did. A step-by-step guide to this process, for this example from Webster, might be appropriate.

The first method of choice, for this particular purpose, is the simplest: one obtains a modern-spelling e-text of *The Duchess of Malfi*, arranged as a single computer file. There is a good modern-spelling e-text of the required sort at http://www.uoregon.edu/~rbear/webster1.html, transcribed by Malcolm Moncrief-Spittle from an 1857 edition of the play. Moncrief-Spittle's transcription is part of *Renascence Editions*, a highly respected project associated with the University of Oregon which aims to develop and distribute usable e-texts of Renaissance literature, so in choosing it I am happy about the likely quality of the transcription (but am still mindful that it derives from a Victorian edition: it is unlikely to include the latest scholarly information, but for a quick look of the sort I have in mind, that is less of a problem). Having opened this file, one uses the 'search' function of one's internet browser (normally ctrl-f, or else found on the 'edit' menu of the browser window), checks the box marked 'match whole word only', and looks for all the occurrences of the exact word 'tyrant' in the play.

This search finds the passage that we started with – which is reassuring – and, in addition, three other hits. When the Duchess is being tormented by her brothers, she speculates about further things they could do to her: 'yond's an excellent property / For a tyrant', she says, before going on to make a suggestion about another torture. Soon, the Duchess' maidservant Cariola has come to consider Ferdinand a tyrant, calling him 'your tyrant brother'. By the time the Duchess dies, even her tormentor Bosola concedes the fact, planning to hand the Duchess' body over to holy women for burial: 'that, the cruel tyrant / Shall not deny me' (4.1.66; 4.2.3; 4.2.364).

This is interesting, because these four references seem to suggest a process in which 'tyrant' starts off as a word used in metaphor, and gradually, through the play, becomes more concrete: and we can obtain more evidence of this, and more evidence that tyrants are something relevant to the play, by widening our search terms. Rather than searching for the exact word 'tyrant', one can uncheck the box marked 'match whole word only', and search for 'tyran', which now will find not merely 'tyrant', but also words like 'tyrants', 'tyranny', and 'tyrannize'. This search gives us eleven results to go at, which enable us to further document the ways in which tyranny is referred to in the imagery of the play.

Similarly, the same very basic technique helps confirm one's strong impression, based on a memory of reading the play, that this speech's reference to the tomb of the Duchess' husband is part of the play's fascination with tombs, graves, and funeral monuments. A search for 'tomb' discovers five appearances of the word through the play, starting again with the passage under discussion. After that we find Bosola warning the Duchess: 'I am come to make thy tomb . . . I am a tomb-maker', and the Duchess replying in kind (4.2.115, 140). Again, widening the search reveals other references through the play to tombs, and (not easily found by electronic searching, but certainly germane to the argument) there is also the fact that in Act Five the whole stage becomes the graveyard in which the Duchess is dead and buried. As with 'tyrant', we see a process in which a word which is introduced as a metaphor gradually turns, in the course of the play, into something much more concrete and actual. The passage with which we started, in short, sets up two words – 'tyrant' and 'tomb' – which repeat through the play.

The search technique described above is obviously a very basic one, but it gives a hint of what can be achieved by more sophisticated methods. The tools of choice here are subscription databases, led by *Literature Online* and *Early English Books Online*, which offer the possibility of far more sophisticated and wide-ranging searches. The two databases I have just named have their searchable texts in old-spelling versions, which are in some respects less convenient for the sort of search we are primarily interested in here (although more powerful for other sorts of searches). In any case, the drawback is partly mitigated by enabling their 'variant spellings' feature, which automatically searches for the most common variations of spelling (so that, for instance, a search for 'jealousy' also finds strings such as 'iealousy' and 'jalousie').

The big advantage of these databases is that they can search dozens, or even thousands, of texts at once. At the time of writing, for instance, *Literature Online* contains ten plays which it attributes, entirely or in part, to Webster: it is possible, by limiting our search to the author 'Webster', to search across these ten plays for a string such as 'tyran*', and note, for instance, that tyrants feature in several other plays with which Webster is connected, especially *The White Devil* and *The Malcontent*. That fact might suggest possibilities for further reading.

What's more, both databases support far more sophisticated search operations than a mere 'find': they support, for instance, the phenomenally powerful 'proximity searching'. For instance, if one searches on *EEBO* for

alabaster NEAR.5 tomb

– then, at the time of writing, the search locates within *EEBO*'s selection of early English printed books seventy-seven occurrences of the word 'alabaster' which are within five words of the word 'tomb'. This is a highly useful, highly detailed starting-point for thinking about what associations alabaster monuments might have for a Renaissance audience. *EEBO* opens up wonderful possibilities for this sort of thematic, historicizing research.

Of course, it is necessary to sound a number of warning notes at this point. First of all, electronic searching does not confer the same sort of knowledge as carefully reading a text. Our electronic search of *The Duchess of Malfi* for references to tyranny might give the impression that the brothers kill the Duchess purely for opposing their political tyranny, when, of course, the picture expressed over the full course of the play is more complex. A mere search for the sequence of letters t-o-m-b misses many things which might be useful in establishing that this is a play interested in tombs, graves, and monuments. There is no substitute for a careful reading of the play as a whole, with electronic search a useful supplement to, rather than a replacement for, this process.

Secondly, for various reasons, the subscription databases can give mislead-ing results. Most obviously, neither of them contains everything even within their self-set limits. *EEBO* contains page images of over 110,000 books, of all sorts from cookery books to sermons, but even this does not represent all of the surviving print culture of the period; its full-text transcriptions, while magnificent, still only cover a minority of the books which it contains as page images; and the problem of old-spelling remains. The Duchess' reference to alabaster, with which we started, is spelt as 'Allablaster' in the first edition, a form which defeats even *EEBO*'s 'variant spellings' feature. Even the attribu-tions of authorship in *EEBO* and *LION*, while not in themselves unreasonable, sometimes (inevitably) obscure the complexities of the evidence. For instance, we saw that *LION* associates Webster with ten plays, among them *The Mal-content*. But *The Malcontent* is usually attributed to John Marston. It is correct to draw attention to Webster in connection with *The Malcontent*, since he pro-vided (it is generally thought) revisions and additions to Marston's original play, revisions and additions that first appeared in the play's third printed edition. But a student unaware of that wrinkle in the evidence, and led to *The Malcontent* by electronic searching for words in the Webster canon, may well be unaware – unless s/he reads around – that much of *The Malcontent* is, fairly clearly, not written by Webster.[4]

With all of these warnings duly observed, though, electronic text remains an astonishingly powerful new tool to investigate a text such as *The Duchess of Malfi*, whether in the simple form of a 'find' feature, or in the more elaborate capabilities of an *EEBO* or a *LION*. One could epitomize this approach by considering two further extensions of the idea more or less implicit, in fact, in all of these electronic searches, that the play can be thought of as a 'pure' alphanumeric artifact. The first of these is Stefan Sinclair's text analysis appli-cation *Hyperpo*, online at http://hyperpo.org/, which can take the webpage of *The Duchess of Malfi* (using, again, the URL of our Renascence Editions electronic text); derive a whole bank of statistics about the text's properties, such as average word length; and display the text in the form of an interactive concordance enabling entirely new searches for patterns and repeating strings within the material.

The second is, at least on the face of it, more simply aesthetic: W. Bradford Paley's program *Textarc*, http://www.textarc.org/, which represents a text as if it were a two-dimensional web of words, with each thread made up by connecting individual appearances of a word within the play. *Textarc* can be set to process the Project Gutenberg e-text of *The Duchess of Malfi* (through the feature at http://www.textarc.org/Thousands.html), and it turns the whole play from being a linear sequence of scenes into a curling rind made up of the thousands of separate blank-verse lines, each interconnecting and echo-ing with others elsewhere in the play, and stretching filaments out into the crowded central space where the words tangle together. The extract we started with, for instance, becomes a tiny section of the outer rim, at around two o'clock, stretching its connections around the rest of the text.

At first glance, *Textarc* seems merely a beautiful novelty, but in fact we can use it to reinvestigate some of the things observed in our simple 'find' search of the play. We observed, for instance, how the Duchess' one metaphorical reference to tyrants foreshadows a series of later uses of the word in the play. But *Textarc* confirms this visually, drawing a line from this passage to the word 'tyrant' in the central space, and showing all the other connections which radiate from that word 'tyrant' to lines around the edge. Strikingly, all the other connections lead to a short section of the play located at about seven o'clock on the text arc: and this is the section of the play where the Duchess dies. We might have noticed this clustering from what we found paging through the Renascence Editions webpage using the 'find' feature, or through our knowledge of the play; but *Textarc* may help us if we missed it, enabling us to gain an instant impression of the word's distribution which is more visual than that gained through the mere 'find' feature. The same is true, even more strikingly, of the other word we looked for using 'find', the 'tomb' that the Duchess also mentions in her speech in this extract. Just as with 'tyrant', *Textarc* shows that this one early occurrence of the word leads to a tight cluster of other uses around the moment of the Duchess' death, and nowhere else in the play. The wooing scene, one might start to argue, functions like an anticipation of the later death scene, planting words which will now lie dormant in the play until they re-emerge at its crisis. Of course, one could gather the same data and reach the same conclusion without *Textarc*, indeed, without electronic search of any sort, simply by attentive and painstaking reading; but *Hyperpo, Textarc*, and their ilk may help us sharpen our instincts in that respect.

These are only suggestions for how such programs might be useful, and how they make explicit and visual things which one might otherwise miss about patterning within the play. Beyond this, what one might as a literary scholar *do* with *Hyperpo, Textarc,* and the rest remains, as yet, largely unexplored: but as a challenge to one's thinking, as a new way of reading an old text such as the wooing scene in *The Duchess of Malfi*, they represent exciting new developments in the available arsenal of techniques for close reading.

And yet treating the play like this, as merely a complex arrangement of alphanumeric characters, would be to miss the point entirely, in the view of the new and growing intellectual discipline of 'performance criticism'.[5] The play, performance critics might argue, is not just a patterned sequence of characters which can be read in any order: it is a script for performance, which the audience do experience in temporal sequence, and do experience not as an abstract electronic idea but as a particular performance, acted by flesh-and-blood actors, in a particular theatre. For performance critics, it is not too much to say, the words of the Duchess are only half the story of this passage: the other half lies in the work to be done by the other actor on stage, the one playing Antonio.

Particularly suggestive, here, is the Duchess' longer speech: a speech which, on the page, one tends to treat almost as a soliloquy, but which, on stage, works more as a duet. That is to say, in performance in a theatre, the audience's attention is partly on the Duchess, and what she is saying, but partly too on the silent Antonio, since his unfolding reaction to her proposition is in some ways as eloquent about the power and gender relations in the world of the play as are her words. Some of those reactions, in fact, are hinted at in the Duchess' lines. The speech pencils in Antonio's growing disquiet, leading perhaps to some sort of effort to leave, upon which the Duchess comments, caustically, 'Go, go . . .'. We may imagine the Duchess putting a hand on his arm, or something similar, to discover that 'You do tremble'. Upon the line 'this is flesh and blood, sir', the Duchess must make some sort of deictic gesture to indicate her own body, whether by merely inclining her head, or by putting her hand to her breast, or by putting Antonio's hand to her breast, or any of a number of other alternatives. But Antonio still must not respond warmly: otherwise her 'Awake, awake man' will not make sense. Thus, written into this speech are instructions for a series of actions. Such 'implied stage directions' – as they are usefully called – provide a skeleton for the acting of the speech, although some are more clear-cut than others.

On top of that skeleton, one can document and analyze the performance choices made by modern productions of the play. For instance, in one production I have seen, the Duchess did press Antonio's hand to her breast on the line 'this is flesh and blood, sir', and the audience laughed at her forwardness contrasting with Antonio's trepidation: is this a common reaction? Is this effect one which has recently been observed or one that has always been present in performances, and can one permit laughter in a tragedy? How would the line have come across on a Renaissance stage where the actor's bosom was not exactly flesh and blood, since the part would have been played by a young boy in a dress, with (possibly) false breasts?[6]

In pursuing such questions, one is bringing in issues of theatre studies, theatre history, and cultural history. Intellectually, this is a long way from the strictly formal analysis encouraged by electronic methods. And yet – as the example of *The Duchess of Malfi* illustrates – both performance criticism and computer-aided textual analysis offer accessible, and rewarding, ways into the very detailed analysis of particular passages of a Renaissance text.

Reading Closely for an Examination

John Milton, *Paradise Lost* (1667, 1674)

In Book X of *Paradise Lost*, Sin and Death, who in Book II remained behind at the gates of Hell when Satan set out on his mission to reach Earth, feel new strength rise within them because they realize that Satan must have succeeded, and that therefore the earth is theirs for the taking. Death, indeed, can smell the opportunities that await him, and the two of them together begin to build a bridge to Earth:

> So saying, with delight he snuffed the smell
> Of mortal change on earth. As when a flock
> Of ravenous fowl, though many a league remote,
> Against the day of battle, to a field,
> Where armies lie encamped, come flying, lured
> With scent of living carcasses designed
> For death, the following day, in bloody fight.
> So scented the grim feature, and upturned
> His nostril wide into the murky air,
> Sagacious of his quarry from so far.
> Then both from out hell gates into the waste
> Wide anarchy of chaos damp and dark
> Flew diverse; and with power (their power was great)
> Hovering upon the waters; what they met
> Solid or slimy, as in raging sea
> Tossed up and down, together crowded drove
> From each side shoaling towards the mouth of hell.
> As when two polar winds blowing adverse
> Upon the Cronian sea, together drive
> Mountains of ice, that stop the imagined way
> Beyond Petsora eastward, to the rich
> Cathaian coast. The aggregated soil
> Death with his mace petrific, cold and dry,
> As with a trident smote, and fixed as firm
> As Delos floating once; the rest his look
> Bound with Gorgonian rigour not to move,
> And with asphaltic slime, broad as the gate,
> Deep to the roots of Hell the gathered beach
> They fastened, and the mole immense wrought on

> Over the foaming deep high arched, a bridge
> Of length prodigious joining to the wall
> Immoveable of this now fenceless world
> Forfeit to Death; from hence a passage broad,
> Smooth, easy, inoffensive down to hell.[7]

So far this chapter has looked at two different types of close reading: close reading for sense, and close reading with a view to further secondary research. What follows considers a third scenario for close reading, one which is both common and important within university systems around the world. This is close reading in an examination situation. The exact rules and practices vary, but typically students are given a 'gobbet' – an extract of twenty or thirty lines – from a longer work that they have studied at length, and are asked to write an answer, under examination conditions, which makes a close reading of that gobbet, relating it to the work as a whole. The extract above, for instance, could well be set as a gobbet for students who have worked on *Paradise Lost*. Sometimes the rubric will set the terms of the close reading, and two sample rubrics which might apply to this passage are:

- How does the presentation of Sin and Death here compare with their earlier appearances in the poem?
- Discuss this passage's imagination of the process of creation. How is it typical, or untypical, of the poem as a whole?

Sometimes rubrics simply invite candidates to 'make a close reading of the above passage', in which case, as a rule, examiners are expecting candidates to, in effect, set their own single organizing principles (along the lines of those implicit in the two sample rubrics) around which to structure their accounts of the passage. To answer any of these exam questions requires skills of close reading, but the precise skills involved are slightly more specialized than those which can be used when one is not under exam conditions, and I will examine these more specialized skills in what follows.

First of all, it is important to get a sense of the literal meaning of the passage, something made easier the better one's knowledge is of the work from which the extract is taken. If one has a familiar grasp of the overall story of *Paradise Lost* and a sense of where this episode fits into it – for instance, that this bridge is a direct consequence of the Fall of Man – one is well equipped from the start, whereas if one doesn't recognize this particular passage, one is in difficulties: this is one of the reasons why examiners favor gobbet questions, because they give opportunities to demonstrate broad knowledge of the poem (rather than just of favored, prepared, sets of exam quotations). One can improve one's chances when preparing for a gobbet-based exam by getting to know *Paradise Lost* as a whole as well as possible in advance. The next step is to use the skills of close reading for sense, discussed above with reference to Donne's 'The Flea', to put together pictures of what is going on in the extract.

The opening part seems straightforward enough: Death sniffs at the air like a dog, picking up the scent of decay wafting from the far-distant Earth, and this leads into the extended metaphor in which Death and Sin are like carrion birds drawn toward the scent of battle (lines 273–280). Then, the two of them venture out into the Chaos that lies outside the gates of Hell and seems to fill the space between Hell and Earth. The Chaos is described as a strangely self-inconsistent space, dank and dark and something between liquid and solid. Hovering there, somehow, the two of them pile together material that they find, like winds driving icebergs together to make bigger icebergs.

Here, in particular, one starts to hit problems of vocabulary. In the above passage, under some examination regimes, annotations might be supplied on the exam paper giving the meaning of phrases such as 'Cronian sea' (Arctic Sea), 'Petsora' (a river in Northern Russia), and 'Cathaian' (referring to an empire in Northern China): the image takes us for a moment to seventeenth-century Earth, to a ship trying to reach a fabled Eastern land, in an Arctic passage now choked with ice. Given that information, one can say (among other things) that it is an apt metaphor for the condition of mankind as a whole in its fallen state, with Death and Sin building the obstacles between humanity and heaven. On the other hand, depending on the examiners, such annotations might not be supplied. Assuming that we do not have the benefit of knowing what these words mean, we will simply have to make the best of the matter. There is (one might conclude) some sort of extended geographic metaphor in lines 289–93, and we can't say more than that about it at the moment. Sin and Death go on aggregating the material they possess, using various building techniques, until suddenly the causeway is 'a bridge / Of length prodigious' extending from the Gate of Hell to Earth.

With the sense more or less established, a second pass through might prompt more detailed responses. For instance, I am struck by that repeated, vivid image of Death smelling the air like a dog. It would be fascinating – difficult in an examination situation, but fascinating – to compare it to other images of smell throughout the poem. Eve, famously, is encountered 'veiled in a cloud of fragrance', as the blind Milton imagines a fragrance so intense that it is visible to the eye. That might, not unreasonably, be the only other olfactory image in the poem that one can bring to mind under exam pressure and without access to books, but it is enough to make an interesting point with: 'here are two moments in which smell, not sight or sound, is the most intense sense in the poem'. And the interest in scent is in fact quite extensive in the passage under discussion, since a second look at the simile which compares

Sin and Death to carrion birds shows that it is more complicated than one first thought. The birds, in the simile, are drawn not by the smell of shed blood, as it first seemed, but by something more subtle: the 'scent of living carcasses designed / For death, the following day'. That is, the carrion birds arrive the day before a battle, able to anticipate what will happen from the very smell in the air. Like Death, they have an astonishingly good sense of what an odor can communicate. And the image offers too, one might note, a vivid sidelight on Adam and Eve back on Earth, now 'living carcasses' doomed by their Fall to suffer eventual death, and clearly already starting to smell of mortality.

Similarly, a second look at the section of the passage where Sin and Death start to build the bridge gives cues for further analysis. For instance, this scene is, in fact, rather hard to visualize in spite of our efforts to do so. Is there a reliable 'up' and 'down' in Chaos? How can one hover on the waters there? That phrase is familiar, and even if one can't offhand give chapter and verse for the line being parodied, one would certainly want to allude to the idea that this is a parody of the act of creation seen both in the Bible and earlier in *Paradise Lost*. Sin, Death, and Satan are often described by Milton critics (and I'd name names, if I could, in exam conditions) as the anti-Trinity, a parody of the Holy Trinity, whose ties to each other take the form of, not an ineffable mystery, but multiple incest. In this scene, it is not unreasonable to say, Sin and Death undertake a form of anti-creation, not unlike the devils' building of Pandemonium in Book I.

To see this scene as a parody of creation is a helpful idea, because it opens up the possibility of seeing it as deliberately disjointed, deliberately absurd. Sin and Death seem to have to pile up sludge to get their bridge started, and to stick it together with 'slime': hardly epic or decorous. There's something comic about the two methods Death has of cementing the soil into place: one is to strike it with his mace, hardly the method of a fine architect; the other is simply to give the sludge a hard stare so that it freezes into solidity.

The phrase used of the stare, 'Gorgonian rigour', exemplifies some of the problems one faces when close reading in an exam. Offhand, I rather think that the Gorgon is a mythical monster who can turn people to stone by look-ing at them: but I can't look it up, and I have doubts about my facts, aware that the Gorgon could be something else entirely. Should I assert that the Gorgon turns people to stone, or should I not comment on it at all so as to avoid committing an obvious factual error? Part of the art of examinations is striking the right balance between making interesting connections and push-ing one's knowledge too far. In this particular case, the decision might depend on how my overall answer is taking shape: if the keynote of the answer is to be, say, the presentation of Sin and Death as monsters, then it would be exceptionally useful, especially if deployed in a slightly non-committal way ('. . . and another connection to a mythical monster occurs when Death's stare is said to possess "Gorgonian rigour", linking him to the Gorgon from Greek mythology'). If, though, the main thrust of the answer is about Sin and Death as parodic creators, I might decide that I don't need to risk exposing my ignorance on what exactly the Gorgon is. In a similar category of uncertainty in these lines, but definitely worth including in a close reading of the treatment of creation here, it'd be worth recording one's suspicion (if one suspects it) that 'soil', in the seventeenth century, could mean 'fecal matter'. This would suggest that, metaphorically at least, Sin and Death are wading in sewage as they build. These are far from heroic figures, and there seems an almost comic mismatch between their groveling around in Chaos and the splendid bridge that emerges from their efforts.

The bridge itself, too, is obviously deceptive. There's something beautifully mimetic about the whole sentence in which it is described, which I'd be keen to try to put into words. The sentence starts in the middle of a verse line ('The aggregated soil . . .'), with the word order inverted, so that the object of the sentence, the soil, comes first, before Death strikes it and fixes it into something more permanent (the 'beach' which appears six lines later into the sentence). The sentence uses enjambment – that is to say, the major pauses don't occur at the line breaks, but rather in the middle of lines (for instance, after 'fastened', after 'high arched'), to build up its emerging momentum, and its emerging clarity, as the bridge arises out of and arches over chaos. The shape of the sentence, in fact, is mimetic of the bridge itself. But it also carries that beautiful sting in its tail, at the moment when the sense and the line finally end together: 'smooth, easy, inoffensive, down to hell'. The deceptiveness is of the sort that Stanley Fish describes in his book *Surprised by Sin*. If readers do not realize that this bridge is fundamentally a thing of evil, for all the magic of its appearance, then ultimately they too may find themselves unwittingly taking the one-way journey along it.

So far, so good, and yet by coming to grips with all these details of the passage, one has still only done half the work of making the answer. The next step is to winnow through the things that one could say, and prioritize those which specifically address the rubric. To return to those two sample rubrics offered above: in the case of the first one offered, on Sin and Death in comparison to their appearance in Book II, then the priority would be to choose material that one could relate to details from Book II that one had at one's disposal. But if writing on this passage's treatment of creation, one might pass over altogether the image of Sin and Death as carrion birds, in favor of closer reading, and more citing of parallels, for the part of the passage that deals with their creation of the bridge. An opening paragraph might begin:

This passage from Book X is a mockery of creation, in which Death tries to assume, almost comically, the role of a creator. My close reading will explore, in particular, the elements of the parodic in Sin and Death's building of the bridge . . .

Reading Closely to Establish an Independent Critical Perspective

William Wycherley, *The Country Wife* (1675)

In Wycherley's archetypical Restoration comedy, Mr. Pinchwife has married late in life. He has selected the bride he feels is least likely to be unfaithful to him: Margery – young, innocent, and country-bred. However, as soon as the newly married Margery is brought to the city, young men try to get to know her, in spite of – and actually helped by – Pinchwife's inept efforts to keep them away. In this scene, Pinchwife has ordered Margery to write an insulting letter rebuffing the advances of one of them, the young rake Horner. This, however, gives Margery other ideas.

MRS PINCHWIFE: 'For Mr Horner –' so. I am glad he [Mr. Pinchwife] has told me his name. Dear Mr Horner – but why should I send thee such a letter, that will vex thee, and make thee angry with me? Well, I will not send it. . . . Ay, but then my husband will kill me – for I see plainly, he won't let me love Mr Horner. But what care I for my husband? I won't, so I won't, send poor Mr Horner such a letter – but then my husband. . . . But oh, what if I writ at bottom, 'my husband made me write it'? Ay, but then my husband would see't. Can one have no shift? Ah, a London woman would have had a hundred presently. Stay – what if I should write a letter, and wrap it up like this, and write upon't too? Ay, but then my husband would see't. I don't know what to do – but yet i'vads I'll try, so I will – for I will not send this letter to poor Mr Horner, come what will on't.

She writes, and repeats what she hath writ.

'Dear, sweet Mr Horner' – so – 'My husband would have me send you a base, rude, unmannerly letter, but I won't' – so – 'and would have me forbid you loving me, but I won't' – so – 'and would have me say to you, I hate you poor Mr Horner, but I won't tell a lie for him' – there – 'for I'm sure if you and I were in the country at cards together' – so – 'I could not help treading on your toe under the table' – so – 'or rubbing knees with you, and staring in your face, till you saw me' – very well – 'and then looking down, and blushing for an hour together' – so – 'but I must make haste before my husband come; and now he has taught me to write letters, you shall have longer ones from me, who am,

Dear, dear, poor dear Mr. Horner, Your most humble friend, and servant to command till death, Margery Pinchwife.[8]

Margery's speech is a lovely piece of writing, halfway between model letter and soliloquy, and its structure repays minute attention. In what follows, I read the speech closely and without preconceptions, as a way of finding a point of view which I can extend into a broader argument about the play.

Firstly, then, one might remark that it is typical of Pinchwife's ineptitude that his very attempts to keep her apart from Horner are the means by which she learns Horner's name. (And Horner's name is of course significant: he is the man who will cause horns to grow upon Pinchwife's forehead, in that he will turn Pinchwife into a cuckold by seducing Margery). 'Dear Mr Horner', which is the formula for starting a letter, becomes the means by which it occurs to Margery that Horner might be dear to her, which she amplifies in her later expansion of the phrase to 'Dear, sweet Mr Horner'. But then she breaks off, and rebels against what Pinchwife wants her to do – 'but why should I?', resolving for a moment on another course of action until another objection occurs – 'Ay, but then my husband . . .'. Throughout the whole of the speech, as if struggling with a good and bad angel, Margery oscillates between considering what she wants to do and considering the reasons why she can't do it. (If you have come across Marlowe's *Dr. Faustus*, with its struggle between good and bad angels, you may recall that the word 'psychomachia' is used by Marlowe critics to describe that effect. I might be tempted to reapply it here.) The effect of this dispute within herself is one of stream-of-consciousness, something amplified by the language and syntax she uses. Look at the way her speech is dotted with interjections ('Ay', 'Ah', 'so'), one comically mild oath ('i'vads'), and a couple of 'tag clauses' which merely repeat what has already been said ('so I won't', 'so I will'). The Duchess of Malfi does not speak like this. Where the Duchess' verse is polished, streamlined, and precise, Margery's prose registers the doubts and uncertainties of a wavering mind.

Furthermore, the stream-of-consciousness effect is especially noticeable in the first edition, now accessible via *EEBO*. In an effort to regularize the presentation, modern editions, such as Dixon's, add quotation marks to differentiate the words that she writes and speaks from those that she merely speaks. Modern editions also introduce full stops, question marks, and ellipses, when in the original, most of the breaks between the fragments of Margery's thought are marked in all the same manner, with a series of dashes. Dixon's modernization imposes on Margery's speech a sense of structure and organization that, in the first printed edition, it does not quite possess.

What's also elegant is the way that each restriction placed on Margery, each reason why she cannot do what seems to her only polite and reasonable, pushes her a little closer toward duplicity. By halfway through the first block of her speech, she is considering that she needs a 'shift'. 'Shift' is the kind of word that repays investigation using the online *OED*, http://www.oed.com. Margery uses the word, initially, in what *OED* labels sense 3: 'an expedient, an ingenious device for effecting some purpose' (*OED, n.* 3). But, as the *OED* also demonstrates, the word quickly tips over into a word for a sort of subterfuge (*OED, n.* 4): and, in particular, for a sexual subterfuge, an overtone enabled here by the reference to the idea that a sophisticated 'London woman' would know what to do (as opposed to the simplicity and ignorance of a country woman).

And this, of course, exemplifies in miniature one of the major oppositions of the play, reflected even in its title: between country and city. This opposition is usually associated with a specific literary genre, the pastoral, in which the countryside is perceived as a place of timeless ideal simplicity, in opposition to the corruption of the city. In a sense, *The Country Wife* can be considered a perverted version of pastoral. In 'normal' pastoral – of which one might take Shakespeare's *As You Like It* as a convenient symbol – sophisticated characters from the city or court come to the country world, and are changed for the better: but in *The Country Wife* a woman from the country comes to the city, and is changed. It is up to the audience (who, since they are watching the play inside a professional playhouse, inevitably belong to the city world) to decide whether she is changed for the worse.

What's more, in early modern literature the very word 'country' carries a lewd sexual pun, as in *Hamlet*'s discussion of 'country matters'. That's not to say that every time the word 'country' is used, it means (and means only) its lewd meaning. The situation is the same as with other Renaissance words with potentially obscene meanings, such as 'die', which can sometimes (but only sometimes) be a synonym for 'achieve orgasm': or, in contemporary use, words such as 'ball', whose potentially obscene meaning is only active in a small subset of the many daily uses of the word. All the same, the obscene meaning of 'country' is potentially present throughout this play, and may sometimes be activated for an audience.

Careful reading of the play (perhaps helped by use of an e-text, as discussed in the previous section) will lead one to many uses of the country/city opposition in the play, and some particularly interesting ones in the context of discussions of sexual relations: for instance, Dorilant's declaration that 'a mistress should be like a little country retreat near the town, not to dwell in constantly, but only for a night and away' (1.1.196–8). In passages like these, the countryside is associated with innocence and exploitability: very much like Margery. Indeed, the speech we're looking at is interesting, since, in a play whose scenes are all set in Restoration London, her account of what she would do with Horner if she were in the country is one of the very few moments in the drama that permits for a moment even an imaginary escape from the high-pressure, high-speed world of central London.

What do we learn about the countryside from her speech? In the country-side, the recreation of choice, it seems, is to sit and play cards, in implicit contrast to the expensive and glamorous city recreations we see in the play, of attending plays and going shopping. Flirtation is at once more direct, more coy, and somehow more wholesome, since what Margery imagines herself and Horner doing, here, seems to stop at the level of rubbing knees and 'blushing for an hour together'. It is hard to imagine one of the town ladies of the play rubbing knees with a suitor, or blushing at anything (and cf. 5.4.110–114). Innocence is lost in Wycherley's London, but in passages like these one might be invited to feel a pang of regret for its passing.

That sense of exploitation is made particularly poignant, one might also observe, by the phrasing of her sign-off: 'Your most humble friend, and servant to command till death'. Clearly, this overenthusiastic phrase is one into which she has been led by her growing sense of Horner's loveliness, itself fed by Pinchwife's prohibitions. But in the wording which so precisely echoes the 'till death do us part' of the marriage service, Margery becomes for a moment a figure like Milton's Eve. We are reminded that what she is being tempted toward, adultery, is a breaking of the holy sacrament of marriage (even though that sacrament is already being abused by Pinchwife's bad behavior to her). This choice of words draws the audience's attention (though not perhaps Margery's) to the seriousness of what is at stake.

And, of course, a final irony – Margery is, initially, right: the insulting letter that Pinchwife has requested *is* an unmannerly letter to send, unmannerly by country manners, unmannerly by town manners. Nonetheless, the con-sequences of her innocent subterfuge to do the decent thing take her further away from her country origins and start to wind her into the deceiving ways of the city.

Hence, one might argue, this speech is double-edged. It is partly a joke on Margery's gaucheness; partly a joke on Pinchwife, whom she nevertheless manages to trick; but partly too an indirect condemnation of London, since her gaucheness throws into sharp relief the wickedness of the city, particu-larly since this speech offers such a minute anatomy of a stage in the process by which she becomes entangled into that wickedness. For 'us', the town-dwelling audience of Margery's speech, the satire here is double-edged. It's not just about how Margery is losing what she had, but about how much we all have lost already.

Having come this far, through close reading, I note that the reading I've developed seems to be at odds with the general thrust of a lot of what is said and thought about the play. In general, most literary criticism of Wycherley is very eager to assert the play's general cynicism and lack of sentimentality. Few modern critics are so helpfully unambiguous as the nineteenth-century writer Macaulay, whose description of the play as 'heartless and profligate' is widely quoted, but it's fair to say that, in general, criticism tends to assume that there's no room for eighteenth-century-style sentiment in Restoration comedy. Nor have the female characters been the center of attention in this play. In recent influential readings, *The Country Wife* is considered, principally, as a play about the men: a play about male friendship or what constitutes the ideal of masculinity, or male competition in which the women aren't much more than tokens whose possession makes a man a winner.

This gives one something with which to disagree. Starting from what one finds in a close reading of this passage, and extending it to the rest of the play, one can look for suggestions that we could and should take Margery a little more seriously as a realistically conceived and sympathetically represented character. One might propose, for the sake of argument, that one should see the play more as if it were like a later 'sentimental comedy', a close-up character study of a falling woman. Of course, fully developing this reading would be an uphill struggle, since much of the play does indeed seem rather indubitably cynical; nor is the reading entirely original, since much Wycherley criticism is already more nuanced, and more interested in Wycherley as a moralist, than the brief summary at the start suggested. But close reading is the technique that can get one started.

In this chapter, then, we have looked at four varieties of close reading: close reading to establish meaning; close reading using analytical tools; close reading as an examination-based discipline, and close reading as a way of starting to establish an independent critical perspective. Each of these approaches is valuable in its own way, and, taken together, all of them suggest the fundamental value of close reading as a basic critical method.

6 Case Studies in Reading Critical Texts: Four Classics of Scholarship

James Hirsh

Chapter Overview

Like human beings, scholarly works have varying life-spans. Some are still-born in that they never have much of an impact on the development of scholarship. Some have an immediate impact but quickly become out-of-date. However, a few works of scholarship provoke lively interest for many years despite very significant social and cultural changes. This chapter will explore four such classics of scholarship.

 Stanley Fish, *Self-Consuming Artifacts* (1972)

Among the classics of audience response criticism are two books by Stanley Fish: *Surprised by Sin: The Reader* in Paradise Lost and *Self-Consuming Artifacts: The Experience of Seventeenth-Century Literature*.[1] There are several subcategories of audience response criticism. Reception studies, for example, focus on evidence of actual responses to a literary work (sales data, book reviews, critical commentary, adaptations by later writers, etc.). Fish's approach, which he labels 'affective stylistics', focuses instead on the responses that particular features of a work seem to have been designed by the author to produce in a reader.

Influenced by Platonic philosophy, Fish builds the conceptual framework for *Self-Consuming Artifacts* on a contrast between rhetoric and dialectic:

> A presentation is rhetorical if . . . whatever one is told can be placed and contained within the categories and assumptions of received systems of knowledge. A dialectical presentation, on the other hand, is disturbing, for it requires of its readers a searching and rigorous scrutiny of everything they believe in and live by.[2]

According to Fish, a dialectical work of literature is self-consuming in two senses. It consumes the *reader's self* that complacently accepted conventional beliefs, and it also consumes *itself*, negates itself, in that it establishes an intellectual structure that it then dismantles. Fish argues that a number of canonical seventeenth-century English works fit his description of self-consuming artifacts.

Death's Duell, the last sermon delivered by the great lyric poet and preacher John Donne before his death in 1631, encourages listeners or readers to exercise their reason, their faculties of making distinctions and organizing ideas in logical sequences, but Donne's eventual goal was to discredit rationality as a way of understanding Christian doctrine, which must be accepted on faith alone. Fish demonstrates Donne's strategy by closely analyzing particular passages, such as the following:

> And therefore as the *Mysteries* of our *Religion*, are *not* the *objects* of *our reason*, but *by faith we rest* on *God's decree* and purpose, . . . so *Gods decrees* are ever to be considered in the *manifestations* thereof.[3]

Even though the passage explicitly denies that the mysteries of God's decrees are approachable by reason, Donne entices listeners to approach the topic in precisely this way by framing the idea as if it were a logical deduction ('therefore', 'as . . . so'). On a larger scale Donne encourages listeners to believe that he will provide a systematic taxonomy of the '*manifestations*' of the biblical decree '*Unto God the Lord belong the issues of death*'.[4] It turns out, however, that all the manifestations are basically the same. Life in the womb is a kind of death, as is each stage of a person's life after birth. Familiar distinctions are made to seem illusory, and logical organization is made to seem inadequate. 'As a result, the experience of the sermon becomes a cycle of frustrations'.[5]

Instead of merely being told about the inadequacy of reasoning as a means of understanding God's decrees, readers are made to experience that inadequacy. According to Fish, the effect of this on Christian listeners would be to reinforce their unconditional faith in biblical teachings.

A problem with Fish's argument is that the contrast Fish initially establishes between rhetoric and dialectic becomes almost reversed in the section on Donne. In this section the opposite of dialectic is not rhetoric as defined earlier by Fish – the complacent acceptance of conventional beliefs – but rationality (which is not necessarily complacent and which might lead one to unconventional conclusions). Also, what Fish calls dialectic in the section on Donne actually fits the definition of rhetoric supplied earlier. As Fish notes, the effect of Donne's sermon depends on his audience's pre-existing faith in Christian doctrine. The beliefs Donne was promoting were not merely conventional in Donne's society but enforced by law; one could be severely punished for refusing to accept the teachings of the Church. Instead of encouraging 'scrutiny of everything they believe in', the sermon, according to Fish, actively discourages scrutiny of the conventional Christian beliefs of Donne's listeners. In the body of Fish's text, dialectic and rhetoric take on rather different meanings than those initially asserted by Fish. Dialectic generally turns out to mean the promotion of an unquestioning transcendentalism, and rhetoric to mean anything that might distract one from such a belief, including not only crass worldly wisdom but also rationality, pragmatism, and empiricism. Several babies get thrown out with the bath water.

In his *Essays* (initially published in 1597 and greatly expanded in editions published in 1612 and 1625), Francis Bacon discusses a wide variety of topics, from love to usury. Fish argues that the real subject of each of these essays is not the topic itself but instead received opinion on the topic. Bacon's purpose is not to supply a reader with a compendium of reliable wisdom about the topic but rather to arouse, on the basis of the reader's own experience, skepticism about received opinions. Typically, Bacon expresses a received opinion as if it were unquestionably valid but then immediately presents evidence or another received opinion that conflicts with the initial opinion. In 'Of Simulation and Dissimulation' Bacon at first seems to endorse conventional morality by making a sweeping condemnation of all forms of concealment and deceit. But the essay subtly undermines this position, as illustrated by the closing sentence:

> Certainly the ablest men that ever were have had all an openness and frankness of dealing; and a name of certainty and veracity; but . . . when they thought the case indeed required dissimulation, if then they used it, it came to pass that the former opinion spread abroad of their good faith, and clearness of dealing made them almost invisible.[6]

This resembles the off-the-record response of a politician when asked to identify the most important character trait for a politician: 'Sincerity – if you can fake that, you've got it made'. The first clause in Bacon's sentence seems an unambiguous and emphatic ('Certainly') affirmation of conventional morality. A subtle shift begins when Bacon notes that 'the ablest men' also have 'a name' (a reputation) for veracity. By the end of the sentence, readers are told that this reputation for honesty is useful when these men decide that it is necessary to deceive people! In some cases, Bacon makes a sentimental assertion and then supplies a supposed illustration that demolishes the assertion with deadpan irony, as in this example from 'Of Goodness and Goodness of Nature':

> The inclination to goodness is imprinted deeply in the nature of man; inasmuch that if it not issue towards men, it will take unto other living creatures; as is seen in the Turks, a cruel people, who nevertheless are kind to beasts . . . a Christian boy in Constantinople had like to have been stoned for gagging in a waggishness [strangling for amusement] a long-billed fowl.[7]

A good title for this chapter of Fish's book would have been 'Surprised by Cynicism'.

Perhaps imitating Donne and Bacon, Fish misleads his own readers in his chapter on Bacon. After demonstrating that Bacon misleads readers and undermines an intellectual framework he himself sets up, Fish ends the chapter by nevertheless excluding Bacon's essays from the category of self-consuming dialectical artifacts. Bacon's intention in undermining conventional wisdom was not to lead readers to a transcendental vision but rather to lead them to a more accurate and sophisticated worldly wisdom, a better understanding of the physical world, human psychology, politics, and so on. Fish disparagingly contrasts Bacon's 'Method' to dialectic:

> Although the object of both is to change the mind, one works a profound, the other a superficial, change. . . . Method, in short, bypasses the soul. . . . Dialectic, on the other hand, is soul-centered. . . . Method reduces all minds to a common level, the level of empirical observation. Dialectic raises the level of the mind, and raises it to the point where it becomes indistinguishable from the object of its search, and so disappears.[8]

According to Fish,

> while the dialogues of Plato and the sermons of Donne are self-consuming, Bacon's *Essays* are merely self-regulating.[9] (154)

By 'self-regulating', Fish means self-correcting. Because science is based on 'empirical observation', the scientific method can correct its own errors. If a new observation is in conflict with a current scientific theory, the theory is corrected to accommodate the new piece of evidence. Dialectic, on the other hand, makes assertions that cannot be tested against evidence and so are unassailable but also incorrigible.

What makes Fish's denigration of scientific method incongruous is that throughout *Self-Consuming Artifacts*, Fish's own method is generally much closer to the scientific method than to dialectic. Unlike Donne, who expected listeners to accept unquestioningly the validity of religious pronouncements, Fish attempts to convince readers of the validity of his assertions about the methods and purposes of literary figures by a systematic presentation of carefully analyzed evidence. In the chapter on Bacon, Fish gives his own readers an experience not of being compelled to accept doctrines on the basis of faith but of the trial-and-error empirical methodology that he explicitly denigrates. Fish first presents evidence that Bacon employed tactics similar to those of Donne, evidence that supports the hypothesis that the two writers belong in the same category. Fish then presents evidence of differences between Bacon and Donne that outweigh the similarities, and as a result Fish and readers correct the faulty hypothesis and arrive at the more reasonable conclusion that the two writers belong in different categories.

As Fish demonstrates, the poetry of George Herbert explores the dilemma of a Protestant who earnestly believes that, as a result of inherent sinfulness, human beings deserve damnation and that salvation, for those who are saved, is entirely the result of Christ's sacrifice. In poem after poem, the speaker seeks to *do* something but realizes that the impulse to exert personal agency or individual identity is not only futile but a potentially sinful assertion of independence from God. The more adept a poet is as a poet the more his poems run the risk of highlighting his poetic skill rather than serving as a transparent medium for the glorification of God. Herbert explores this dilemma not merely by depicting a speaker who is ensnared in it, but by ensnaring a reader (at least a reader who already shares Herbert's Protestant faith). The appearance on the printed page of one of Herbert's most famous poems, 'The Altar', takes the form of an altar. Even before reading the first line, a reader is tempted to admire the poet's ingenuity. As the poem progresses, however, a reader is carried along by the speaker's passionate attribution of agency to God. The reader begins with a perception of human agency but is led to alter his or her perception. Fish correctly notes that a pun on altar/alter 'is not beyond Herbert',[10] but he fails to note that a reader's recognition of a clever pun that alludes to his own experience in reading the poem might paradoxically swing the balance back toward an admiration of the poet's skill.

Fish argues that the title of the allegorical narrative *Pilgrim's Progress* (1678–1684) by John Bunyan is ironic. Like Herbert, Bunyan believed that human beings are incapable on their own of making 'progress' toward salvation. In the narrative itself, characters often do seem to be making spiritual progress: they seem to learn from their mistakes. But in subsequent episodes, the same characters make the same mistakes again. A reader who assumes that on a given occasion the character has finally learned his lesson has not learned his lesson. Like the characters, readers repeatedly experience their own fallibility. According to Fish, Bunyan's strategy instills in readers 'a *blind* trust in God' (Fish's emphasis).[11] It discredits 'the evidence of things seen in favor of the inner light of faith'.[12]

In 1642 John Milton published *The Reason of Church Government*, which attacked the episcopal organization of the Anglican Church. Fish argues that the title of this tract, which suggests that it will present a reasoned argument, is (like the title of Bunyan's allegory) intentionally misleading. Milton believed that the Presbyterian form of church government is prescribed by the Bible, the infallible word of God, and so must be accepted as a matter of faith that is not open to reasoned debate. According to Fish, Milton sought to arouse expectations of reasoned discourse only to discredit reasoning as a method of deciding the issue. This argument is unconvincing. Fish points out numerous logical fallacies in the treatise and passages in which Milton engages in name-calling and ascribes guilt by association. Rather than discrediting reason, the treatise discredits these flagrantly irrational tactics. According to Fish, the treatise is 'insulting' to readers, who are 'bullied'.[13] In each of the other works discussed by Fish, the author plays tricks on readers, but the tricks are artistically sophisticated, whereas the tactics of *The Reason of Church Government* described by Fish seem crude, heavy-handed, and clumsy. Fish was perhaps lured into convincing himself that Milton intentionally employed a strategy similar to that of Bunyan simply because Milton's title makes a false claim. Fish also fails to explore the problem posed by the fact that the blind faith Milton sought to arouse was at odds with the blind faith Donne sought to arouse. Because blind faith is not 'self-regulating', one must choose on the basis of blind faith which blind faith to choose.

As Fish entertainingly shows, in *The Anatomy of Melancholy*, a treatise first published in 1621, Robert Burton keeps promising a systematic account of forms of madness but pervasively undermines his own assertions, conventional wisdom, and the complacency of readers. The enormous book is dense with quotations from authorities that conflict with one another and so lose authority (as occurs on a much smaller scale in Bacon's essays). Although seemingly restricted to a limited area of human behavior, the work turns out to encompass all of human behavior because all human beings (Burton excludes neither himself nor his readers) are fools and madmen, as illustrated by everything they do. Burton divides and subdivides madness into countless types and subtypes, but this structure is itself demonstrably mad because, it turns out, forms of madness cannot be neatly differentiated from one another. Burton encourages readers to hope that some exception – some form of sanity – exists, but this hope is repeatedly dashed. Fish argues, however, that (unlike Donne, Herbert, Bunyan, and Milton) Burton arrives at utter 'negativity'.[14] According to Fish, Burton mentions the supposed 'consolation of Christian doctrine' but then 'dismisses it as one more ineffectual remedy against an irresistible disease'.[15] Although Fish does not explicitly deny the *Anatomy* a place among self-consuming, dialectical artifacts, his claim that it dismisses Christian consolation would seem to disqualify it because (like Bacon's essays) it does not lead readers to a transcendental vision.

In *Religio Medici* (the Latin title means 'the religion of a doctor'), published in 1643, Thomas Browne explores a series of questions that have no rational answers, paradoxes that have no rational resolutions and mysteries that have no rational explanations. Each of these explorations 'winds, obliquely, but predictably, toward a reaffirmation of the immanence of God's presence'.[16] Like other writers Fish discusses, Thomas Browne often 'impugns the credibility of his sources'[17] and often arouses a reader's expectations of rational development only to undermine rationality. According to Fish, however, the chief effect of the treatise is to arouse admiration for Browne's ingenuity rather than to provide a reader with 'an uncomfortable and unsettling experience' leading to greater self-knowledge and a transcendental vision.[18] According to the criteria Fish sets out in the chapter on Bacon, this implicitly disqualifies Browne (along with Bacon and Burton) from the dialectical club.

Fish's governing metaphor of self-consuming artifacts is misleading. A genuinely self-consuming artifact would be one that negates itself by defeating its own purpose. But this is not what Fish has in mind, as the following comments about *Death's Duell* make clear:

> It is here that *the true object* of Donne's concern and *the true object* of the sermon's assault are openly identified. The undermining of *the original plan*, and the disallowing of its claims (to explain the mysteries of our religion) is a strategy . . . directed . . . at the presumption inherent in the act of reasoning itself. . . . the focus of attention changes from the *supposed subject* of the sermon to ourselves, who become (as we always have been) *the true subject* [emphasis added].[19]

According to Fish himself, none of the artifacts he analyzes is actually self-consuming. Each defeats its apparent purpose merely as a strategy to accomplish its actual purpose. Fish himself employs this strategy. The title announces a treatise about self-consuming artifacts, but it turns out that the artifacts analyzed are only *apparently* self-consuming. Just as the authors he discusses initially mislead their readers about the actual subjects and purposes of their writings, Fish misleads his readers about the actual category of artifacts he will analyze. Instead of entitling his book *Apparently Self-Consuming Artifacts* or *Intentionally and Temporarily Misleading Artifacts*, Fish creates his own apparently self-consuming artifact, a critical treatise apparently about one kind of literary work (self-consuming) that turns out to be about a different kind of work (apparently self-consuming).

Fish claims that his 'method of analysis . . . focuses on the reader *rather than the artifact*' (emphasis added).[20] Just as Fish's analyses belie the word 'self-consuming' in the title of his book, this denial that he focuses on artifacts belies the word 'artifacts' in the title. Perhaps Fish meant the reference to 'artifacts' in the main title of a book in which he claims he is not focusing on 'the artifact' to be ironic (self-consuming?) and the reference to 'experience' in the subtitle to be a corrective (such ingenuity is not beyond Fish). But, in fact, Fish's denial that the study focuses on artifacts is (intentionally or unintentionally) misleading. The book focuses on specific features of each artifact that can be explained, he argues, only as attempts by the author to arouse a particular experience in a reader. Most of the actual readers Fish mentions in the text are other critics who did not have the experiences Fish describes.

A key strategy of each of the works Fish discusses is that it overtly sets up an intellectual framework that it covertly or ultimately dismantles. As suggested in the present essay, the intellectual framework of Fish's own book, in which he extols transcendentalism and denigrates empiricism, is undermined by Fish's methodology and much of his analysis. Is it possible that Fish was imitating the apparently self-consuming strategy of the works he discusses? Is it possible that he overtly promotes transcendentalism but covertly seeks to undermine it? This seems unlikely. In the course of the book Fish contrasts transcendentalism not only with rationality and empirical observation (both of which he himself employs pervasively) but with crass self-interest. The most plausible explanation is that Fish adopted a simple either/or dichotomy as a convenient framework but that this crude structure did not accord with his own sophisticated recognition of the subtleties and complexities in cultural history.

This account of *Self-Consuming Artifacts* may have given the misleading impression that it does not deserve its status as a classic of scholarship. Its value does not lie in its flawed grandiose theory but in its generally convincing and often brilliant practical criticism. *Self-Consuming Artifacts* illuminates important, complex, and fascinating literary techniques that had not previously received due attention.

Barbara Lewalski, *Protestant Poetics and the Seventeenth-Century Religious Lyric* (1979)

In her monumental study *Protestant Poetics and the Seventeenth-Century Religious Lyric*, Barbara Kiefer Lewalski demonstrates 'that the spectacular flowering of English religious lyric poetry in the seventeenth century occurred in response to a new and powerful stimulus to the imagination – the pervasive Protestant emphasis upon the Bible as a book, as God's Word'.[21] She focuses attention on five poets: John Donne, George Herbert, Henry Vaughan, Thomas Traherne, and Edward Taylor. Although earlier scholars traced certain elements in the works of these poets to Catholic sources (medieval or Counter-Reformation), Lewalski argues that Protestant poetics had a more important and more direct influence.

A major feature of the Protestant Reformation was the effort to make the Bible available in vernacular translations to listeners and readers in order to foster a direct relationship between each Christian and God unmediated by priestly intervention. Protestant theologians placed less emphasis on the community of believers than did Catholic theologians and more on the religious experience of individuals. Lewalski finds in the work of each of the poets she discusses elements of what she calls the 'Protestant paradigm of salvation'[22] articulated by the sixteenth-century French theologian John Calvin. Key elements of this paradigm are that all human beings are sinners; that no human being is capable of earning salvation by his or her own efforts; that certain individuals nevertheless are granted salvation because Jesus allowed himself to be crucified for their sake; that God chooses these individuals at random in advance of their birth (predestination); and that an individual could detect signs of his or her 'election' by engaging in introspection. 'This emphasis upon the constant scrutiny of personal emotions and feelings is a primary cause of that introspective intensity and keen psychological awareness so characteristic of seventeenth-century religious lyrics'.[23] Each poet explored particular ramifications of the paradigm. Donne's Holy Sonnets, for example, 'focus especially upon the beginnings of the process, dramatizing the speaker's pleas for justification and regeneration'.[24] Herbert adopted the metaphor of building a temple for the lifelong process of sanctification, while Vaughan employed the metaphor of a pilgrimage. Traherne's poetry all but denies original sin and thus 'seems to diverge very far from the Protestant paradigm', and yet it focuses on 'the thoroughly Protestant experience of discovering the Bible to be a full commentary on his own life and spiritual condition'.[25] The dominant theme of Taylor's poems is 'the unfathomable gulf between God's greatness and goodness and the speaker's abject depravity, a gulf which can be bridged only by irresistible grace'.[26]

Four books of the Bible – the Psalms (attributed to David), Proverbs, Ecclesiastes, and the Song of Songs (the latter three attributed to Solomon) – consist entirely of lyric poetry. 'The Book of Psalms was widely recognized as the compendium *par excellence* of lyric poetry'[27] in that it 'presented an epitome of human emotions'[28] and an anthology of diverse subcategories of lyric poems, including supplications, hymns, laments, complaints, rejoicings, ballads, and love songs. The Psalms provided a model for a Christian poet who wished to create a collection of religious poems in diverse lyric genres. The Book of Proverbs conveyed moral lessons in poetic form. Protestant poets were especially attracted to Ecclesiastes because they regarded the author of this poetic sermon 'as a repentant sinner preaching out of his own life's experience'.[29] Although both Catholic and Protestant theologians interpreted the relationship between the Bride and Bridegroom depicted in the Song of Songs as a spiritual allegory, Catholic theologians regarded it primarily as a representation of the relationship between Christ and the Catholic Church, while Protestant theologians regarded it primarily as a representation of the relationship between Christ and each individual Christian.

The biblical metaphors most often invoked in seventeenth-century religious lyrics focus on the spiritual experiences of individuals: sin as sickness, death, darkness, blindness, indebtedness, or bondage; God's Word as light; God's grace as a release from debt or freedom from slavery; the life of a Christian as warfare, a pilgrimage, chastisement, or trial; a Christian as a child, sheep, plant, temple, heart, or wife; God or Jesus as a father, shepherd, gardener, builder, or husband. Lewalski acknowledges that these metaphors occur in Catholic poetry of the period but argues that they occur 'more intensively' in Protestant poetry.[30] Each poet had a set of favorite biblical tropes. Donne chose metaphors of chastisement, servitude, violence, and bondage. Herbert's governing metaphor describes the speaker's heart as a temple of God, and many of his poems portray the speaker as a child or servant. Vaughan's characteristic tropes – pilgrimage, light, darkness, bondage, exile, childhood, and husbandry – are often intricately interwoven. Although Traherne dismissed 'curling Metaphors' and 'painted Eloquence' and sought 'naked Truth' by means of 'transparent Words',[31] his poetry memorably employs the tropes of childhood and light. As the child of God, Traherne's speaker is the heir to the kingdom and glory of God. In some of Traherne's poems, 'the source of light suffusing all things with glory is not God directly but the image of God in the speaker'.[32] According to Lewalski, Taylor merely comments on biblical metaphors rather than adapting them to new uses and his 'inability' to do the latter signals 'an end of an era'.[33]

Another aspect of biblical poetics that had a major influence on seventeenth-century poets was typology. Ancient and medieval Christian commentators developed a scheme of interpreting episodes in the Old Testament whereby each episode conveyed several spiritual meanings as well as a literal meaning. These commentators believed, for example, that the escape of the Israelites from bondage in Egypt also served as a kind of prototype or foreshadowing of the redemption of sinners by Christ's sacrifice, the conversion of an individual Christian to a state of grace, and the passing of a soul from the corruption of this world to the glory of heaven. Most important for Protestant lyric poets was 'the Reformation emphasis upon the application of all scripture to the self, the discovery of scriptural paradigms and of the workings of Divine Providence in one's own life'.[34] According to Lewalski, typological symbolism is 'absolutely central' in Herbert's poetic vision.[35] The speaker of the collection of lyrics in 'The Church' portion of *The Temple* progresses from an identification with Old Testament types to a perception of an affinity with Christ's fulfillment of those types.

In an earlier study, Louis L. Martz noted striking similarities between seventeenth-century religious lyrics written by Protestant poets and the Catholic tradition of spiritual meditation.[36] Lewalski argues, however, that by the early seventeenth century a distinctly Protestant tradition of meditation had arisen and that the poets she examines were more aligned with this tradition than with medieval and Counter-Reformation traditions. Distinctive elements of Protestant meditations were 'a focus upon the Bible' and 'a particular application to the self'.[37] This intense self-examination led to 'a new depth and sophistication of psychological insight'.[38] These elements of prose meditations found their way into Protestant meditative poetry.

Seventeenth-century religious lyrics were also influenced by sacred emblem books. An emblem consisted of a religiously symbolic picture accompanied by a motto and poem. Although emblem books were a prominent element in Jesuit religious instruction, Lewalski points out that there was a distinct tradition of Protestant emblem books based on the premise that natural objects were imbued by God with religious symbolism that could be discerned by viewing nature through the lens of scripture. Donne appropriated the common emblem of a wreath or crown (with its multiple significances, including Christ's crown of thorns and the crown of glory of a saved sinner) in the sonnet series 'La Corona'. Many of Herbert's lyrics have clearly been influenced by the *Schola Cordis* (school of the heart) subgenre of emblem books, in which a heart is depicted in various situations that, as explained in the accompanying poetic commentary, represent a soul's spiritual trials and purification. Some of his most famous poems, including 'The Altar' and 'Easter-wings', resemble emblems even more closely since they combine verbal expression and a visual image formed by the appearance of the lines of the poem on the page. Lewalski quotes numerous poems in which Taylor uses some form of the word 'emblem' – for example, a lily 'doth Emblemize' Jesus (*Preparatory Meditations*, II.98.9),[39] but she regards these self-conscious references to the emblem tradition as a sign of 'the exhaustion of a literary mode'.[40]

Lewalski argues that the practices of Protestant poets were also strongly influenced by Protestant sermon theory. But the element of sermon theory on which Lewalski focuses attention is the appeal 'to Biblical texture and style as the model for ... the preacher's appropriate art'.[41] This makes it extremely difficult to distinguish the particular influence of sermon theory on poetry from the influence of the more general and pervasive Protestant fixation on the Bible. In this chapter, Lewalski does demonstrate that different poets were able to locate in the Bible rather different models for their own poetic practices. Donne found precedents in the Bible for the far-fetched metaphors and other kinds of elaborate and witty artfulness he employed in both his sermons and his poetry:

> My *God*, my *God*, Thou art a *direct God*, may I not say a *literall God*. . . . But thou art also . . . a *figurative*, a *metaphoricall God* too', a god who conducted '*peregrinations* to fetch remote and precious *metaphors*' (*Devotions upon Emergent Occasions*).[42]

Although Herbert chastises himself for 'Curling with metaphors a plain intention' ('Jordan II'), he could curl with the best of them. Traherne adhered more strictly to a plain style. Taylor expressed awe of biblical eloquence but regarded himself as incapable of imitating it.

After describing one distinct component of Protestant poetics in each of a series of chapters, Lewalski provides in each of her final five chapters a detailed analysis of the complex intertwining of these components in the work of a single poet. These chapters demonstrate that, although all of these poets were influenced by Protestant poetics, each responded to that collection of attitudes in an idiosyncratic way. That Lewalski devotes the final 170 pages of her book to the creative output of individual poets indicates that the main purpose of the book is not to illuminate the cultural dynamics of the period by citing a representative sample of poetry (although the book certainly accomplishes that secondary purpose) but rather to illuminate the literary artistry of individual poets by providing information about the cultural context. The primacy of artistry over sociology is evident in such passages as the following:

> The 'Hymne to God my God, in my sicknesse' is perhaps Donne's most brilliant and most moving religious poem. It has been much commented on, and much admired, though, without full consideration of the way in which genre theory and typology contribute to its stunning effect.[43]

Lewalski's subordination of cultural context to individual artistry rhymes with the poetry she analyzes, which focuses intensely on a speaker's individual spiritual condition.

By describing the work of each poet with loving care and by delineating differences among the techniques employed by different poets, Lewalski conveys what was distinctive in the way each poet gave voice to Protestant attitudes. While Donne and Herbert each imitated the wit he discovered in the Bible and transformed meditation into personal drama, 'We do not . . . find in Herbert the agonized outcries by which Donne dramatized the early stages of the process of regeneration'.[44] Donne's verse was often intentionally jarring, and his jaded and combative speakers often call on God to inflict violence on them. Herbert's verse is generally harmonious, and his often naive speaker is treated with tenderness by God. Vaughan explicitly, repeatedly, and emphatically declared himself to be Herbert's disciple, and yet Vaughan's poetic collection '*Silex Scintillans* is a brilliantly original volume . . . shaped by Vaughan's unique religious and poetic sensibility'.[45] Vaughan's poetry focuses less often on the depiction of a personal relationship between the speaker and Jesus and much more often on the interpretation of quoted biblical texts and on 'his sense of the wonder and mystery of God's creation'.[46] Vaughan's poetry is more often rhapsodic and apocalyptic than that of Herbert. Traherne's 'most striking departure from the Protestant consensus is his ecstatic celebration of infant innocence, which all but denies original sin'.[47] Unlike Donne, Herbert, and Vaughan, whose poetry is dense with metaphysical conceits (self-consciously far-fetched metaphors), Traherne used figurative language sparingly. While Donne focused almost entirely on the early phase of the Protestant paradigm, in which the individual experiences a sense of guilt and an abject fear, Traherne focuses mainly on the 'last phase: . . . what it means to be, by creation and then by restoration, God's image, child, and heir'.[48] Taylor's poetry is 'quite distinctive'.[49] Many of his poems are built upon the contrast between the grandeur of God and his own utter vileness, but unlike Donne he did not typically focus a poem on a single unifying metaphor. Instead, he supplied catalogues such as the following, in which the speaker describes his heart as

> A Sty of Filth, a Trough of Washing-Swill
> A Dunghill Pit, a Puddle of mere Slime.
> A Nest of Vipers, Hive of Hornets Stings.
> A Bag of Poyson, Civit-Box of Sins.
> (*Preparatory Meditations, First Series* I.40, 3–6).[50]

Taylor's 'poetry deliberately enacts failure, as a means to glorify God'.[51]

The notion that five poets all qualify as distinctly Protestant and yet also exhibit profound differences from one another is not a contradiction. Lewalski isolates many poetic practices that can be traced to Protestant sources. Each poet engaged in several of these practices regularly and with great intensity but engaged in others only rarely or half-heartedly. What this means is that two poets might both be intensely Protestant and yet have very little in common with one another and even be strikingly different in some respects.

Lewalski acknowledges earlier studies that noted similarities between elements of the poems she discusses and Catholic cultural artifacts, and she herself traces some elements of Protestant poetics to pre-Reformation sources. But she argues convincingly that specifically Protestant attitudes had not been given sufficient attention in earlier studies, and she provides a systematic survey of many different kinds of evidence to support her argument.

 ## Jonathan Dollimore, *Radical Tragedy* (1984, 1993)

In *The Elizabethan World Picture*, a famous and influential book first published in 1943, E.M.W. Tillyard argued that Elizabethans saw the cosmos as hierarchical.[52] God occupied the highest rank, and lower levels were occupied (in order of decreasing status) by angels, human souls in heaven, human beings on earth, animals, plants, inanimate nature, damned souls, devils, and (at the very bottom) Satan. By analogy, the proper organization of society was a hierarchy in which the monarch occupied the highest rank and lower levels were occupied (in descending order of social status) by aristocrats; gentry; merchants and artisans; peasants, servants, and laborers; vagrants and most criminals; and (at the very bottom) traitors and heretics. This cosmic hierarchy or Great Chain of Being was maintained by divine providence. According to Tillyard, this scheme was implicitly or explicitly promoted in most literary works of the period. In *Radical Tragedy: Religion, Ideology and Power in the Drama of Shakespeare and His Contemporaries*, Jonathan Dollimore points out that the hierarchical world view served the narrow interests of the upper classes.[53] The notion that their social positions were ordained by God was an important element of social control. Anyone who disrupted or questioned the social hierarchy could be accused not only of treason but of a crime against God. Dollimore argues that, rather than being universally accepted, the hierarchical world view was counteracted by a number of cultural forces. One such force was what Dollimore labels 'radical tragedy', a dramatic genre that exposed the hierarchical world view for what it was, the self-interested ideology of the powers that be. According to Dollimore, these plays were a contributory factor in the fomentation of discontent with the social order, discontent that erupted in the English Revolution of the 1640s. As Dollimore notes, in the sixteenth century and early seventeenth century, orthodoxy was subjected to rigorous scrutiny and overt attack from a variety of directions. Martin Luther and John Calvin condemned the hierarchical organization of the Catholic Church; Francis Bacon advocated the testing of received opinion against evidence; Niccolò Machiavelli demystified politics and suggested that politicians cynically exploited religion to acquire and maintain power; Michel de Montaigne suggested that conscience is not a divinely implanted morality but the result of social indoctrination; and so on.

Dollimore is a self-described cultural materialist. It is misleading to call cultural materialism a form of literary criticism since its main goal is not to illuminate works of literature themselves. It is more accurate to describe this approach as an attempt to illuminate social conditions by examining literature and other cultural artifacts from a Marxist perspective. Although Marx's predictions about the future were flawed, his analyses of the methods by which ruling classes maintain their power were trenchant and have been refined and carried in new directions by later social theorists and cultural historians. Dollimore finds fault with early twentieth-century literary historians and critics for sentimentalizing the hierarchical order that relegated most members of society to material deprivation and subservience while maintaining the wealth and power of a few.

Most of *Radical Tragedy* is devoted to a series of case studies, examinations of various techniques by which certain dramatists exposed flaws in the dominant ideology, including its internal contradictions, its inadequacy as a description of human beings and society, and the injustices it entailed and obscured. Because the government could censor or punish opponents of the existing political order, 'we find in the drama not simple denunciation of religious and political orthodoxy . . . so much as underlying subversion'.[54] A radical insight might escape censorship by being put in the mouth of a villain but might nevertheless provoke subversive thought. In the prologue of Christopher Marlowe's *Jew of Malta*, a fictionalized Machiavelli (who was widely demonized by conventional moralists of the time) shockingly describes religion as a means of social manipulation. Rather than refuting this notion, the play confirms it by episodes in which nominally Jewish, Islamic, and (most disturbingly for Marlowe's original audience) Christian characters use religion for Machiavellian purposes. A play set in a foreign country, the distant past, or a fantasyland might escape censorship for that reason but still might subversively dramatize a hierarchical social system analogous to that in England at the time of the play's performance as contingent and unjust, not divinely ordained.

One of the most common subversive techniques Dollimore finds in these tragedies is a contradiction between, on the one hand, speeches in which characters invoke divine providence (or fate, an analogue of providence in plays set in non-Christian societies) to explain the disasters that befall them and, on the other hand, the action of the play, which shows that those disasters were actually produced by the unjust social system in which the characters themselves are implicated. Although characters in Shakespeare's *Troilus and Cressida* 'repeatedly make fatalistic appeals to an extra-human reality or force',[55] for example, the action dramatizes their own complicity in the injustices and dislocations of their societies. The play is an examination of how 'people brutalise themselves in order to survive in a brutal world'.[56] Victims in Ben Jonson's *Sejanus* attribute their misfortunes to fate, but playgoers are shown how these misfortunes are actually brought about by the machinations of Sejanus, a powerful henchman of the ancient Roman emperor Tiberius. The destruction of Sejanus himself in the final act does not eliminate the disillusioning effect of the play's realistic depiction of cynically pragmatic political machinations (*realpolitik*) earlier in the play. In *The Revenger's Tragedy* (probably written by Thomas Middleton), providentialism is subverted by parody. Vindice bitterly asks, 'Is there no thunder left, or is't kept up / In stock for heaven's vengeance?' (4.2.198–99). At that precise moment, stage thunder is heard. Vindice's facetious response, 'There it goes!' (1. 199), mocks his own invocation of divine providence.[57]

Dollimore argues that Jacobean tragedy also dramatized the 'decentring of "man"'.[58] According to Dollimore, the early seventeenth century occupied a gap between two epochs of thought. The medieval world view, in which man occupied the central position in a stable, hierarchical universe, was collapsing, but 'essentialist humanism',[59] the notion that society is composed of autonomous individuals, did not rise to cultural dominance until the Enlightenment of the late seventeenth and early eighteenth centuries. According to Dollimore, the basic premise of essentialist humanism is false. Individual autonomy is an illusion; the consciousness of each human being is actually constructed by social indoctrination. Paradoxically, since the late seventeenth century people have been brainwashed into believing that they are autonomous. Dollimore's argument that individual autonomy is a myth is at odds with his frequent extolling of profound, original insights of individual thinkers (Calvin, Machiavelli, Montaigne, Thomas More, Francis Bacon, Thomas Hobbes, Marx, Friedrich Nietzsche, Louis Althusser, Walter Benjamin, Bertolt Brecht, Antonio Gramsci, Michel Foucault, Raymond Williams, et al.). Dollimore does not explain how these individuals were able to think outside the social-indoctrination box of their times. In any case, according to Dollimore, the widely held notion that Jacobean tragedy dramatized the individuality of protagonists is actually a projection back onto this drama of the Enlightenment world view. Dollimore argues that Jacobean tragedy actually resembles the post-Enlightenment, socialist drama of Brecht, which, according to

Benjamin, presents 'an "untragic hero" who is "like an empty stage on which the contradictions of . . . society are acted out"'.[60] Jacobean tragedy reveals 'that identity is a fiction or a construct', that an 'essential self' is an 'illusion'.[61] 'It seems more useful to talk not of the individualism of this period', argues Dollimore, 'but its self-consciousness, especially its sense of the self as flexible, problematic, elusive, dislocated – and, of course, contradictory: simultaneously arrogant and masochistic, victim and agent, object and effect of power'.[62] According to Dollimore, Marlowe's *Dr. Faustus* is neither an orthodox affirmation of Divine Law nor an affirmation of 'the heroic aspiration of "Renaissance man"'.[63] The divine power that punishes Faustus is dramatized as unjust and cruel, but Faustus' sale of his soul to Lucifer is not sentimentalized – it is 'masochistic and despairing'.[64] The title character of *Bussy D'Ambois* by George Chapman is a courtier whose supposedly innate nobility of character is dramatized as not merely an illusion, but an illusion encouraged and exploited by those in power.

Dollimore finds inadequate both the Christian and the 'humanist' interpretations of Shakespeare's *King Lear*. The Christian interpretation claims that 'the suffering of Lear and Cordelia is part of a providential and redemptive design'[65] not evident in the action of the play. The humanist interpretation claims that suffering reveals 'man's intrinsic nature – his courage and integrity'.[66] According to Dollimore that interpretation 'mystifies suffering and invests man with a quasi-transcendent identity whereas the play does neither of these things'.[67] By regarding suffering as a universal and ineradicable component of the human condition, humanism inhibits practical efforts to make changes in social organization that might alleviate suffering. Instead of endorsing providentialism or humanism or sinking into nihilism, *King Lear* illuminates 'social process and its forms of ideological misrecognition'.[68] Lear's madness, for example, is linked to his loss of a sense of identity, and that identity, which Lear naively imagined was intrinsic, is revealed to have been a social construct that can be withdrawn by his two eldest daughters once they acquire power. Edmund's 'illegitimate exclusion from society gives him an insight into the ideological basis of that society', but he 'does not thereby liberate himself from his society's obsession with power, property and inheritance'.[69]

Dollimore examines two other plays by Shakespeare that dramatize the decentering of man. Shakespeare's *Antony and Cleopatra* demystifies honor and sexual love by revealing that each is a social construct rather than a manifestation of individual autonomy. Grand speeches about military virtue and love are undermined by a 'counter-discourse'.[70] In an exchange between two of Antony's lieutenants, Silius congratulates Ventidius on recent military victories and urges him to seek further glory by pursuing the enemy forces. Ventidius rejects this advice on the cynically pragmatic grounds that a subordinate who outshines his leader would receive not honor but the antipathy of his superior. The grandeur of the love of Antony and Cleopatra is dramatized as inextricable from their positions of power, and Cleopatra manipulates her lover as a Machiavellian politician might manipulate public opinion. The title character of Shakespeare's *Coriolanus* is an ancient Roman patrician and warrior whose belief in his innate military virtue has been nurtured by his mother Volumnia. To acquire a consulship, however, he is obligated to ask for the support of the plebeians. By pressuring her son to engage in this public performance, Volumnia represents 'not motherhood so much as socialisation'.[71] Coriolanus rejects the implication that his honor is somehow dependent on the goodwill of the rabble. And yet, as Dollimore suggests, Coriolanus 'needs the plebeians . . . as objects of inferiority without which his superiority would be literally meaningless'.[72] The play 'does not show the defeat of innate nobility by policy, but rather challenges the very idea of innate nobility'.[73] Shakespeare does not sentimentalize the plebeians but shows how oppression inhibits their ability to take effective political action.

In writing *The White Devil*, the final play to which Dollimore devotes an entire chapter, John Webster found ways of 'demystifying state power and ideology'.[74] 'The crimes of Flamineo and Vittoria reveal not their essential criminality but the operations of a criminal society'[75] in which the strong exploit the weak. Without sentimentalizing Vittoria, Webster suggests that she is a victim of a hypocritical and unjust social system. Women are subordinated by patriarchal ideology, and any hint of assertiveness by a woman arouses male insecurity and misogyny. The social system also inflicts suffering on most males. Flamineo is unable to find a satisfying outlet for his talents and so is forced to perform immoral and demeaning tasks for a powerful lord. The play undermines the concept of individuality: 'In no other play is the identity of the individual shown to depend so much on social interaction'.[76]

In several important respects cultural materialism resembles new historicism, an approach whose most famous practitioner is Stephen Greenblatt. Both methodologies examine literary works in order to illuminate the social conditions in which the works were produced. Like cultural materialists, new historicists expose the inequities of the hierarchical system of values and the sentimentalization of that system by certain scholars of earlier generations. Both cultural materialists and new historicists find fault with the early twentieth-century New Critics for analyzing works of literature in isolation from the particular social and political contexts in which the works were produced and for obscuring and perpetuating the social inequities of the status quo by glamorizing harmony, unity, order, and stability. But there are important differences between cultural materialism and new historicism. Cultural materialism arose in England as an offshoot of a well-established and continuous tradition of Marxist social commentary that tends to be optimistic, at least in the long term, about the replacement of cut-throat capitalism by a more equitable social system. New historicism arose in the United States, where Marxism had been successfully demonized during the Cold War, and has been strongly influenced by the pessimism of Michel Foucault. In Foucault's nightmare vision, power necessarily corrupts, and history is the record of a continuous succession of unjust systems of power. Once established, a system of power is generally able to contain subversive forces. If subversive forces succeed in overthrowing a particular unjust system of power, the result is merely the installation of a new and often more efficient unjust system of power. In a section on 'Containment/Subversion' in the Introduction to the second edition of *Radical Tragedy*, Dollimore differentiates his own position from that of Greenblatt by (somewhat lamely) declaring that the radical tragedy of the early seventeenth century represented a 'substantial challenge' to the hierarchical power structure.[77]

 Leah Marcus, *The Politics of Mirth* (1986)

In *The Politics of Mirth: Jonson, Herrick, Milton, Marvell, and the Defense of Old Holiday Pastimes*, Leah Marcus explores a set of intricate and fascinating interconnections among social customs, politics, and literature in early seventeenth-century England.[78] At that time, a variety of traditional festivities, many of which were tied to the agricultural calendar, were held on a regular basis in rural England. From the first of May to Midsummer (the 24th of June), for example, activities included games, sports, frolicking in the woods, and the erection of maypoles adorned with garlands. Dancing around the phallic maypole supposedly enhanced the fertility of a young woman. Celebrations also occurred at harvest time and during the Christmas season. Other festivities included country fairs, Morris dancing, and church 'ales' (also known as 'wakes'), annual feasts at which the sale of beer raised money for the upkeep of the church. Although they may now seem innocuous, in the early seventeenth century these festivities became the focus of bitter strife. Puritans and other radical Protestant reformers objected to such festivities on several grounds: they originated in pagan customs; they were associated with Catholicism; they encouraged sinful behavior; and they diverted people's attention and energies away from spiritual matters. These traditional, rural, feudal, and communal activities were also at odds with commercial values of the growing metropolis of London. To the city fathers, revelry was a threat to public order. Defenders of festivities included royalists, who saw attempts to proscribe festivities as a veiled attempt to limit the feudal power of the monarch. The Anglican Church establishment saw efforts to restrict traditional pastimes as part of a campaign to subject the Church to radical reform. King James I, who ruled from 1603 to 1625, regarded the issue as so important that in 1618 he himself published a defense of holiday festivities, the *Book of Sports*. His son, Charles I, reissued this document in 1633. The struggle over holiday pastimes and public recreations was an element of a much larger political struggle that eventually led to the English Civil War, the decisive defeat of the Royalist forces in 1647, and in 1649 the execution of King Charles.

In a series of royal masques and plays from 1612 to 1633, Ben Jonson focused attention on the contentious issue of holiday pastimes. A royal masque was designed for performance at the court and was expected to culminate in praise of the monarch. Characters were often mythological or allegorical, and plots were fanciful. Set decoration, music, and dancing were major elements, and the royal and aristocratic spectators themselves often participated as characters or dancers. Although Jonson's masques contained the obligatory praise of the monarch, they also included critiques of the policies and behavior of the royal court. Performed at court on Twelfth Night, 1612, Jonson's masque *Love Restored* dramatizes a conflict between Plutus, who as Marcus notes, is 'not exactly' the Roman god of wealth, but rather 'The Making of Money a God'.[79] He represents rich but stingy urban capitalists who fail to supply King James with revenues needed to foster communal revelry. Plutus is opposed by Robin Goodfellow, 'the humble representative of traditional country loyalty'.[80] But Robin also rebukes courtiers who engage in extravagant and wasteful displays of wealth. Self-referential elements of the masque implicitly find fault with James for allowing the focus of masques to shift from the serious issues raised in Jonson's dialogue to spectacular sets designed by the architect Inigo Jones. Both forms of extravagance, Jonson warned, alienated the court from the common people.

A form of popular entertainment is an even more overt issue in Jonson's play *Bartholomew Fair*, performed at the Hope Theatre in 1614. Taking place in Smithfield on the outskirts of London, Bartholomew Fair was savagely condemned by Puritans, represented in the play by Zeal-of-the-Land Busy, as a site where visitors were tempted into committing sins of the flesh. The Fair was also condemned by London authorities, represented in the play by Justice Adam Overdo, who decides to attend the fair in disguise in order to root out criminal activities. Jonson develops an analogy between the fair and the public theaters, for it was in one of those theaters that the play about the fair was being dramatized. Puritans regarded theaters as dens of iniquity, and civic leaders of London regarded them as threats to public order. By opposing these forms of popular amusement, Puritans and London authorities set themselves in opposition to the monarchy. The King actively encouraged traditional pastimes, and members of the royal family were the nominal patrons of the theater companies. Marcus points out that in 1614 Parliament was 'openly critical' of the king's extravagance and his promotion of what they regarded as 'popish' pastimes.[81] The killjoys in the play, who fail to heed the biblical warning 'let him who is without sin cast the first stone' (see John 8:7), are ultimately humiliated.

Over the course of the early seventeenth century, polarization intensified. Puritans and London capitalists, both of whom were well-represented in Parliament, were frequently allied against the King, the Anglican Church establishment, and the feudal traditions of rural England. Marcus notes that James 'issued frequent proclamations prohibiting new building in London and ordering gentry and aristocrats back to their country estates'.[82] In a 1616 speech to the Star Chamber, James condemned judges who interfered with his policies, especially those who tried to suppress holiday pastimes. In *The Vision of Delight*, a masque performed at court in January 1617, Jonson depicted an imaginary world in which the King's policies bring about a magical transformation: 'The masque moves from a corrupt and disordered city environment out to an idealized, revitalized countryside'.[83] Although 'The character of Fant'sy . . . is Jonson's tribute to the creative imagination of James, who was able to diagnose abuses and to propose noble and harmonious correctives', the masque also implicitly chastised the King since 'Fant'sy is implicated in the very vices it castigates'.[84] Another masque performed in the same Christmas season, *Christmas His Masque*, dramatizes the King's complaints that, instead of maintaining the communal celebrations of Christmas on their country estates, aristocrats spent Christmas in London, where traditional Christmas festivities were discouraged by Puritans and city officials. In *The Devil Is an Ass*, first performed by the King's Men in late 1616, Squire Fitzdottrel abandons his country estate and compulsively adapts his clothes and behavior to the ever-changing fashions of London, where individual rapacity has destroyed community spirit. But Jonson also implies that the King himself may be partly responsible for the problem: a con artist in the play describes a project for making money that would have reminded playgoers of James' sale of commercial monopolies.

After James was succeeded on the throne by his inept son and especially after William Laud became Archbishop of Canterbury in 1633, positions hardened. Jonson's play *A Tale of a Tub*, performed at court in 1634, dramatizes a fanciful victory of the royalist supporters of festivity:

> a series of malapert local officials abuse the law in order to prevent the enactment of an old holiday custom. . . . Fertility and well-being win the day, and the play ends with the beginnings of a Bride-Ale feast.[85]

But Jonson also includes a parody of court masques. He was dismayed by the increasing tendency in masques produced during the reign of Charles I to consist simply of extravagant spectacle and undiluted praise. The spectacular elements were antithetical to the homespun festivities advocated in the *Book of Sports*; the flattery encouraged royal self-delusion; and both isolated Charles and his court from the common people.

Many of the poems in Robert Herrick's *Hesperides* celebrate rural festivity. In 'The Wake', Herrick suggests that such festivities diffuse discontent that otherwise might lead to social disorder. According to Marcus, in 'Corinna's Going A-Maying', Herrick comes close to endorsing the sexual license for which Puritans denounced maypole celebrations. The association of festivity with paganism was one of the grounds for Puritan condemnation, but Herrick 'steeps his pastimes in paganism in order to affirm their primordial, indigenous nature'.[86] Herrick's poems often have a nostalgic and elegiac tone because, by the time they were written, mainly in the 1630s, the traditional festivities were dying out, in large part because of the growing antipathy and assertiveness of the Puritan movement.

John Milton, a strong advocate for the purification of the English Church, eventually rose to high station in the Commonwealth government that replaced the monarchy, and was the author of that government's rationale for the execution of King Charles I. It is thus superficially incongruous that one of Milton's early masterpieces is *A Mask* (that is, a masque). Written and performed in 1634 and usually referred by the title *Comus*, this work is not as incongruous as it seems. It was not a royal masque but instead celebrated the family of the Earl of Bridgewater, who actively opposed some of the policies of Archbishop Laud. And Milton took this opportunity to express his own opposition to the royal promotion of popular festivities. Comus is an enchanter and spokesperson for festivity who entices his victims to drink a potion that replaces their human heads with those of beasts. When the Lady, who was played in the first performance by the daughter of the Earl of Bridgewater, refuses to cooperate, he immobilizes her. Marcus argues that Comus' 'language and his argumentative style are those of a pro-Laudian spokesman in the manner of Robert Herrick'.[87] According to Marcus, Milton 'lays bare the stark mechanisms of power which underlie' the 'images of rural celebration' in Caroline political and poetic rhetoric.[88] The enforcement of communal festivity was a threat to the conscience of individuals. The association between festivity and coercive royal power is reinforced when Comus transports the Lady to a stately palace. Unlike some Puritans, Milton did not denounce all forms of revelry. The figure of Sabrina 'offers a healing middle territory between the absolute rejection of the Lady and the extreme indulgence of Comus'.[89]

The final chapter of *The Politics of Mirth* focuses on poetry written after the defeat and execution of Charles I. In their attempts to come to terms with this defeat, Cavalier poets such as Richard Lovelace inscribed images of a royal court and Anglican ritual in the landscape of the countryside. These poems often employed allusions to Druidism and Hermetic philosophy to represent 'an Anglicanism gone underground'.[90] Until the hoped-for restoration of the monarchy, Cavaliers had to make do with private revelry among like-minded friends. Andrew Marvell appropriated some of the imagery and poetic motifs of Cavalier poetry. His Mower poems, for example, suggest 'connections between holiday and violence that the Laudian pro-sport policy had been designed to suppress'.[91] But Marvell also exposes unrealistic elements in the Cavalier image of a sacred space in the country in which royalism, Anglicanism, and traditional feudal relationships were maintained. Marvell's 'Mower against Gardens' undercuts this sentimental fantasy by creating a speaker who objects to enclosure, the process whereby landlords privatized what once had been common fields, a process that drove peasants off the land. Marcus argues (not entirely convincingly) that the facetious military metaphors in 'Upon Appleton House', Marvell's poetic description of the country estate of Lord Fairfax, develop a serious theme: 'The old Stuart valorization of country life becomes increasingly comic as it is stripped of the ideals of peace and collective social renewal to which it had traditionally been bound'.[92] According to Marcus, the poem suggests that 'the old seasonal pastimes . . . were played out and exhausted'[93] but that the program of the Levelers, radical opponents of enclosure and social hierarchy, would produce a self-destructive anarchy. After the restoration of the monarchy, which was accompanied by a revival of traditional pastimes, Marvell turned to social satire, which he compared to the social custom of the Skimmington, whereby countryfolk shamed misbehaving neighbors by subjecting them to a raucous parade through the village.

Some cultural historians assume that writers in a given age are mere conduits through which the spirit of the age speaks, but Marcus' research subverts that assumption. The seemingly simple issue of mirth raised complex social, moral, religious, and political questions. The individual authors she discusses were psychologically complex and their talents were diverse. It is not surprising that this combination of the complex ramifications of the issue and the complexity and diversity of individuals led to a wide diversity of viewpoints. As J. Hillis Miller has wisely noted, 'Periods differ from one another because there are different forms of heterogeneity, not because each period held a single coherent view of the world'.[94] Even the concept of a 'period' is an artificial concept because social changes are not synchronized with one another. Jonson, Herrick, Milton, and Marvell each responded to the politics of mirth in a unique way, so each chapter tells a different story.

Indeed, Jonson requires three chapters because he adopted different stances toward the issue of mirth at different times in his career. Marcus discusses only a single work by Milton, written when he was a young man. If she had chosen to discuss his later works, he too would have required more than one chapter.

Concluding Comments

Despite profound differences, these four classics of scholarship do have some common elements. Each study reflects the author's personal point of view, but that personal point of view is the result not of a mere whim but of a painstaking analysis of relevant evidence. Each study also illustrates the notion that (to paraphrase Donne) no work of scholarship is an island. Each establishes a network of relationships to earlier studies both by acknowledging debts to precursors and by meticulously delineating differences between the author's interpretations of evidence from those of other scholars. Although each of these classics is a work of non-fiction, it is nevertheless itself a work of literature. Each study tells a series of stories about the complex interactions among writers (each with a unique set of inclinations and talents), the state of art forms in the period during which those artists worked (current genres, literary conventions, etc.), and social, economic, and political conditions. These non-fiction narratives take some curious twists and turns and can be as fascinating to a reader interested in literature or cultural history as the plot of a good work of fiction. Most importantly, each of these studies was the product of the author's creative imagination, which enabled the scholar to perceive patterns and relationships in the literary and historical record previously undetected or only dimly perceived by others.

7 Key Critical Concepts and Topics

Nancy Mohrlock Bunker and James S. Baumlin

Chapter Overview

Blank Verse/Heroic Couplet

Unsuited to the quantitative meters of Greece and Rome (as an experiment in quantitative verse, Jonson's 'Celebration of Charis' proves a rare exception), English Renaissance and Restoration poetry remained accentual-syllabic and predominantly iambic in its prosody. While lyric poets played with the panoply of accentual meters, line lengths, and stanzaic forms (in these respects, no two of Donne's *Songs and Sonnets* are identical), 'blank verse' – unrhymed iambic pentameter – provided the prosodic backbone of seventeenth-century English drama and epic. 'Marlowe's mighty line', as Ben Jonson describes it, first demonstrated the sonority, power, and flexibility of English blank verse; Shakespeare followed Marlowe's example, as did Milton.

In his prose preface to *Paradise Lost* (1674), Milton writes that 'the Measure is *English* Heroic Verse without Rime, as that of *Homer* in Greek, and Virgil in Latin; Rime being no necessary Adjunct or true Ornament of Poem . . . but the Invention of a barbarous Age, to set off wretched matter and lame Meter'.[1] Dryden and later Restoration/eighteenth-century poets thought otherwise. The prosodic foundation of English 'neoclassicism' became the 'heroic couplet', a rhymed couplet in iambic pentameter. Whereas blank verse made free use of 'run-on' lines or enjambment (the opening sentence of *Paradise Lost* traverses ten lines), the 'heroic couplet' tended to be end-stopped, each line offering a complete grammatical/rhetorical unit. The opening of Dryden's 'Mac Flecknoe' (1683) illustrates: 'All humane things are subject to decay, / And, when Fate summons, Monarchs must obey' (1–2). The end-stopped, rhymed couplet reinforces the formal balance and symmetry prized by 'neoclassicism'.

Caroline Comedy

During the reign of Charles I (1625–1642), Cavalier and Puritan sensibilities both inflected the age's drama. While a sense of melancholy weighs over the whole, its plays tend to depict an idealized society grounded in moral and aesthetic certainty. 'Caroline comedy' shows the triumph of love over (Jonsonian) satire, as exemplified in John Fletcher's *The Woman's Prize, or the*

Tamer Tamed (1625) and John Ford's *'Tis a Pity She's a Whore* (1628). In depicting a conflict between family generations, Richard Brome's *The Weeding of Covent Garden* (1632) returns to the Jonsonian 'comedy of humours'.

City Comedy

The Jacobean dramatists, writes Gail Kern Paster, are 'deeply preoccupied with the conditions and meaning of urban life'.[2] London's burgeoning growth, new and old money, marketplace expansion, flourishing guilds, post-Reformation religious uncertainty, and political anxieties gave rise, thus, to 'city comedy'. Francis Beaumont's *The Knight of the Burning Pestle* (1609) and Ben Jonson's *Epicoene, or the Silent Woman* (1609) exemplify this subgenre, which takes the city as its subject, stereotypes its characters, and draws on London audiences' own social/economic fantasies as a source of energy. In its moralizing tendencies, 'high-minded theory confronts low-life experience',[3] as Brian Gibbons notes. George Chapman's *May Day* (1611) and Thomas Middleton's *A Chaste Maid in Cheapside* (1613) express anxiety over the social consequences of urban cultural/economic change. Hence city comedy charts the social conflicts existing outside the theatre.[4]

Closet Drama

Intended for reading in small groups or privately, 'in one's closet' (or sitting room), the 'closet drama' was not composed for public performance. Lofty in rhetoric and intended for declamation or reading aloud, the Roman Seneca's *Hercules Furens* provided a classical model. With the closing of the theatres during the Civil Wars and Interregnum (1642–1660), there was an increased interest in closet drama. Given their exclusion (prior to Aphra Behn) from the public theatre, female authors often engaged the form.[5] In *Plays Written by . . . the Lady Marchioness of Newcastle* (1662), Margaret Cavendish published a score of light-hearted closet dramas celebrating women's freedom in education, cross-dressing, and sexual intrigue. The age's most famous example remains Milton's *Samson Agonistes* (1671).

Comedy of Humours

A mode of satiric comedy drawing liberally from the Romans Plautus and Terence, 'comedy of humours' assumes a physiological theory of human personality, wherein an individual's character derives from the predominance of one of four bodily fluids: black bile (earth), cold and dry; yellow bile (fire), hot and dry; blood (air), hot and moist; and phlegm (water), cold and moist. Sending vapors to the brain, the predominant humor thus governed one's habitual emotions – whether fiery and angry, cold and cowardly, and so on. Ben Jonson's *Every Man in His Humour* (1598) and *Every Man Out of His Humour* (1599) provide seminal examples of the subgenre. Full of eccentric, 'humourous' characters, Jonson's *Alchemist* (1611) fuses themes of 'city comedy' with 'comedy of humours'.

Comedy: 'old' *vs.* 'new'

A dramatic 'genre' whose pedigree reaches back to the Greek Aristophanes, comedy treats its subject matter lightly, happily tying up the loose ends of its plots with marriage, rebirth, and optimism – often in fantastic, improbable fashion. Amusement, humor, and laughter are its watchwords.[6] In his *Poetics*, Aristotle describes comedy as the ' "imitation" of inferior people' (in contrast to the nobler characterizations of 'tragedy'): comic characters tend to behave badly even when of higher status, making 'the laughable an error or disgrace that does not involve pain or destruction'.[7]

The protagonists of 'old comedy' find themselves involved in incongruous, disconnected or diverse events, and they often manipulate or simply resolve situations. Capable of intricate machinations, they may be predictable, confused, overwhelmed, or mistaken; furthermore, their actions may derive from overreaction, a loss of control, or irrationality. Such characters express their lively and vital interaction with the world: often we laugh 'with' or 'at' comedic characters but refrain from moral judgment about their means. This is not the case with Aristophanes, whose *vetus comoedia* or 'old comedy' seeks to 'reform manners' by lampooning, 'satirizing', or ridiculing foibles of human character.

The Greek Menander influenced later Romans Plautus and Terence, whose *comoedia nova* or 'new comedy' retained the stock characters (gull, braggart, clown, trickster) and themes (young love, interfering parents, marriage matches, financial difficulties) of *vetus comoedia*; indeed, these stock themes and characters remain well into the seventeenth century. While missing the old comedy's 'wild flights of fancy', the 'new comedy' raises socio-economic issues, addressing the 'relation of wealth to loose habits'.[8]

The plots of 'new comedy' move swiftly; their speed and dialogue offer opportunities for surprising twists and mistakes. The characters of 'new comedy' are judged implicitly against a moral norm identified with the larger society – which, presumably, represents the audience's own (morally, socially, economically conservative) values. Two thematic types evolved: 'romantic comedy', which treats of love and marriage and turns to the natural world for its backdrop; and 'city comedy', which satirizes the manners and eccentricities (and money schemes) of city-dwellers. Both types allow audiences to see themselves in the 'mirror' of drama.

Commedia dell'arte/commedia erudita

Two Italian renaissance comedic forms recur in seventeenth-century English garb.[9] 'Commedia dell'arte' is an improvisational slapstick comedy (with beatings and pratfalls) originally performed by street entertainers. Dell'arte's characters Pantalone and Harlequin find counterparts on the Jacobean stage in low-comedy figures who engage in buffoonery, coarse jesting, or drunkenness. At the same time, the 'commedia erudita' flourished: a 'learned' comedy written for educated, courtly audiences and based upon Roman models, it observed the classical unities of action, time, and place. Jonson's *Volpone* (1607) draws liberally from both these traditions.

Country House Poem

A variety of 'occasional', topographical lyric, the country house poem intermingles epicurean and stoic themes in ways typical of the age's courtly, Cavalier literature. Lavishing Nature's bounty (in epicurean fashion) upon its owners, the land rewarded the home's possessors for their (stoic) virtues, their commitments to duty, labor, justice, and generosity toward guests – as well as toward servants, whose devotion to their superiors completes the 'genre's' idealizing projections of social, ethical, natural, and familial harmony.[10] Written in praise of Sir Robert Sidney's ancestral estate, Jonson's 'To Penshurst' (1616) is the most influential Jacobean example. Marvell's 'Upon Appleton House' (ca. 1652) offers a complex Interregnum example. Aemilia Lanyer's 'Description of Cooke-ham' (1611) – whose praise of the Countess of Cumberland actually predates Jonson's poem – celebrates a uniquely woman's courtly/literary world.

Elegy

In classical antiquity, 'elegy' referred originally to a metrical form (the elegiac distych or couplet, which alternated dactylic hexameter and pentameter lines). As practiced by the Greeks Theocritus and Bion and the Romans Propertius, Catullus and Ovid, the elegy evolved into a lyric 'genre' used to express intense personal emotions, one whose subjects ranged from funereal mourning to erotic longing and complaint. Donne's youthful *Elegies* offer a late-Elizabethan example of the Ovidian erotic elegy, while Milton's 'Lycidas' (1637) exemplifies the tradition of funeral elegy. Following Theocritus' *Idylls*, Milton cast his elegy into the pastoral mode, its speaker assuming the persona of a shepherd whose song laments a lost friend or beloved.

Behind its 'pretty tales of wolves and sheep', the pastoral mode (as Sir Philip Sidney writes in his *Defence of Poesy* [1595]) raises 'considerations of wrongdoing'.[11] In Stuart literature, pastoral became a vehicle for 'encoded' or cryptic social, religious, political criticism: Milton's 'Lycidas', thus, 'fore-tells the ruin of our corrupted Clergy then in their height'. Thus the poet writes in the 1645 edition of his *Poems*,[12] presenting his anti-Episcopal attack in 'prophetic' terms.[13]

Formal Satire

A vituperative 'genre' that 'lashed vice' through mockery, exaggeration, and caricature (often leading to thinly-veiled personal attack), 'satire' is character-ized by its distinctive styles and range of personae or literary masks. Two classical models predominate. The Roman Horace's ironizing *sermo* style used light-hearted laughter to reform opponents' manners. In contrast to Horace's 'comic' satire, Juvenal's 'tragic' satire vented its anger – its *saeve indignatio* or 'wild indignation' – against criminals and human vice.[14] Whereas the Horatian satirist seeks to educate, the Juvenalian satirist seeks to punish. (Known for his difficult, 'crabbed' style, the stoic Persius proved a third albeit less influen-tial Roman model.) Stuart and Restoration satire alternated between the Horatian 'low style' and the Juvenalian 'mixed style' (whose quasi-epic rhetoric reaches indecorously down to the gutter in attacking its enemies). Given satire's penchant for personal libel and political-religious dissent, the Tudor/Stuart monarchs often prosecuted its authors. Ecclesiastical authorities burned Marston's late-Elizabethan *Scourge of Villainy* (1598); Marston, Jonson, and Chapman (among others) were imprisoned for their satiric dramas. After the Restoration (when Stuart despotism lost much of its power of political/ religious censorship), satire became the predominant literary genre. As Leo Braudy writes,

> In the absence of a traditional language of political argument, it was literature . . . that principally supplied the armoury of discussion. With uncertain steps, political language was distinguishing itself from what we would call literature, as well as gathering strength from it. New styles of controversy had emerged from the Civil War, and during all the most important political situations of the period, . . . the use of literary language . . . to change minds was crucial.[15]

Hence the prominence of literary satire in Restoration politics. John Dryden's *Discourse Concerning the Original and Progress of Satire* (1693) presents the major English Augustan criticism, while his 'Mac Flecknoe' (1682) is Restoration literature's most brilliant example of Juvenalian character-assassination. Samuel Butler's *Hudibras* (1660–1680) and Andrew Marvell's 'Last Instructions to a Painter' (1667) are other popular, influential satires.[16]

Genre

As Barbara Lewalski, Heather Dubrow, and John T. Shawcross[17] (among numerous critics) affirm, Stuart literature is governed by notions of 'genre', wherein individual works conform to the conventions or 'rules' identified with their respective forms or 'kinds'. Though some forms are post-classical in origin (the sonnet, for example), the age's genre theory remains 'neoclassical' in its commitments to the separation and 'purity' of each form and to the 'rules' governing each: as Homeric-Virgilian practice governs epic and the Aristotelian 'rules' govern drama, so the age's classically-based lyrics conform largely to principles outlined in the Roman Horace's *Ars poetica*. Each genre has its unique decorum (or 'seemliness', as the Elizabethan George Puttenham Anglicizes this Latin term), which stipulates its range of subjects, structures, and styles. Major genres, too have a range of subgenres, as comedy divides into 'romantic comedy' and 'city comedy', 'comedy of humours' and comedy of manners.

According to Horace, a poet's work aims to be *utile et dulce*, 'useful and sweet': in effect, 'to teach and delight'. Yet, literature 'teaches' in various ways, in accordance with the varieties of genre. To this Horatian precept, the age's genre-theorists added the function of *epideixis*: derived from classical rhetoric, this further 'use' or aim expressed itself in strategies of 'praise and blame'. The vituperative genres – 'formal satire', epigram, 'satiric comedy' among others – teach by lashing vice, giving negative examples of human character. The more laudatory genres – which include epic, the ode, 'elegy', and most epistolary or 'occasional' verse – teach by giving praise. The praise becomes extravagant in much of the age's courtly literature, reflecting the social inequalities of aristocratic literary patronage.

Heroic Drama

With the English court's return from exile, Restoration drama developed a unique hybridized form inspired by classical epic, influenced by the grand style of Continental-French 'neoclassicism' and reflective of the old Cavalier ethos. The twin, typically competing claims of love and honor fuel the age's 'heroic drama'. Heroes and heroines alike provide models of idealized behavior: unfailing courage, complete fidelity and devotion, strict adherence to the old Cavalier code of honor. Dryden's *Tyrannic Love, or the Royal Martyr* (1669) exemplifies the form, as does his *Conquest of Granada* (1670). Exotic settings and epic power struggles (typically against tyrannical rule or Oriental despotism) mark the plots of Elkanah Settle's *The Empress of Morocco* (1673), John Crowne's *The Destruction of Jerusalem by Titus Vespasian* (1677), and Nathaniel Lee's *Tragedy of Nero* (1674). Aphra

Behn's prose tale *Oroonoko* (1688) draws freely from the conventions of 'heroic drama'.

Ignatian Meditation

Fusing native and Continental sources, the devotional lyric – as exemplified by Donne's *Holy Sonnets* (1633) and George Herbert's *The Temple* (1633) – remains one of the great Jacobean contributions to English literature. The devotional poet drew, first, from Scriptural tradition, the Psalms especially, adapting David's prayerful, penitential, celebratory stances. The poet drew as well upon the Anglican service, liturgical calendar, and *Book of Common Prayer*. Addressing God in intimate terms, the poet incorporated Petrarchan *topoi* or commonplaces, turning the traditionally secular love sonnet into a vehicle for religious praise, complaint, prayer, and supplication to God. The devotional poet met the age's religious controversies head-on, addressing Calvinist themes of election, predestination, and the problem of personal salvation. But, as Louis Martz argues, the defining influence is Catholic, specifically the meditative tradition as outlined in the *Spiritual Exercises* (1548) of Ignatius Loyola.[18]

Reflecting Counter-Reformation emphases upon iconography – the use of lively images to stir the passions – the 'Ignatian meditation' seeks to recreate Scriptural scenes imaginatively, leading to emotionally-intense interior dialogue. His 'First Exercise' gives the model:

> Imagine Christ our Lord present and placed upon the Cross, let me make a colloquy, how from the Creator He is come to Making himself Man, and from life eternal is come to temporal death, and so to die for my sins.
>
> Likewise, looking at myself, what I have done for Christ, what I am doing for Christ, what I ought to do for Christ. . . .

'The Colloquy is made', Loyola adds, 'as one friend speaks to another, or as a servant to his master'. Donne's Holy Sonnet XI ('Spit in my face you Jews, and pierce my side') imagines the poet participating and sharing in Christ's crucifixion.

In its iconographic emphases, 'Ignatian meditation' reflects the age's use of emblem. Often allegorical and drawn from the 'Book of Nature', books of emblems presented a series of visual images that served as both interpretive puzzles and 'aides to memory'. The visual image was, in fact, part of a complex visual/textual programme that included an *impresa* or cryptic motto and a lengthier poem that offered to interpret the whole. Yet the Catholic, Counter-Reformation emphases of Ignatian meditation have seemed, to some critics (Barbara K. Lewalski most notably), an imposition upon English Protestant poetry.[19] (For an alternative tradition, see 'Protestant poetics'.)

Imitation

Lecturing the 'players' or actors come to Elsinore, Hamlet advises them to 'suit the action to the word, the word to the action, with this special observance, that you o'erstep not the modesty of nature: for anything so o'erdone is from the purpose of playing, whose end . . . is, to hold as 'twere the mirror up to nature'. In so saying, Hamlet gives a rough-and-ready definition of dramatic decorum ('suit[ing] the action to the word'), as well as of 'imitation' – that is, the 'mirror[ing]' or faithful representation of reality. Specifically, Shakespeare invokes the Aristotelian doctrine of *mimesis*. In his *Ars poetica*, the Roman Horace gives a second, more 'literary' meaning: the classicizing poet's art remains imitative, but his 'mirror' shifts from 'nature' to the subjects, structures, and styles of previous poets. English literature from Jonson to Milton to Dryden commits to both Aristotelian *mimesis* and Horatian *imitatio*. A foundation of 'neoclassicism', *imitatio* emphasizes literary echo and allusion – the incorporation of the classics as literary subtexts. For a Christian poet like Milton, classical imitation becomes eristic or competitive: even as he invokes Homer and Virgil, his own epic seeks to 'soar / Above th' Aonian mount', thus surpassing its classical-pagan models. Miltonic allusion and 'source study' is a vast subject, to which Barbara K. Lewalski has made significant contributions.[20]

Jacobean Comedy

As part of the age's repertoire of dramatic forms, Jacobean comedy 'found itself actively inventing answers to questions of social import', as Douglas Bruster notes, its plays exploring the nuanced relationships 'between the theatre and extra-theatrical reality'.[21] Questioning the age's evolving market economy, Ben Jonson's *Bartholomew Fair* (1614) exposes the division between those who trade, purchase and consume and those who serve and work, thus highlighting conflicts between socioeconomic classes.

Love and marriage (rather, love *vs.* marriage) bring feminist themes into Jacobean comedy. As Mary Beth Rose argues, Jacobean comedy provides an 'index of the progressive valorization of social and political roles of woman and wife': henceforth, 'eros, courtship, marriage' are 'no longer peripheral but at the center'[22] of life. Both plot and subplot critique the politics of gender as it intersects with performance and dramatic representation.[23] Philip Massinger's *A New Way to Pay Old Debts* (1625) portrays a heroine's resistance against arranged marriage into the aristocracy.

Jacobean Tragedy

Depicting humanity at its most pessimistic, Jacobean tragedy explores (without naming) the moral/spiritual crises fueled by Calvinism, wherein evil is real, human nature inherently fallen, and damnation a certainty for many.[24] George Chapman's *Tragedy of Bussy d'Ambois* (1608) takes place in the French court, depicting a world of intrigue and corruption. John Webster's *Duchess of Malfi* (1614) takes place in a vice-ridden Italian palace, presenting a plot of sensational intrigue wherein deeply perverse energies of the mind govern. In Thomas Middleton and William Rowley's *The Changeling* (1622), the characters DeFlores and Alsemero construct their lives out of cruelty, duplicity, degradation, and intimidation of others. Tragedies such as these are often thought to reflect the darkening mood of the Jacobean period. They often offer grim depictions of human nature and corrupt behavior.

Masque

Henry VIII's Epiphany spectacle of 1512 (in which the king participated) is often called the first English masque; the 'genre' boasts a regal history, indeed. Shakespeare's betrothal masque in *The Tempest* (1611) offers an early Jacobean example. Prior to the Civil Wars, the masque became the showpiece of court entertainment and one of the primary instruments of royal propaganda. In partnership with architect Inigo Jones, whose elaborate stage sets featured spectacular *trompe l'oeil* effects, Ben Jonson developed the masque into a celebration of Stuart royal ideology.

Whereas London's professional companies played in public theatres, the Stuart masque was staged privately at court, most often at Whitehall. While joining poetry and music, its primary effect (to Ben Jonson's literary chagrin) was visual – a series of rapidly changing scenes crowded with gods and monsters, heroes and villains, fairies and witches. Exquisite costumes and elaborate masks concealed actors, who were often amateurs drawn from court society. Jonson and Jones' *Masque of Blacknesse* (1605) exemplifies the masque's major conventions: its imaginative world reflects the moral/spiritual cosmos, whose competing forces – of light *vs.* 'blackness' – vie against each other, only to be brought back into harmony by the king's benign presence. This Platonizing movement (from masque to anti-masque to kingly resolution) culminates in a formal dance, when members of the courtly audience come down to join masquers in the dancing. In effect, the boundary between court and stage spectacle is dissolved: the masque not only celebrates but incorporates the Stuart court in its idealized projections of social harmony.[25] Milton's *Comus* (1634) presents a curiously Protestant, Puritan version of this otherwise Platonizing form.[26] The Inns of Court frequently staged their own private entertainments, as well, but the era of the Stuart masque ended in 1642, with the onset of the Civil Wars.

Neoclassicism

An aesthetic based in the 'imitation' or decorous recreation of Greco-Roman models, 'neoclassicism' assumes that human knowledge and its cultural-artistic products reached their height in classical antiquity. In literature as in art and architecture, 'neoclassicism' values symmetry, balance and unity of composition, formal restraint, clarity of sense and 'purity' of expression. Its value system, thus, is conservative: faithful to its models, 'neoclassicism' rejects the 'barbarisms' of medieval literature and the excesses/innovations of modernism. (Parodied in Swift's *Tale of a Tub* [1704], the 'Battle between the Ancients and the Moderns' pits 'neoclassicism' against modernism in the arts, philosophy, and science.) Ben Jonson's plain style is an early Jacobean expression; refined by Dryden and brought to perfection by Pope, 'neoclassicism' became the reigning aesthetic of Restoration and early eighteenth-century Augustan literature. Synonymous with 'neoclassicism', Augustanism invokes the highest standards (and generic/stylistic models) of Latin poetry, as developed during the reign of Caesar Augustus: Virgil in epic, Horace in satire and literary epistle, Martial in epigram, and Ovid in erotic elegy.

Pamphlets

Throughout the seventeenth century, printing presses scattered across the kingdom (and on the Continent) poured out a flood of English broadsides, polemical tracts, and short prose treatises, most of them unlicensed by government censors. Much of the Reformation controversy (and its political fallout) proceeded by pamphleteering.[27] The age's formal, 'high' art – its poetry – cannot be separated from the 'popular' prose genres, with which it dialogues. Milton's career gives the proof: he was known (though largely scorned) in his own age as a pamphleteer, not a poet. For a most famous example, see Milton's *Areopagitica* (1644).

Prophetic Mode

With government censorship having broken down, the 1640s represented an 'age of kerygma', of active preaching and claims of prophesying by non-conformist/sectarian authors. From the prose 'pamphlets' of Abiezer Coppe and Anna Trapnel to the allegories of John Bunyan to the sophisticated treatises and poems of John Milton, claims of prophetic authority and visionary prophecy mark the age's sectarian polemics. 'Enthusiasm', one's claim of a private, unmediated, extra-Scriptural revelation from the Spirit, posed severe challenges to the public institutional authority of the Established Church; despite his own 'inner Word' theology, Calvin himself rejected the enthusiasts' claims. Whereas the classical poet declared his inspiration from the pagan Muses, seventeenth-century English authors – Milton especially – put a sectarian spin on such conventional claims.[28] Identified with the Holy Spirit, Milton's 'Heavenly Muse' poses unique problems of interpretation.

Protestant Poetics

As described by Barbara K. Lewalski, English devotional poets of the seventeenth country (Donne, Herbert and Vaughan, among other poets) developed a distinctive Christian aesthetic that asserted, first, the Bible's poetic excellence.[29] 'There are in all the world not so eloquent books as the Scriptures', preached Donne: 'if we would take all those figures and tropes, which are collected out of secular poets . . . we may give higher and livelier examples . . . out of the Scriptures'.[30] Mistrustful of Counter-Reformation emotionalism, English poets replaced 'Ignatian meditation' (and its emphasis upon lively images) with a less dramatized, more rational meditation upon the Word. Contrasting the four-fold *allegoresis* of medieval Catholicism, English poets adopted the Scriptural hermeneutic of typology, often used in 'Protestant poetics', wherein Old Testament characters and events prefigure their New Testament anti-type or 'fulfillment' in Christ. Above all, the English devotional poet adopted the so-called Pauline 'paradigm of salvation', whose separate stages are election, calling, justification, adoption, sanctification, and glorification.[31] Individual poems explore the diverse psychology of these stages in the Christian's progress toward God.

Restoration Comedy

The folly (and pitfalls) of city life provides the subject matter of Restoration comedy, while fluctuating relationships (both amorous and mercantile) provide its plot lines. George Etherege's *She Would if She Could* (1668) and John Dryden's *Marriage A-la-Mode* (1672) suggest increased attention to the love match.[32] At times nostalgic for the old social order, Restoration playwrights aim their satire at the ruling class. The age's distinctive character type, the Restoration rake (partly indebted to the Cavalier hero) thrives in his libertinism by means of wit and social savvy – keys to success into this new secular, Whiggish world.[33] The fop, silly and artificial but not without power, becomes the new object of satire. William Wycherly's *Country Wife* (1675) and George Etherege's *The Man of Mode* (1676) are famous examples of the Restoration comedy of manners, which reveled in sexual license and witty repartee.[34]

Audiences, however, would eventually react against the Restoration play-wrights' depictions of libertine superficiality (including hostility toward parents) and blatant sexual bawdy, and the king himself came to decry the age's ribaldry, indecorum, and penchant for political attack. Thomas D'Urfey's *Squire Olsapp* (1678) and *The Royalist* (1682) represent the more socially (and morally) conservative, Whig responses.

Restoration Drama

Returned to the throne in 1660, Charles II granted William Davenant (who had gone into exile with the Stuart court) and Thomas Killigrew a temporary monopoly on theatrical performances. Restoration drama reflected the Continental influences that had crept into the English court during its French exile: anti-Puritanism (as in John Tatham's *The Rump* [1660]), a taste for Spanish romance (as in Thomas Tuke's *Adventures of Five Hours* [1663]), scenic and musical refinements (previously associated with 'masque'), the introduction of actresses (with avoidance of boy-actor scandals), and a general cleaning-up of older plays. Above all, 'Restoration drama' sought a refinement of language associated with the age's 'neoclassicism'. As Robert D. Hume has chronicled, 'Restoration drama' brings character into the study of 'genre' and its political undercurrents.[35] Politics comes into close proximity with plot and style also, as J. Douglas Canfield has argued. It is the cultural work of the 'Restoration tragedy' (a subgenre that surfaced at the transition to a bourgeois sensibility)[36] to legitimize the upper class' right to rule. Examples of this subgenre include John Dryden's *All for Love* (1677) and Thomas Otway's *Venice Preserved* (1682).

Revenge Tragedy

Inspired by the Roman Seneca and made popular by Thomas Kyd's *Spanish Tragedy* (1586), revenge tragedy often depicts revenge for a murder, the murder sometimes having been revealed to the protagonist by the victim's ghost. The plot may include the hero's hesitation, his insanity (either real or pretended), his contemplation of self-murder or suicide, intrigues of plot, a preponderance of soliloquies, and sensationalized horror (such as on-stage murder or presentation of dead bodies). Cyril Tourneur's *Atheist's Tragedy* (1611) is a Jacobean example.[37]

Romantic Comedy

This thematic subgenre takes the triumph of love as its subject: projecting an idealized heroine, its lovers win over all obstacles (typically parental and socioeconomic) and retreat from the city's woes to an idyllic natural setting. Its happy endings are typically simplistic and improbable. Shakespeare's *As You Like It* (acted c.1603) remains a brilliant late-Elizabethan example. Jacobean dramatists such as Ben Jonson preferred this subgenre's thematic rival, 'city comedy'. Romantic comedy would, however, provide characters, plots, and themes for the age's prose romance (which, in turn, fueled the development of the modern novel).[38]

Tragedy

As Aristotle pronounces in his *Poetics*, tragedy is an ' "imitation" of an action that is serious, complete, and of a certain magnitude' containing six elements: plot, character, thought, diction, music, and spectacle.[39] The protagonist of classical tragedy exhibits personal strength, courage, and tenacity while manifesting some tragic 'flaw', leading to an error in action or judgment. As the plot unfolds, the protagonist meets with some 'reversal' of fortune, comes to some moral/spiritual 'recognition' or self-discovery (often regarding his or her identity and/or fate), and undergoes an intense suffering. In turn, the protagonist's suffering awakens fear and pity in audiences. Aristotle's pronouncements were highly respected in the seventeenth century and became especially influential in the second half, with the rise of neoclassicism.

Aristotle's declaration that tragedy was 'complete, and of a certain magnitude' became ossified in the later, 'neoclassical' doctrine of dramatic 'unities', wherein a plot would depict a unified (hence, single) action occurring in one place (hence, allowing for no scene changes) and transpiring within a narrow time frame (typically the span of a day). While reflecting aspects of the Aristotelian definition, Shakespeare clearly ignored 'neoclassical' 'unities' in such tragedies as *Othello* (1604), *Macbeth* (1605), and *Antony and Cleopatra* (1606) – while Ben Jonson's *Volpone* (1607) follows them more or less faithfully.

Tragicomedy

Commingling tragic grandeur with low comedy, Giovanni Battista Guarini's pastoral drama *Il pastor fido* (1598) provided a Continental model for John Fletcher's pastoral tragicomedy *The Faithful Shepherdess* (acted 1608–1609). Francis Beaumont and Fletcher developed this subgenre, which is marked by improbable plots (as in their *Philaster* [1610], whose unexpected turn of events shifts from tragedy to a happy ending), radical contrasts between villainy and virtue (also, between pure love *vs.* gross lust), blatant treacheries, and rescues in the nick of time.[40] George Chapman's *The Widow's Tears* (1612) and John Webster's *The Devil's Law Case* (1623) are further Jacobean examples; Thomas Heywood's *A Challenge for Beauty* (1634) and Thomas Killigrew's *The Prisoner*

(1638) offer Caroline examples. Tragicomedy retained its popularity after the Restoration, as exemplified by Thomas Shadwell's *Royal Shepherdess* (1669), William Davenant's *Fair Favorite* (1673), and John Dryden's *Secret Love* (1667).

Wit

Defying precise definition, wit remained foundational to seventeenth-century literature, describing both a faculty of mind and its imaginative/stylistic creations. In its late Elizabethan formulation, wit expressed itself in courtly *sprezzatura* – which the Italian Castiglione described as 'a certain nonchalance, so as to conceal all art and make whatever one does or says appear to be without effort'.[41] Pope's eighteenth-century formula, 'What oft was thought, but ne'er so well Expressed',[42] places emphasis upon the surprising or well-turned phrase – in sum, upon style. For Donne and the so-called metaphysical poets, wit came to define mental more than stylistic agility. 'We are thought wits, *when 'tis understood'*, wrote Jasper Mayne in his 1633 elegy on Donne, thus alluding to the intellectual/epistemological/rhetorical complexity of the Donnean conceit.[43] In his *Life of Cowley* (1779), Samuel Johnson pronounces against Donnean wit (which contradicted the clarity and simplicity of Johnson's 'neoclassicism'):

> The most heterogeneous ideas are yoked by violence together; nature and art are ransacked for illustrations, comparisons, and allusions; their learning instructs, and their subtlety surprises; but the reader commonly thinks his improvement dearly bought and, though he sometimes admires, is seldom pleased.[44]

The Donnean conceit – an extended metaphor, whose elaboration spread across stanzas and whole poems – was grounded in paradox: hence, 'the most heterogeneous ideas are yoked by violence together'. Based in the ancient/medieval cosmology of 'occult resemblances', Donne's arguments by analogy drew heavily upon traditions of alchemy, Neoplatonism, and hermeticism (hence the deliberate obscurity of his thought). The extended metaphor driving Donne's lyric, 'The Flea', illustrates these many features of metaphysical wit.

8 Fourteen Ways of Looking at Literature: A Survey of Current Approaches

Robert C. Evans

In the introduction to his classic study *The Mirror and the Lamp*, M.H. Abrams argued that any literary theory that tries to be complete must account for four basic aspects of literature: the author, the text, the audience, and the universe (or 'reality'). Abrams' list can be usefully supplemented by adding a fifth category: the role or function of the critic herself. Any reasonably well developed literary theory, in other words, will be a theory about all these factors and the relations among them. The assumptions a theorist makes about the author, for example, will inevitably affect (and be affected by) the assumptions he makes about the text, the audience, 'reality', and the purposes of criticism. Indeed, Abrams argues that each theory will tend to emphasize one of these aspects as the crucial or most important factor – the one that colors and helps define all the others.[1]

In the survey below, which is organized in rough chronological order (from older approaches to the most recent), the basic assumptions of each theory are sketched extremely briefly, and the crucial or defining emphasis of each theory is italicized. Each theory is then used to help explicate a single poem – Ben Jonson's famous lyric 'On My First Son', which records the poet's reaction to the sudden death of his seven-year-old namesake. By looking at one poem in detail from fourteen different angles, readers will (it is hoped) not only gain a fuller appreciation of that poem itself but will also see how any work can be illuminated by examining it from a variety of theoretical perspectives. The main purpose of this chapter, then, is not to explain in any detail the basic tenets of recent theories (that has been done quite well many times before) but to show how the various theories can actually be *used* to come to grips with an actual literary text.[2] The chief goal of this chapter, then, is to exemplify the theories by showing them in action and practice as they help shed a variety of different kinds of light on a single important text.

Ben Jonson (1572–1637)
'On My First Son'

Farewell, thou child of my right hand and joy.
My sin was too much hope of thee, loved boy.
Seven years thou'ert lent to me, and I thee pay,
Exacted by thy fate, on the just day.
O, could I lose all father now! For why
Will man lament the state he should envy?
To have so soon scaped world's and flesh's rage,
And, if no other misery, yet age?
Rest in soft peace and, asked, say: here doth lie
Ben. Jonson his best piece of poetry,
For whose sake, henceforth, all his vows be such
As what he loves may never like too much.[3]

Traditional Historical Criticism

Because traditional historical critics tend to emphasize the ways social *realities* influence the writer, the writer's creation of a text, and the audience's reactions to it, they stress the critic's obligation to study the past as thoroughly and objectively as possible to determine how the text might have been understood by its original readers.

Confronted with a text such as 'On My First Son', a traditional historical critic would immediately want to learn everything possible about the man, the boy, the poem's genre, the particular works it may echo, and the specific poem itself, especially its historical circumstances. Knowing facts about Jonson's other works and about his career would obviously help a historical critic interpret this particular text. For example, the mere fact that Jonson was writing an epigram would be historically important, especially given his interest in classical culture and his role as a prime transmitter (and transformer) of that culture during the English Renaissance.

The fact that Jonson echoes previous texts (such as the Bible and also poems by the Roman author Martial) would be significant, especially if it could be shown that contemporary readers would have been likely to recognize such allusions. Many original readers would have known, for instance, that the opening line, by referring to the boy as a 'child of my right hand', translates the biblical name 'Benjamin' and that the phrase generally suggests a position of special favor. Many modern readers, less familiar with the Bible and with Jacobean English than the original audience, will depend on notes (products of historical research) to learn such crucial information.

A historical critic would also want to answer such questions as how Jonson's poem compares and contrasts with previous epigrams in general; whether Jonson is likely to have intended the similarities and differences; and how (or even if) the poem reflects his general style or usual habits of thinking. Such a critic would even look for evidence to confirm the factual details the poem openly asserts and would also explore the historical significance of such 'facts'. Is it important, for example, that Jonson describes the death of a boy? (A historical critic might argue that in a largely patriarchal culture, a son's death would be far more significant than a daughter's.) Is it significant that the boy lived to be seven? (A historical critic might contend that because a boy of that age, in Jonson's times, had survived the generally high rates of infant mortality, his death would come as a greater shock than if he had died at six months.)

A traditional historical critic might also want to explore how Jonson's attitude toward his son compares or contrasts with the attitudes of other parents of his period. For example, would a father in Jonson's times have been as emotionally attached to his children as a father in later eras? Perhaps most significantly, a historical critic might want to know how Jonson's poem reflects his personal religious stance. Did the Christian perspective implied by so much of the poem's phrasing provide genuine consolation? How did Christian attitudes toward death compare with the classical attitudes Jonson knew so well? Does the poem favor one attitude or another, or does it reveal unresolved tensions between the two? How might Jonson's personal, religious or philosophical position help us to interpret the famously ambiguous final couplet?

Jonson's epigram, in short, raises many questions that a traditional historical critic might valuably attempt to answer. Although the poem deals with such a common problem that it might seem to transcend differences of time and place, a historical critic would argue that even this poem demands to be read in its original context(s). A father's reaction to his son's death might seem to be primal or universal, but a historical critic would argue that it is precisely in such circumstances that a historical perspective can be most helpful.

Thematic Criticism

Because thematic critics stress the importance of ideas in shaping social and psychological *reality*, they generally look for the ways those ideas are expressed by (and affect) the texts that writers create. They assume that audiences turn to texts for enlightenment as well as entertainment and that writers either express the same basic ideas repeatedly or that the evolution of their thinking can be traced in different works.

A thematic critic approaching 'On My First Son' might focus on any number of important ideas the poem explores. These might include, for instance, Christian vs. non-Christian responses to death; the ideal of moderation; the distinction between fate and free will; the relations between self and other; the conflict between grief and consolation; the difference between liking and loving; or the problem of loss. Another significant theme the poem treats is fatherhood: the epigram depicts Jonson not only as a father to his son but as a son to his own heavenly Father, as well as implying his role as a father or author of poems. As various critics have shown, fatherhood is often a central topic in Jonson's writing and could be linked closely to aspects of his own life, including his prenatal loss of his own father through death; his ambivalent experiences with his new stepfather; his relations with such noteworthy father-figures as his schoolmaster, William Camden; and his own role as 'father' to younger poets. However, still another important theme explored in this epigram is also an idea central to much Renaissance literature – the conflict between reason and passion. According to many early modern writers, reason should control and master the passions. Jonson's epigram can be seen as an attempt to do just that – to impose order on some of the most unruly passions a person might imagine. Throughout the poem the speaker struggles to achieve a disciplined emotional response to his son's death, and it is precisely the evidence of this struggle that helps lend the poem so much of its power.

Even the poem's first word – 'Farewell' – can be read as an expression either of emotion or of reason (or of both at once). On the one hand, the speaker's willingness to say goodbye might indicate his rational acceptance of his son's death; on the other hand, the fact that he writes as if his son is still living might imply an emotional reluctance to let go. Similarly, whereas the description of the son as the speaker's 'right hand and joy' might suggest properly restrained emotion, the sudden self-accusation of 'sin' might seem to express painfully intense feeling (including self-contempt), even as it implies a verdict rooted in reasonable judgment. Paradoxically, perhaps, the speaker's severely rational self-judgment might then be read as excessively emotional and hyperbolic (and therefore as unreasonably unjust). Meanwhile, phrases such as 'loved boy' imply a properly balanced emotion, while a phrase such as 'too much hope' combines a double emphasis on emotion ('hope') and rational assessment ('too much'). In addition, the shift from l. 3 to l. 4 might be seen as epitomizing the poem's larger tension between reason and emotion. And (to give the screw one further twist) this outburst itself might seem in some ways perfectly 'reasonable' (that is, inevitable or predictable) under the circumstances. A thematic approach, therefore, can help explain not only the poem's larger structures and meanings but also its smallest details. Such an approach, furthermore, need not be reductive but can help highlight the complexity of the speaker's response.

The relevance of the theme of emotion vs. reason to a larger audience than the speaker himself is suggested in ll. 5–6. Here the speaker's question seems addressed not only to himself but to his readers. Moreover (and para-doxically), whereas the purpose of the question is to encourage a reasonable answer, the question itself is posed in highly emotional terms: it can be read as another self-accusation, similar to the earlier reference to 'sin'. Here, however, the speaker has moved away from the limited self-judgment of l. 2 to a much wider indictment – one applicable to any reader.

Ironically, even in making the ensuing case for a reasonable response to early death, the speaker resorts to strong emotion not only in his diction ('rage'; 'misery') but even in his syntax (ll. 7–8 technically constitute a frag-ment). All in all, the poem enacts a miniature mental battle between the forces of reason and passion, and when the speaker finally imagines his son's 'Rest' (l. 9), he is signaling his own desire for (and unstable achievement of) mental and emotional 'peace'. The questioning and response that help constitute the poem (especially in ll. 5–6 and 9–12) mirror the emotional questioning and attempts at rational response within the speaker's own mind. The final coup-let, for instance, seems also a final effort to assert reasonable self-control, yet even here the language can seem heartfelt and perhaps a bit excessive: the speaker insists that from now on, in 'all' of his 'vows', he will 'never' again make the mistake of valuing a thing 'too much'. Thus, in the very attempt to control or deny emotion, the speaker is expressing it, and if the final couplet can seem in one respect consoling and reasonable, in another respect it may also still imply tinges of pain, frustration, and anger. Even in the final lines, then, the tension between reason and passion may still be unresolved.

Formalist Criticism (Anglo-American 'New Criticism')

Because formalists value the *text* as a complex unity in which all the parts contribute to a rich and resonant effect, they usually offer highly detailed ('close') readings intended to show how the work achieves a powerful, compelling artistic form. Formalist critics help audiences appreciate how a work's subtle nuances contribute to its total effect.

A formalist critic would find much to appreciate in Jonson's epigram 'On My First Son'. Every element of the poem would seem potentially worthy of close attention. Such a critic might begin, for instance, by noting that the opening word, 'Farewell', is itself a kind of complex unity, since it suggests not only an ending (of the boy's life) but also a beginning (of his journey to, and new existence in, heaven). In the very first word, then, Jonson already suggests that the boy is not really dead, yet the fact that the son has indeed died makes the word ironic and contributes to a larger poignancy. The opening word also implies direct address, not only suggesting a personal connection between speaker and subject but also foreshadowing the boy's imagined reply in ll. 9–10. 'Farewell' captures both the speaker's sense of loss and his hope of renewed contact. It thus epitomizes some of the tension inherent in the poem as a whole.

If the phrase 'thou child' seems at first a bit distant and formal, the ensuing phrase 'loved boy' soon balances that impression (and is intensified by it). This oscillation between distanced and emotional responses, in fact, will become part of a larger pattern. This balance is also evident even in such a small detail as the phrase 'child of my right hand and joy', since it is not immediately clear whether the final two words extend the first clause ('child of my . . . joy'), start a new one (i.e., you are 'my joy'), or do both. Formalists often look for such meaningful ambiguities since these imply skill and craftsmanship.

Although the immediate allusion to the Hebrew etymology of 'Benjamin' (meaning 'of the right hand') might seem unnecessarily learned, a formalist could retort that the allusion is not obtrusive: the line works even if the etymology is unknown, and the etymology, if known, already implies the 'hope' mentioned in l. 2, since the son had been given the name in (ironic) anticipation of his good fortune. Meanwhile, the reference to the 'right hand' (the hand with which Jonson presumably wrote) already anticipates his later reference to the boy as his best poem (l. 10), just as the very phrase 'My right hand' also sets up the balancing phrase in the very next line: 'My sin'.

'My right hand' suggests good fortune; 'My sin' suggests not only bad fortune but personal culpability. Although a formalist would generally appreciate the poem's clear and simple diction (which is preserved even when Jonson is punning), such a critic would also appreciate the work's subtle nuances.

A formalist would value both the poem's rich diction and its complex structure. He might note, for instance, how the opening reference to 'too much hope' anticipates the closing reference to 'lik[ing] too much', or how the early reference to the past 'seven years' is balanced by the closing emphasis on an unlimited future. A formalist might also note how the father's humble willingness to accept blame in the second line nicely balances the subtle pride implied in the first. Yet even such pride doesn't seem truly blameworthy, since it expresses genuine love. A formalist might also note that while the poem's first line focuses on the present tense, its second line focuses on the past. Likewise, 'Loved boy' also implies both past and present tenses. 'Hope', meanwhile, implies a future expectation which is (ironically) already past, while the reference to 'sin' in l. 2 already subtly implies the existence of God, who is then explicitly introduced in l. 3.

In addition, a formalist would note how the plain and declarative diction of the opening lines helps prepare (by contrast) for the emotional outburst of line 5. Even the apparently simple word 'O' would, for a formalist, carry multiple implications, including anger, astonishment, frustration, desire, surprise, pain, desperation, and need (to mention just a few). In short, a formalist would move carefully through the poem, word by word and even sound by sound (as in the juxtaposed 'f's' of 'fate' and 'father'), trying to determine how all the poem's parts contributed to a total impact that is, at least in a truly great work, finally indefinable.

Psychoanalytic Criticism

Freudian or psychoanalytic critics emphasize the key role of the human mind in perceiving and shaping *reality* and believe that the minds of writers, audiences, and critics are highly complex and often highly conflicted (especially in sexual terms, and particularly in terms of the moralistic 'super-ego', the rational ego, and the irrational 'id'). They contend that such complexity inevitably affects the ways texts are written and read. The critic, therefore, should analyze how psychological patterns affect the ways in which texts are created and received.

'On My First Son' offers many opportunities for psychoanalytic exploration. Thus the father's 'hope' and 'sin' (l. 2) toward his son can be seen as expressions of his selfish id – his desire for private or individual satisfaction. In this sense the child (a product of a sexual act) becomes an expression of personal self-assertion. This argument is strengthened by the fact that the poem nowhere mentions the child's mother. The fact that the lamented child is a boy might also seem significant, since the speaker has invested much masculine pride in his son, who (if he had lived) would presumably have perpetuated both the father's genes and name through his own sexual prowess. According to such a reading, the epigram might thus be interpreted as a product of the ego's attempt to find order and meaning in (or to impose them on) a loss that seems all the more painful because it seems so meaningless.

From this perspective, the poem is forceful precisely because it so convincingly embodies the conflicts between the speaker's id, ego, and super-ego. Whether the epigram ever really resolves these tensions is debatable, but the fact that it epitomizes them would (for a Freudian) help explain the poem's force.

A psychoanalytic critic might find evidence of the id's strongly emotional impulses in such words or phrases as 'too much hope' and 'loved boy', and especially in the heart-felt outburst of 'O, could I lose all *father* now!'; emphasis added). In addition, such a critic might see the rational ego operating in such words or phrases as 'lent', 'I thee pay', and 'just day' (since these words imply consciously chosen acts and rational understanding of regulated behavior; ll. 3–4). Finally, a Freudian might see evidence of the super-ego entering the poem in such language as 'sin' (which implies a moral failing, a transgression against God the Father) or 'father' (which implies one's responsibility to fulfill an important social role). By escaping the 'flesh's rage', the boy has escaped (among other troubles) the forceful sexual urges accompanying puberty, and indeed the poem itself can be seen as expressing rage at the flesh – our inevitable frustration at realizing the limits and impermanence of the individual body, as well as the inevitable frustration of the desires of the id. In this respect, 'age' is a 'misery' partly because it is a time when fleshly pleasures and strengths weaken, as do the desires and satisfactions of the id. In finally vowing that he will never again 'like too much', the speaker tries to control his future. The poem can therefore be seen as an attempt to respond reasonably (by exercising the ego) to a painful emotional loss (felt mainly by the id). By creating a masterfully effective poem out of his loss, the speaker attempts to reaffirm his rational mastery over himself and over his troubling circumstances.

Psychoanalytic critics might also respond to Jonson's poem in various other ways. They might see it, for instance, as a typical expression of his strongest emotional impulses: his desire to create, to be a father, to assert himself and leave something permanent behind, and to impose and display self-discipline. Or they might see the poem as reflecting Jonson's own experiences with fatherhood, including the early loss of his own father; his presumably uneasy relations with his stepfather (a bricklayer); his bonds with beloved surrogate fathers such as his teacher William Camden; his search for such father-figures in his own pursuit of worthy patrons; and his desire to act as a father-figure to others (such as younger poets).

Psychoanalytic critics might also ponder the ways the poem appeals to the subconscious desires of readers, especially their private desires for love in general, for a father's love in particular, for personal immortality, for parenthood, or for personal self-control. Indeed, in responding to the poem, a reader can subconsciously imagine himself either as the grieving father or as the victimized son. Furthermore, a psychoanalytic critic influenced by the writings of Jacques Lacan might argue that the year of the son's death is particularly significant, since the seven-year-old boy was about to enter most fully the symbolic realm of the father – the realm of language, law, and social competition. To lose a son at this age might seem particularly difficult for a man like Jonson. Having lost his own father to death, he now similarly loses his own chance at fatherhood. Nevertheless, in writing his poem he not only expresses the emotions of his id and displays the rationality of his ego but also, by enacting the culturally prescribed role of an ideal father, satisfies the social and moral expectations associated with the super-ego.

Archetypal (or 'Myth') Criticism

Because archetypal critics believe that humans experience *reality* in terms of certain basic fears, desires, images (symbols), and stories (myths), they assume that writers will inevitably employ such patterns; that audiences will react to them forcefully and almost automatically; and that critics should therefore study the ways such patterns affect writers, texts, and readers.

An archetypal critic might explain part of the power of 'On My First Son' by noting that it confronts several key human fears, including death, separation from a loved one, fear of the unknown, and fear of having offended a higher power. The poem draws on widespread human desires for security, love, control of the future, and immortality – desires which are all strongly threatened by the son's death. Children traditionally symbolize new beginnings; thus the death of a child is usually seen as especially tragic. Children also tend to be seen archetypally as innocent, so a child's death somehow seems particularly unfair. In this case, the death of a child of the 'right hand' seems especially ironic. Hands traditionally symbolize power; they are the prime human tools, by which we literally manipulate the world. The right hand, especially, has been seen as the active hand, while 'right' is the side archetypally associated with numerous positive qualities. To lose the child of one's 'right hand' might therefore seem, symbolically, as devastating as losing that hand itself.

The fact that the child here is a son is archetypally significant, since sons (especially first sons) have often been seen as crucial to their parents, particularly to their fathers. A son's death therefore also implies the inevitable death of oneself, and since the birth of a child is one way of defeating mortality, the death of one's child can make mortality seem doubly destructive. Moreover, the fact that this poem emphasizes a father's loss is archetypally significant, since fathers have often been associated with dominion, control, order, wisdom, and authority. This father, however, must confront a loss of control and must struggle to assert (or accept) wisdom; he must in a sense face becoming a son again by not only acknowledging but also accepting God's greater wisdom. He must struggle to understand how a heavenly father who supposedly loves him can take away the son whom the earthly father loves. The poem, then, draws on traditional stories of tensions between parents and children. By accepting God's decree, Jonson himself enacts the archetypal role of good son. The poem thus shows that one way of dealing with the common fear of lack of control is to concede control to (through trust in) one's parent. The power of the earthly father seems undermined, but the power of the heavenly father is thereby affirmed; and it is the power of God that ultimately guarantees Jonson's eternal security and survival, as well as the eventual renewal of his connection with his own son. Just as his own son undergoes an archetypal process of initiation and rebirth, so in a sense does the poet. In a poem so much concerned with loss of control and fear of an unknown future, Jonson appropriately ends by attempting to reassert his control of the future (and of himself) by vowing self-restraint and an avoidance of excess.

Marxist Criticism

Because Marxist critics assume that conflicts between economic classes inevitably shape social *reality*, they emphasize the ways these struggles affect writers, audiences, and texts. They assume that literature will either reflect, reinforce, or undermine (or some combination of these) the dominant ideologies (i.e., standard patterns of thought) that help structure social relations. Marxist critics study the complex relations between literature and society, ideally seeking to promote social progress.

Jonson's epigram 'On My First Son' might seem at first to offer few opportunities for Marxist analysis. Part of the effectiveness of the poem would seem to lie in its appeal to an apparently basic human emotion (the love of a parent for a child) that might seem to transcend differences of class. A Marxist reading, of course, will seek to show how even such an apparently 'apolitical' poem has definite political dimensions. Such a reading might begin by noting that part of the speaker's attachment to his son derives from his strong sense of owning and possessing the boy: his son seems to belong to him alone (not even the boy's mother is mentioned), and yet the poem shows how even our most prized and private possessions can suddenly be snatched away. A Marxist reading might also emphasize the economic metaphor used in ll. 3–4: the son is a loan that must be repaid, and in this case the lender is a being who, by definition, possesses total power over His dependents and who can revoke any contract at any time and for any reason. Of course, the Christian God is imagined as a creditor who never abuses His power (unlike His earthly counterparts) and whose repossessions are inevitably beneficial. Nevertheless, the poem's speaker still has trouble coping with his loss, perhaps in part because he lived in a world in which power relations routinely proclaimed as 'just' must often have seemed arbitrary, capricious, and self-serving, especially to someone of Jonson's relatively low social status.

A Marxist reading might emphasize, in fact, that a boy like Jonson's would have been far more likely to die of disease and other causes than the scion of a more prosperous family. Jonson himself, of course, was away from London when his son died: he was visiting the country home of a wealthy patron, an absence dictated by economic need. If he felt at all guilty about such distance, however, he probably would not have blamed the contemporary social system. Instead, the poem encourages him (and us) to accept infant mortality as an inevitable part of God's plan. Thus, instead of seeking to overturn unjust social conditions, Jonson accuses himself of 'sin' for having felt 'too much hope' of his son's future (l. 1). Although Marxists would not deny the inevitability of death, they might emphasize that early death and suffering are more likely to afflict some classes than others. A Marxist might also contend that a society devoted to scientific understanding (rather than preoccupied with supernatural consolations) would be more likely to discover and eradicate the material causes of deadly diseases.

Not only would a person of Jonson's class have been less capable of preventing a son's early death; he would also have been less capable of dealing with its consequences. During Jonson's day, a son would have helped prevent an aging parent's poverty or sickness – concerns less likely to trouble the wealthy, who would also have had more plentiful consolations in dealing with a child's death. Lacking a son, Jonson would himself have been more exposed both to the 'world's and flesh's rage' and to that 'other misery [of] age' (ll. 7–8). By dying early, his boy escaped the raging, worldly competition for status and scarce resources – a competition Jonson and others of his class could never afford to forget. The death of his dependent son, therefore, would probably have made Jonson worry about eventually depending on others himself (as in fact he did in old age).

Even the poem in which Jonson laments his private loss inevitably functioned as a public, commercial product – as an advertisement of the poet's abilities (especially with potential patrons) and as an incentive for purchasing the books in which the poem appeared. Written by a man who was himself slightly privileged (since his livelihood no longer depended on physical labor), this learned, sophisticated epigram appeals to other readers of the same class, status, and level of literacy. As a poet, Jonson enjoyed uncertain social standing and economic security, both of which depended on his ability to please a paying audience by working with words. He was one of the first members of a 'new class' of professional humanists, yet the poem presents him not as the spokesman of a specific interest group but as a voice of widely shared ethical and religious values.

In this poem as so often elsewhere, religion becomes a means of reconciling a frustrated man (and his readers) to the wretched conditions of earthly existence, so that instead of trying to change the world he learns to accept it. Rather than seeking to correct society or improve the economic system, Jonson seeks instead to correct himself. Rather than truly envying or even threatening the rich, he urges himself to 'envy' his son's new prosperity in heaven. Although real money might actually have helped to prevent his son's death and defeat similar miseries, money is mentioned merely as a metaphor. Although the epigram ends by acknowledging that private property can never be securely possessed, and although it implicitly warns both speaker and readers never to take earthly prosperity for granted, a Marxist critic might argue that it never openly advocates the sort of social change that could have made the need for such poems less likely.

Structuralist Criticism

Because structuralist critics assume that humans structure (or make sense of) *reality* by imposing patterns of meaning on it, and because they assume that these structures can only be interpreted in terms of the codes the structures embody, they believe that writers will inevitably rely on such codes to create meaning, that texts will inevitably embody such codes, and that audiences will inevitably use such codes to interpret texts. To understand a text, the critic must be familiar with the systematic codes that shape it; he must master the system(s) the text implies.

'On My First Son' offers various possibilities for structuralist analysis. A structuralist might begin by noting, for instance, the many binary oppositions embedded within the poem. These paired opposites (such as 'male/female') have tended to be defined in our culture in terms of their differences from one another. Thus we have tended to think of males as essentially 'not females', and vice versa. Other binary oppositions that help structure the meanings of Jonson's poem include the following: Christian/pagan; father/son; parent/child; English/Latin; English/Hebrew; adult/child; son/daughter; reason/emotion; acceptance/resistance; right/left; lyric/narrative; brevity/length; justice/injustice; subject/object; I/thou; love/sin; lending/payment; father/mother; first/subsequent; life/death; boy/girl; knowledge/uncertainty;

heaven/earth; present/future; peace/rage; innocence/corruption; loving/ liking. Such a list could easily be extended, and links between the listed pairs could easily be made (for example, the boy/girl opposition is inherent in the larger contrasts of male/female and adult/child). The most important point, however, is that in order to interpret Jonson's poem, a structuralist would first want to determine which binary oppositions were most relevant to the poem and how those contrasting pairs functioned in Jonson's culture.

Most of Jonson's contemporaries would have assumed, for instance, that Christianity is superior to paganism; that a father has a special relationship with his son, especially his first; that a parent should respond in certain ways to a child and should react differently to misfortune than a child might react; that a male should behave differently than a female; that a son might have one kind of social value and a daughter another; that reason is a better rule of conduct than emotion; that accepting the inevitable makes more sense than resisting it; that right is somehow preferable to left; that heaven is superior to earth; that peace is better than rage; etc. The meanings just attributed to any of these pairs might easily be challenged, but determining the precise functions or meanings such pairs have (at a particular point in time and space) is precisely the goal of structuralist analysis. Once such larger meanings have been determined, the meaning of any single text that relies on them, including a text such as Jonson's poem, can be determined. Moreover, every word of the poem is part of a larger code in which things are defined by what they are not. Structuralists, then, do not so much 'read' a work of literature as 'decode' it, and to do so they must examine the larger systems of meaning the work implies. It is significant, for instance, that Jonson's poem is an epigram rather than an epic: knowing just this much about the work can help us properly assess its meaning(s). Structuralist analysis, therefore, inevitably tells us not only about an individual text but about the larger culture (or system of codes) in which that text has meaning.

Feminist Criticism

Because feminist critics assume that our experience of *reality* is inevitably affected by categories of sex and gender (such as divisions between male and female, heterosexual and homosexual, etc.), and because they assume that (heterosexual) males have long enjoyed dominant social power, they believe that writers, texts, and audiences will all be affected (usually negatively) by 'patriarchal' forces. The critic's job will be to study (and even attempt to counteract) the impact of patriarchy.

A feminist analysis of Ben Jonson's epigram 'On My First Son' might begin by emphasizing the very lack of implied or explicit references to women in this poem. From the title to the final line, the epigram emphasizes male experience and male perception. The poet's wife (and son's mother) is now-here mentioned, and when Jonson speaks of the boy's creation (in l. 10), he does so metaphorically, never alluding to actual physical birth. The son, significantly, bore the father's first and last names, and if he had lived he would have perpetuated the Jonson family 'line' in a larger system of cultural patriarchy. At some point, indeed, the grown son would have possessed more legal rights and power than his own mother; the age of the parent would have mattered less than the sex and gender of her offspring. Women enter the poem at most through implication – as, perhaps, in the reference to the 'flesh's rage' the boy has mercifully escaped (l. 7). In one sense this phrase refers to all the physical liabilities of being human, but in another sense it alludes to the (presumably) heterosexual desire that the pre-pubescent boy has avoided by dying young.

In this poem, the most important relations are links between fathers and sons – not only the speaker and his dead boy, but the speaker and his Heavenly Father, who has revoked His precious loan. In Jonson's culture, fathers possessed enormous power, and this was especially true of God the father. Indeed, part of the poignancy of Jonson's epigram derives from the speaker's recognition that although, in worldly terms, he himself was a father who enjoyed the right to determine his son's future, in another sense both he and his son are sons of a (male) God who truly enjoys absolute control of both their fates. In trying to cope with the death of his son, then, Jonson attempts to enact the culturally prescribed roles of both a good son and a good father. Even human beings are generically defined in this poem as males: 'why / Will man lament the state he should envy?' (ll. 5–6). The fact that Jonson probably intended no conscious sexism in so writing may, paradoxically, make the poem's embedded sexism all the more significant.

By creating a poetic tribute to his son, Jonson attempts to give both the boy and himself a kind of immortality that neither one could derive from mere fleshly mothers: the poem, in one sense an acknowledgment of the defeat of his male 'hope' or ambitions (l. 2), in another sense enacts such hope on a different, 'higher' level. Moreover, it might even be argued that there is a sense in which Jonson himself in this work enacts the stereotypical behavior of both mother and father, of the reasonable man and emotional woman, especially in the tenderly (almost stereotypically feminine) injunction, 'Rest in *soft* peace' (l. 9; emphasis added). Perhaps the boy's mother is absent from the poem precisely because she would have had no role to perform: her role has been preempted by her husband. In this epigram, the poet acts as both father and mother, sensible patriarch and grieving parent. The poem might be interpreted, indeed, as a means of perpetuating patriarchal values (despite the speaker's explicit desire to 'lose all father'; l. 5). The speaker's idealization of the son is made all the easier, in fact, because the boy died long before he could seriously threaten (or disappoint) his father's masculine values or challenge his father's domination. Although in actual fact the father was physically absent when the boy died, the poem implicitly commemorates and perpetuates their relationship. Young Ben's mother (old Ben's wife) goes unnamed and unmentioned, just as she generally went unnoticed in Jonson's life and in Jonson's culture. Few records of her life survive; no record of her mourning survives; and in the poem as elsewhere she literally has no voice.

Deconstructive Criticism

Because Deconstructive critics assume that *'reality'* cannot be experienced except through language, and because they believe that language is inevitably full of contradictions, gaps, and dead ends, they believe that no writer, text, audience, or critic can ever escape from the unsolvable paradoxes language embodies. Deconstruction therefore undercuts the hierarchical assumptions of any other critical system (such as structuralism, formalism, Marxism, etc.) that claims to offer an 'objective', 'neutral', or 'scientific' perspective on literature.

A deconstructor confronted with 'On My First Son' might begin by interrogating some apparently simple words. Thus 'My' already involves a contradiction, since the poem will show how the dead son both is and is not the speaker's possession. Similarly, 'Farewell' suggests both a leave-taking and a refusal to take leave or let go: like the whole poem, it implies a (doomed) desire to maintain control. Similarly, while the word 'child' suggests the speaker's superiority to the boy, the whole poem implies the new advantages the boy achieves through death. The word 'joy' is similarly unstable, since it immediately implies its opposite: the child, once a source of pleasure, but now a source of pain, should still inspire pleasure, but still inspires pain. Likewise, 'sin' suggests its opposite: in the very act of confessing sin, the speaker seems to escape it: his self-indictment encourages our (and God's?) forgiveness. Even the phrase 'child of my right hand' embodies a paradox: the boy is both the speaker's son and God's; his death is both fortunate and not; the name suggests both the dead boy and the risen Christ.

By addressing the dead boy as if he is still present, the speaker suggests how the boy is both present and absent, implying that his absence signifies an eternal presence from which the speaker himself is absented. Mortality has made the boy immortal, just as the father's strength now leaves the father vulnerable and weak. Although the death is likened to a 'just' repayment, the analogy seems unstable, since in earthly contracts the terms (and times) of possession are spelled out and both the borrower and lender are theoretically equal. Equally paradoxical is the exclamation in l. 5, since the expressed desire to 'lose all father' is also the poem's strongest assertion of fatherly feeling. Yet, Jonson's strong self-assertion also implies weakness; the exclamation undercuts the very desire for detachment it seeks to express; the very outburst suggests the impossibility of 'los[ing] all father'. Similarly, even as the speaker concedes that his son is now an immortal spirit, he speaks as if the boy were still a thing of flesh (1. 9), and the poem itself can be seen as expressing the very rage it openly condemns.

In short, for a deconstructor few things here (or in any piece of language) are simple or straightforward; every apparent meaning is tinged by its opposite. Perhaps this is most obviously true in the poem's final lines. Thus in the very act of disavowing extreme reactions, the speaker shows his still-extreme attachment, while the last line, so perfectly balanced in rhetoric and sound and so seemingly definite in its distinction between liking and loving, is also notoriously difficult to interpret. What seems clear is also confusing; what seems neat is also messy; what seems simple is also complicated; what seems a resolution may be unresolved. The poem enacts a defeat that is also a kind of victory: the speaker cannot finally lose all sense of 'father'. Try as he might to play the role of trusting child to a heavenly Father, the final lines suggest that he cannot completely give up a need for control.

Reader-Response Criticism

Because reader-response critics assume that literary texts are inevitably interpreted by individual members of the *audience* and that these individuals react to texts in ways that are sometimes shared, sometimes highly personal (and sometimes both at once), they believe that writers exert much less control over texts than we sometimes suppose and that critics must never ignore the crucial role of audience response(s).

Reader-response critics reacting to 'On My First Son' might obviously adopt various approaches. They might focus, for instance, on the actual or possible responses of Jonson's immediate circle, especially responses by anyone who may have known the boy directly. Or they might explore how reactions to the epigram might vary depending on readers' own experiences, especially their experiences with children or with parenthood. For example, how might a reader who is childless through choice react, as opposed to one childless through sterility or one who has lost a child to death? How might readers who are too young to have yet had children react, and how might their reactions differ from those who presently have (or who once have had) children the same age as Jonson's son? How might a mother react differently than a father? In one sense, the number of possible responses is almost infinite, for despite the poem's very heavy autobiographical emphasis, each reader will (arguably) read it in light of his or her own personal experiences. Phenomenological critics, on the other hand, might argue that the poem allows us to enter Jonson's head and heart, to think and feel as he did and make his experiences our own.

Other reader-response critics might emphasize the poem's existence as a process unfolding in the reader's mind or as a shared experience. They might especially stress, for instance, the sudden jolt that occurs in the transition from ll. 4–5 or the less violent transition that occurs between ll. 6 and 9. Or reader-response critics might focus on how the final couplet focuses on the speaker's imagined future response and on how that response (without being overtly didactic) perhaps encourages us to respond likewise to life's hopes and disappointments. They might also argue that the apparent genuineness of the speaker's reaction to his son's death helps encourage a similar deeply-felt response in the audience. The speaker himself might even be seen as a 'reader' who must respond to (and interpret) the fact of his son's death. From this perspective, part of the effectiveness of the poem might derive precisely from the fact that it includes within itself a diversity of sometimes conflicting reactions.

Other reader-response critics might contend that part of what makes Jonson's poem effective is that we respond to it slightly differently each time we read it. Each reading, arguably, will also be affected by the circumstances of the moment: the poem is likely to have different effects depending on how the reader, at any given point in time, is feeling. A reader-response critic might argue that the poem is effective precisely because it is open to a variety of readings and does not dictate a simple, unambiguous reaction. In reacting to such a highly personal poem, of course, readers are also likely to grant the legitimacy of the speaker's response and are likely to regard any opposed reaction as intrusive or inappropriate.

Reception theorists might emphasize how Jonson's first readers might have been shaped by different assumptions and sets of values (such as a strong commitment to Christianity or an easy familiarity with classical culture) than subsequent readers. In any case, reader-response critics might see the diverse interpretations the poem has already generated as evidence of the validity of their basic theory, since their approach might be seen as explaining both the interpretive agreements and disagreements the poem has notoriously provoked.

Dialogical Criticism

Because dialogical critics assume that the (worthy) *text* almost inevitably embodies divergent points of view, they believe that elements within a text engage in a constant dialogue or give-and-take with other elements, both within and outside the text itself. The writer, too, is almost inevitably engaged in a complex dialogue, through the text, with his potential audience(s), and the sensitive critic must be alert to the multitude of voices a text expresses or implies.

A dialogical critic confronted with Jonson's epigram 'On My First Son' might argue that the poem articulates a variety of sometimes competing voices and shows the speaker engaged in explicit or implicit dialogue with himself, with God, with his son, with his readers (including other fathers, other parents, other Christians, etc.), and with a variety of literary, poetic, and philosophical traditions. The tones of voice the poem expresses are sometimes gentle and loving (e.g., ll. 1 and 9), sometimes self-accusing (e.g., l. 2), sometimes logically rational (e.g., ll. 3–4), sometimes exasperated and frustrated (e.g., l. 5), sometimes self-consoling (e.g., ll. 7–8), sometimes modestly proud (e.g., ll. 9–10), and sometimes resolutely stoic (e.g., ll. 11–12). The interaction among these voices and tones might sometimes be described as a civilized dialogue, sometimes as a heated debate. Although in one sense the poem is highly personal, in another it is insistently rhetorical, as the speaker seeks to persuade both his readers and himself, and the failure of one voice to triumph may actually be a sign of the poem's moral and intellectual integrity and artistic success.

Since dialogical critics assume that all language is addressed to someone, they might be particularly interested in the moments in Jonson's poem when such address seems to become explicit, as in the very opening words (l. 1), the anguished exclamation (l. 5), the incredulous question (ll. 5–6), the return to gentle solicitation (l. 9), and even the poignant invitation for the son himself to respond, from beyond the grave and through the father's poem, to an imagined interlocutor (l. 9). Even the last couplet of the poem imagines future projected speech-acts (l. 11). From start to finish, then, the poem is obsessed with speech – with questions, answers, exclamations, declarations, and vows.

Although the entire epigram is explicitly addressed to Jonson's dead boy, it must obviously have been written also with other audiences in mind, including the poet's friends, family, patrons, and God. Part of its pathos, indeed, derives from the fact that in some sense the direct address to the son can only be imaginary, for on one level, at least, all dialogue between Jonson and his son has now obviously ended. Ironically, the boy has been cut off just as he was about to enter the realm of real, full dialogue and verbal exchange – just as he was beginning to master language in a way that would have signified his transition from simple childhood. By the same token, Jonson also seems to feel cut off from full dialogue not only with his son but also with his heavenly father, whose motives he can only imagine rather than certainly know. Again, part of the poem's pathos derives from the impossibility of receiving clear responses to the questions the work asks and the problems it poses. Words such as 'fate' and 'just' (l. 4) imply that there can be no further debate or negotiation, and yet obviously the poem continues for another eight lines. In composing the poem (it might be argued), Jonson fashioned a dialogue between himself and his son, between himself and God, between himself and his readers, between the conflicting values of his culture, and between divergent aspects of himself.

New Historicist Criticism

Because new historicist critics assume that our experience of *reality* is inevitably social, and because they emphasize the way systems of power and domination both provoke and control social conflicts, they tend to see a culture not as a single coherent entity but as a site of struggle, negotiation, or the constant exchange of energy. New historicists contend that no text, audience, or critic can stand apart from contemporary (i.e., both past and present) dynamics of power.

A new historicist confronted with 'On My First Son' might perhaps argue that this is one of Jonson's most powerful poems precisely because it seems least obsessed with power. It presents one of the most attractive and irresistible images of the poet precisely by seeming oblivious to the usual social concerns about self-presentation. The poem's practical, social effectiveness is enhanced by our sense of being privileged to a very private moment. Although an epitaph does have, by its very nature, a social purpose, and although this poem does reflect the larger values of Jonson's society, to a new historicist the work might seem so powerful precisely because its public, didactic function does not seem primary.

Set among the satiric squibs and poems of praise that constitute Jonson's volume of *Epigrams*, this epitaph on his son (a new historicist might contend) lends his voice a tone of sincerity and powerful feeling. It expresses a deep yet delicate love that enhances the intensity and credibility both of the courtly compliments and of the cynical satires that surround it. Whereas Jonson can sometimes seem most interested in praising the powerful, in commending the people best positioned to help him, this poem and his other epitaphs, especially the ones on children, display his commitment to values higher than power alone. For that reason, however, they help promote his pragmatic appeal and social status. Ironically, this poem confessing his deeply-felt lack of power is one of his most powerful in every sense. Rooted in a profoundly personal loss, it nonetheless depends on its ability to make us share that deprivation, to empathize and identify with the poet to an extent never quite aroused by the satires or complimentary works. Although in the epitaph Jonson speaks most intensely for himself, he also voices common feelings and fears.

In other works, Jonson denies being ambitious or envious. Here, however, he confesses a kind of 'hope' and desires a kind of 'envy' we can only admire.

His confession of private weakness, by enhancing our sense of his inner strength, can only promote his wider social standing. Even the severest rival (and Jonson had many) would be hard put to attack this poem, which is indeed (in every sense) nearly impervious to criticism. It practically forces readers to take it on its own terms and not to second-guess it; it implicitly challenges them to respond with the same tact and subtlety the poem itself embodies. Any approach that seemed to sully the work by raising issues explicitly ignored by the poem itself would run the risk of seeming crass and crude, threatening the interpreter's standing and (even worse) perhaps his self-regard. In its own way, the epitaph is far more powerfully intimidating that any of Jonson's blustering self-defenses or satirical barbs.

A new historicist might claim that 'On My First Son' celebrates a relationship rooted in love and therefore all the more appealing in a society in which such relations would have been complicated or rare. It exalts a relation free of any hint of envy or rivalry, one in which the poet himself was the superior, the giver and provider. Clearly the poem also recognizes the speaker's subjection to a greater power (God), but that power is not presented as exploitative or self-serving. The Lord who exacts tribute is himself a loving Father with only the best interests of his sons at heart.

A new historicist might argue that Jonson's epitaphs (especially the ones on children) enhance his power by wrestling with issues that seem to transcend the political. Such poems help us temporarily forget the ambitions and struggles of the here and now, reducing these concerns to their 'proper' importance and offering a reprieve from the necessity of thinking about them. Thinking about death can prove a great antidote to ambition, but it can also spur the desire to achieve temporal fame. In either case, however, the poems in which Jonson confronts death help promote his social standing, making him a spokesman for values that seem at once intensely private and socially important. This, at least, is one way in which a new historicist might approach Jonson's poem – one way of explaining how the poem is entangled in its contemporary context(s) of power relations.

Multicultural Criticism

Because multicultural critics emphasize the numerous differences that both shape and divide social *reality*, they tend to see all people (including writers, readers, and critics) as members of sometimes divergent, sometimes overlapping groups. These groups, whether relatively fluid or relatively stable, can include such categories as races, sexes, genders, ages, and classes, and the critic should explore how such differences affect the ways in which literature is both written and read.

At first glance, Jonson's epigram 'On My First Son' might seem to offer few opportunities for multicultural analysis. The poem seems to draw on (and appeal to) emotions so basic and fundamental – so simply 'human' – that political or social differences might almost seem irrelevant. Yet, the very difficulty of bringing a multicultural perspective to bear on Jonson's poem helps highlight some of the work's distinctive traits and may also help to explain some of its traditional popularity. Although this might seem a poem that transcends racial, sexual, national, or sectarian tensions, this very appearance paradoxically confirms how inescapable such tensions usually are in other literary works or in other aspects of life. In this poem, it might be argued, Jonson seems to transcend such 'marginal' concerns precisely because he situates himself near the center of some of his culture's dominant values.

Obviously, for instance, Jonson speaks in this poem in the voice of a successful (if momentarily disappointed) heterosexual male; however, one need not assume, for this reason, that his poem would prove unappealing to homosexual men or women. (Indeed, such persons might even be especially attracted to a work celebrating a love that combines deep affection and wholehearted cultural approval, or they might be particularly sympathetic to a speaker who feels painfully cut off from the object of his affection, or they might feel special empathy for a speaker whose desire to raise a child has been denied by 'fate' or a higher power.) Although there seems little reason to doubt Jonson's own strong heterosexual inclinations, the fact remains that in his time, as later, a standard way to attack another male was to impugn his sexual orientation, and even Jonson had been taunted this way on the public stage in the famous 'poetomachia', a conflict between rival dramatists conducted in the years shortly before his epigram was composed. (He himself, in turn, often engaged in such satire of others.) His epigram inevitably functions, then, as an implicit advertisement of his heterosexuality, even though this function may have been the farthest thing from his mind when he wrote it. The poem also takes for granted (as heterosexuals in Jonson's time easily could) the possibility of having more children (particularly more sons) to compensate for the loss of the 'first'. Certainly most heterosexuals in Jonson's culture would have been able to identify strongly with the speaker of this poem, and any bisexuals would presumably have had even more complicated reactions to the epigram than 'straights' or 'gays'.

Although Jonson was probably a member of his culture's dominant sexual majority, he was very definitely, at the time he composed this poem, a member of a persecuted religious minority. The fact that the poem betrays little evidence of his Roman Catholic faith may merely reflect, again, its indifference to 'irrelevant' distinctions, its focus on more 'basic' emotions and values. There can be no doubt, however, that Jonson would generally have been able to write more freely if his Catholicism had been tolerated (or even sanctioned) by his larger culture. We can only imagine how this epigram might have differed if Jonson had enjoyed the right to practice open Catholicism (or Judaism, or Hinduism, or any other non-Christian faith) in the England of his day. Surely a Jew or Muslim would be able to identify with the sentiments Jonson expresses, but just as surely those sentiments would have been expressed in subtly different ways. Of course, if Jonson had lived in London as an African slave, or as an American Indian, or even as an English atheist, his life and work would probably have differed greatly. Although the epigram on his son rarely emphasizes such distinctions, a multiculturalist critic would nonetheless explore the ways Jonson's poem and life silently took them for granted. And such a critic might be especially interested in how the political, sexual, racial, and religious values the poem implies helped it both attain and maintain its status as a 'classic' of the English literary canon.

Postmodernist Criticism

Postmodernists are highly skeptical of large-scale claims to objective 'truths' and thus doubt the validity of grand explanations. They see such claims as attempts to impose order on a *reality* that is, almost by definition, too shifting or fluid to be pinned down. Postmodernists assume that if writers, readers, and audiences abandoned their yearning for such order, they would more easily accept and enjoy the inevitable paradoxes and contradictions of life and art. The postmodern critic will look for (and value) any indications of a text's instabilities.

Although at first 'On My First Son' would seem to offer few openings to a postmodern critic, and although Jonson himself might initially seem the exact opposite of a postmodern writer, both the text and the author yield intriguing responses to postmodern questions and assumptions. Thus the poem obviously illustrates the difficulty of adhering strictly and unambiguously to any single-minded philosophy, and indeed much of its power arguably derives from the conflicts between the different world-views (such as classical and Christian or rational and emotional) embedded in it. Although the poem's speaker clearly wrestles with his conflicting reactions to his son's death, a postmodernist would feel no need to reconcile or harmonize these conflicts. Indeed, doing so would mean doing an injustice to the chaotic feelings and experiences from which the poem was born. A postmodernist might especially appreciate, in fact, the very abruptness of the shift in emotion between lines 4 and 5, and such a critic might argue that the whole poem reveals the inevitable failure of coherent systems of thought (such as Christianity) when confronted with such an ultimate negation of meaning as death.

Precisely because he was not a postmodernist, Jonson seems to be bothered by, rather than accepting of, his incoherent reactions to his son's demise and to the chaos the boy's death seems to symbolize. He experiments unsuccessfully with various large-scale explanations in order to help make sense of the death, at one moment referring to 'fate' and at another calling the death 'just' (l. 4). Ironically, however, his most passionate outburst occurs immediately after this attempt at reason (l. 5). Likewise, at the beginning of the poem, he rebukes himself for his past excesses (l. 2), and at the end he promises to avoid such excess in the future (l. 12). He thus implicitly seeks an attitude of balanced moderation, but the poem paradoxically displays many efforts to impose control through excess: the speaker wants to 'lose *all* father' and promises to supervise '*all* his vows' (ll. 5; 7; emphasis added). The speaker has been taught a metanarrative that '*should*' help him cope with (and even welcome) his son's death (l. 6; emphasis added), but his direct experience conflicts with such pat and simple stories. Heaven is implicitly imagined as a place that transcends change and chaos (ll. 5–7), but the poem (to its credit) does not try to falsify the speaker's actual experience.

From one perspective, then, Jonson's poem seems anything but postmodern: it seems a serious, sincere, intricately crafted work of high art that seeks to find some meaning, order, and stability in response to one of the most chaotic experiences a human can face. Little about the poem seems pervasively ironic, decorative, playful, or purposefully subversive. Even this poem, though, yields intriguing insights when viewed through a postmodern lens.

Changes in the Canon

Bruce Boehrer

Over the last thirty to forty years, the study of seventeenth-century English literature has redefined itself largely by redefining its object of inquiry: that is, by changing our ideas of what belongs in the category of 'seventeenth-century English literature' itself. Scholars typically refer to this process as reconfiguring the canon.

Literary studies inherit a notion of 'the canon' – what *The New Princeton Encyclopedia of Poetry and Poetics* defines as 'a list of texts believed to be cultur-ally central or "classic"'[1] – from Biblical studies, where the term refers to 'the collection or list of books of the Bible accepted by the Christian Church as genuine and inspired'.[2] Following George Orwell's claim that 'there is no test of literary merit except survival, which is itself merely an index to majority opinion',[3] one may think of the canon as essentially a catalogue of survivors. But one must also recognize that the list of survivors tends to change with time, and that while canonical authors may indeed be accepted as such by the majority of readers, it is not necessarily 'majority opinion', in any broad sense, that invests them with their canonicity.

As the study of English literature has grown into a free-standing academic discipline, it has claimed much of the responsibility for maintaining the canon of English classics, a task its members perform largely through teaching and related activities: not just classroom instruction, but also curriculum design, thesis supervision, public lectures, scholarly publications, and other activities, among which textbook production and assignment assume a prominent role.

Thus, to get a rough sense of how the canon of seventeenth-century English literary works has changed over the past three or four decades, one could do worse than to consider the case of *The Norton Anthology of English Literature*. Since 1962, this has probably been the single most influential anthology of English literature in print. The collection's website credits it with 'over 2700 [course] adoptions worldwide',[4] while in an interview recorded on January 19, 2006, National Public Radio commentator Tom Ashbrook declared that 'When it comes to defining the canon of English literary greats, *The Norton Anthology of English Literature* is the world's big gun'.[5]

So, how has 'the world's big gun' changed its approach to seventeenth-century literature over the past four decades? To begin with, consider the following. In 1968, the *Norton*'s second edition devoted 441 pages to 'The Seventeenth Century (1603–1660)'; in 2000, the *Norton*'s seventh edition gave 835 pages to the same period, now identified as 'The Early Seventeenth Century (1603–1660)'. The 1968 *Norton* divided its 440-odd pages between twenty-six authors (and one anonymous ballad); the 2000 *Norton*, with almost twice the amount of space, also increased the number of authors represented from twenty-six to thirty-four.

One normally expects a group of survivors to diminish over time. This group, on the contrary, has not just resisted diminution; it has actually grown, and by no mean measure. If we have some broader experience in literary studies (or if we have read around some more in different editions of the *Norton Anthology*), we might extend this observation into a general hypothesis: *All things being equal, changes in the canon will move in the direction of greater inclusivity.*

But of course, all things are not always equal. Even if one doubles the anthology space given to the seventeenth century, that space still has its limits. Human attention is by nature also limited; if one admits new writers to the canon, they will sooner or later lay claim to attention that therefore cannot be devoted to more established authors. As the *Norton*'s coverage suggests, this fact does not generally pose a threat for the period's most respected writers; the *Norton*'s seventh edition features much-expanded coverage of major figures like Milton, Jonson, and Donne. But second-tier luminaries can and sometimes do suffer; while the later *Norton* contains coverage of fifteen seventeenth-century writers not featured in the 1968 second edition, seven authors and one anonymous ballad featured in the earlier edition have disappeared from the latest.[6] In its most recent incarnation the *Norton* may admit Aemilia Lanyer and Lady Mary Wroth to the canon, but it does so at the expense of figures like Richard Corbet, Henry King, Joseph Hall, Sir Thomas Overbury, and Sir William Davenant.

If these latter figures may in some sense be understood as casualties of canon-change, it nonetheless remains that the new canon creates more winners than losers. In what follows, I shall focus on three of the major strategies whereby scholars have effected this widening of the canon over the past thirty to forty years: (1) by devoting new attention to the traditionally minor works of major authors; (2) by lending new consideration to genres of writing that have not always been regarded as properly literary; and (3) by resurrecting literary authors who for one reason or another have gone largely unnoticed in the recent past. Taken together, these strategies account for much that has changed in the landscape of seventeenth-century English literature since the last quarter of the twentieth century.

New Attention to the 'Minor' Works of Major Authors

The process of canon-change rarely forces first-rank authors into obscurity, but it can on occasion promote a previously obscure author to the highest levels of visibility. The fortunes of John Donne provide a classic example of this process; generally neglected from the eighteenth to the early twentieth centuries, his work was strikingly rehabilitated by the enthusiasm of scholars like T.S. Eliot and the American New Critics. Likewise, while canon-change seldom leads to the devaluation of major authors, it can and often does force a reconsideration of the relative merits of their individual works. Shakespeare provides the most obvious recent example of this process; in the past forty years, a whole series of Shakespearean plays once dismissed as 'stupid . . . and uninspired' (*Titus Andronicus*)[7] or 'loose and desultory' (*Troilus and Cressida*)[8] have come in for sustained reappraisal.

Other major authors of the seventeenth century – I take Milton, Jonson, and Donne as prime examples – have undergone the same kind of reevaluation in recent years. While the general ascendancy of these authors remains unimpaired, scholars have revisited parts of their *oeuvre* once dismissed as inferior or unrepresentative. This process has generally taken two complementary forms, one focusing upon the so-called 'minor' poems and plays of these major authors, the other dealing with works that have been overlooked because of their supposedly non-literary nature.

In the case of Milton, the former tendency has led from the poet's great epics toward a body of less celebrated and accessible, but equally intriguing work. A rich lode of this material resides in the poet's non-English verse, which encompasses Greek, Italian, and most of all Latin, and includes sonnets, odes, epistles, epigrams, personal statements of literary vocation, a miniature epic that anticipates *Paradise Lost* in various ways, and a pastoral elegy that demands comparison with 'Lycidas'. While none of this poetry has yet earned a place in the *Norton Anthology* (which, after all, is mainly devoted to writing in English and mainly aimed at an introductory undergraduate-level readership), it has come in for increasing scholarly attention, as exemplified by the work of Stella Revard, Stephen Guy-Bray, and others.[9]

Still and all, Milton's verse represents a fraction of his overall literary productivity, and his non-English verse represents merely a fraction of that. Any serious move to revise the Milton canon has to address the vast body of his prose works, done in both English and Latin and primarily occasioned by matters of political and theological controversy. The second edition of the *Norton Anthology* includes excerpts from *Areopagitica*, but its editors declare that 'of Milton's complex and troubled career in controversy we need not say too much'.[10] It remains for later editions like the seventh, perhaps moved by an increasingly politicized ethos of scholarship, to include some small examples of the poet's more bare-knuckled controversial prose. Likewise, in the exalted regions of advanced literary studies, recent decades have witnessed a marked increase in scholarship on Milton's prose, including influential books by Keith Stavely and Thomas Corns, and a trend-setting 1974 essay collection edited by Michael Lieb and John T. Shawcross.[11]

This scholarship provides a special case of the more general tendency to be explored in the next section of this essay: the impulse to perform critical analysis of works that have not always been understood as properly literary. While I reserve more detailed treatment of this propensity for later, it bears noting that each of the three major authors I discuss here has been made subject to this kind of reappraisal.

In the case of Ben Jonson, for instance, scholars have again moved simultaneously toward a reconsideration of the poet's literary failures and toward increased discussion of his ostensibly non-literary writings. In the former case, new attention has been lent to Jonson's most famous flops: the plays (*The Staple of News, The New Inn, The Magnetic Lady*) with which he sought late in life to make a comeback on the public stage, and the much earlier plays (*Cynthia's Revels, Poetaster*) that he composed as part of the so-called Poets' War.[12] But the real revolution in Jonson studies has occurred in connection with that part of his work traditionally slighted as sub-literary. Stephen Orgel's groundbreaking 1965 study *The Jonsonian Masque* led the way here by directing unprecedented attention to the magnificent body of courtly entertainments Jonson composed in his capacity as patronage poet.[13] Following Orgel's lead, scholars have produced a massive amount of work on the masques over the past four decades, including but by no means limited to influential volumes by Orgel and Roy Strong, by Joseph Loewenstein, and by Dale Randall.[14] Nor have scholars limited themselves to re-investigating Jonson's masques and pageants. The poet's translations and commonplace book have come in for renewed critical attention, and even the marginal scribblings in the surviving books of his library have received exhaustive study.[15]

With Donne, the story is much the same; from the conventional standpoint of the mid-twentieth century, his literary reputation rested upon his English poems as published posthumously in 1633 and again in 1635. In the words of one commentator, 'One very striking aspect of the critical treatment of Donne until quite recently has been its concentration upon his poetry (and within the poetry, on the *Songs and Sonnets*)'.[16] However, this emphasis has gradually changed as research has focused (1) on certain of his more obscure poems, and (2) upon the rich variety of his prose works. The former include his *Elegies* (long dismissed as leering juvenilia), the *Epicedes and Obsequies* (equally disregarded as sterile exercises in courtly compliment), and such other works as the *Satires* and the unfinished 'Progress of the Soul'. Likewise, the full range of Donne's prose – from sermons to spiritual meditations and religio-political satire – has earned sustained reassessment. Thus John Carey, in an influential study published in 1981, refused 'to assume that the worthwhile element in Donne comprises the poems and a few rousing bits from the sermons, and that the rest of his *oeuvre* can be safely consigned to the rubbish tip of history'.[17]

Apart from Shakespeare, the three cases presented here – Milton, Jonson, and Donne – probably represent the most solidly established bits of the seventeenth-century English literary canon, and over the past few decades, specialists have reconfigured the study of these authors in markedly consistent ways. Moreover, were we to turn our lens on Shakespeare, we would discover similar changes in how criticism has approached him as well. These changes – the renewed interest in minor works and the study of literary genres not traditionally identified with belletristic writing – provide a basis for similar shifts in emphasis throughout the broader range of the canon. The rest of this essay aims to show how these shifts have affected our approach to relatively minor authors and works.

New Consideration of 'Non-Literary' Genres

When Terry Eagleton begins his influential *Literary Theory: An Introduction* by asking 'What is literature?',[18] he raises one of the most exasperating questions in the field of literary studies. It is also the central question of debates about the canon; after all, it is through our 'list of texts believed to be culturally central or "classic" ' that we gain an intuitive sense of what counts as literature. Eagleton's conclusions in the first chapter of his book – (1) that there is no 'inherent quality' essential to literature; (2) that instead the category of literature defines the ways 'in which people *relate themselves* to writing';[19] and (3) that this mode of relationship involves 'value-judgements' with 'a close relation to social ideologies'[20] – hold serious consequences for our understanding of literary genres. As a result, over the past thirty to forty years these ideas have produced an expanding sense of what we study when we study seventeenth-century English literature.

Such expansion has been driven in part by the growing belief that conventional hierarchies of genre – for instance the medieval *rota Virgilii*, or Milton's description of his prose works as products, 'as it were, but of my left hand'[21] – are an extension of the social hierarchies in which they were produced rather than of any consistent critical logic. If Milton's epics are worth study, the argument goes, why are his controversial prose works any less so? These latter were produced by the same mind and drawn from much the same sources; they occupy more space in the poet's collected works and they took up more of his professional time. And if Milton's *Doctrine and Discipline of Divorce* is not intrinsically less worthy of study than *Paradise Lost*, what of Gervase Markham's *Country Contentments*, or Thomas Wright's *Passions of the Mind in General*, or John Lilburne's *Picture of the Council of State*? In fact, the traditional canon has always made at least some room for works in so-called sub-literary genres – for instance Izaac Walton's *Compleat Angler*, Sir Thomas Browne's *Pseudodoxia Epidemica*, and Robert Burton's *Anatomy of Melancholy*. It has simply done so on a selective and more or less unreasoned basis.

By placing a broader range of such works under critical scrutiny, scholars gain a more complete understanding of the literary marketplace that produced such traditional classics as *Paradise Lost* and *King Lear*, and in the process, they can find themselves forced to reassess their intuitive sense of how the seventeenth-century English literary world worked. As Peter Blayney has recently noted, a literary curriculum that focuses on the plays of Shakespeare and Jonson is forced, by its very nature, to ignore the fact that '[c]ustomers in early modern bookshops chose to spend far more of their money on religious books than they did on playbooks and other "literary" publications'.[22] From this standpoint, at least, even Shakespeare's canonicity would appear to be a retroactive construct. And by the same token, the responsible practice of literary history arguably should not limit itself to what later generations have come to regard as the 'classics' of seventeenth-century writing, but should also attend to those literary works and genres that seventeenth-century readers themselves deemed especially worthy of their cash and attention.

When viewed from this perspective, even the most traditionally canonical authors can begin to look non-canonical. We have already noted that most of Milton's surviving work is prose on religious subjects: precisely the kind of thing for which seventeenth-century readers seem to have had an inexhaustible appetite, but also the sort of work that has been pushed to the margins by his reputation as England's foremost epic poet. Likewise, it was Donne's early forays into religious controversy, not his *Songs and Sonnets*, that impressed King James I enough to steer the poet toward his ultimate vocation within the Anglican Church. And even if we self-consciously confine ourselves to so-called 'literary' writing – poems, plays, and fictional narratives in prose – we may be surprised at how much attention these works devote to non-belletristic matters. After all, perhaps the most conventional feature of early modern imaginative writing is its placement within the context of literary patronage; to publish a poem without its attendant panoply of epistles dedicatory, prefaces to readers, dedicatory poems, proems, glosses, marginalia, and envois was as unthinkable in the seventeenth century as it would be now to release a Britney Spears single without the accompanying video. How are these features of the text to be approached? To regard them as mere excrescences does an injustice not only to the frequency with which they appear but also to the fact that they reveal most clearly the material purpose of the publications in which they occur. Insofar as the object of *The Faerie Queene* was to secure favor at court, the poem itself is arguably an appendage to its front-matter, rather than vice versa.

This insight, in turn, suggests that epistles dedicatory, prefaces, dedicatory poems, proems, glosses, and marginalia comprise a distinct literary genre with its own objectives, conventions, and implied readership: yet another sub-literary genre that demands unprecedented critical attention. Accordingly, recent scholarship has devoted increasing study to the forms assumed by seventeenth-century literary patronage; in a landmark 1981 article, Frank Whigham performed close reading on early modern English suitors' letters while observing that they 'display much self-conscious artistry', employ conventions that 'had long been organized by a poetics', and make an appropriate object of literary analysis simply because 'they are made of words'.[23] The precedent thus established has led to further work in a similar vein, most recently David Bergeron's *Textual Patronage in English Drama, 1570–1640*, which examines all the epistles dedicatory and addresses to readers appearing in English playbooks and entertainments printed between its target dates. For Bergeron, these texts function as unique 'authorial *soliloquies*',[24] and as such they acquire their own internal coherence and formal integrity, emerging as literary works in their own right that demand to be read on their own terms.

The conventions of patronage also inform other traditionally sub-literary genres, perhaps most spectacularly the amalgam of text, music, dance, costume, and stage architecture that comprises seventeenth-century masques and pageantry. Thus it should be no surprise to find that scholarly attention to these works has grown exponentially over the past thirty to forty years, with studies of Jonson's entertainments leading the way. Even in their own day these dramatic productions were scarcely accorded the status of literature, a fact attested by Jonson's famous struggle with Inigo Jones over the artistic ontology of their collaborative projects. But Jonson's efforts to claim the masques as his own work also bear witness to the fact that such productions *could* be conceived as literary in nature. Indeed, Jonson's struggle for a literary conception of the masque-form may have been ahead of its own time, but it has arguably born fruit in current critical practice, for one could view the contemporary admission of masques and pageants to the canon of seventeenth-century literature as in fact a reversion to seventeenth-century critical precedent as established by Jonson himself.

If seventeenth-century poets had courtly aspirations which led them into the territory of patronage discourse, the court had its own aspirations too, particularly to expand and consolidate its sphere of political influence. These ambitions imprint themselves on the English literary landscape through yet another set of generic affiliations to come in for close recent study. The project of defining English rule is inseparable from that of defining Englishness itself, and this latter project, in turn, demands the serious attention of anyone seeking a reputation as an English author. Patriotic sentiments and ventures are of course widespread in early modern English literature, ranging from Gaunt's 'sceptered isle' speech in Shakespeare's *Richard II* to Spenser's wholesale celebration of Elizabethan autocracy in *The Faerie Queene*, from Jonson's panegyric on Britannia in *The Masque of Blackness* to Milton's projected epic on King Arthur. Some of these works concern themselves quite specifically with the geographical and historical derivations of Englishness. As Richard Helgerson observes, Michael Drayton's *Poly-Olbion*, William Camden's *Britannia*, and John Speed's *Theater of the Empire of Great Britain* are works belonging 'to different fields', but 'they also belong together' as volumes 'devoted to England'.[25] For Helgerson, this affinity also connects them to a wide range of other works by authors such as Shakespeare, Spenser, Hooker, Coke, and Hakluyt.

Thus seventeenth-century literary studies have witnessed a rebirth, over the past two decades, of interest in the genre of chorography, a literary form that transcends the distinctions between verse and prose in its focus upon the delineation and description of geographical regions – most importantly, for present purposes, those comprising England and Britain. As Helgerson demonstrates in his trend-setting study of English literary nationalism, a focus on, say, Shakespeare's conception of England in the second tetralogy can lead irresistibly toward a study of that most 'non-literary' of print forms: the atlas. From the Elizabethan county maps of Christopher Saxton and John Norden to the Jacobean efforts of Camden and Speed, such works 'had an inescapable part in creating the cultural entity [i.e., England] they pretended only to represent'.[26] Likewise, the geographical delineation of Englishness anticipates and in a sense calls for the geographical *projection* of Englishness into foreign and inhospitable spaces. On this level, the maps of Saxton and the antiquarianism of Camden find their counterpart in the exploration narratives assembled by Richard Hakluyt and Samuel Purchas. In the face of growing

English self-definition, these latter works encounter the unfamiliar and sub-due it, 'colonizing the marvelous' on paper even as England embarks upon its long history of more literal colonization.[27]

For scholars like Stephen Greenblatt and Richard Helgerson, exploration narratives not only provide essential insight into the growth of English nationhood and imperialism; they also provide essential background for understanding the traditional canon of English literary greats. A play like *The Tempest* demands to be read alongside William Strachey's account of the dis-covery of Bermuda; a play like *Othello* requires placement alongside the Moorish captivity narratives recently edited by Daniel Vitkus.[28] By the same token, still other genres of non-belletristic writing can be imbricated in the production of first-magnitude English classics. It has long been acknow-ledged, for instance, that early modern humors comedy owes a debt to Galenic medical theory, but within the past two decades scholars have begun to argue that this influence extends beyond the so-called humors plays to affect the fundamental ways in which early modern theater understands the human body. Leading the way here, Gail Paster has brought medical texts like Helkiah Crooke's *Microcosmographia* and Nicholas Culpeper's *Directory for Midwives* into conversation with major early modern plays like Jonson's *Alchemist* and Middleton and Rowley's *Changeling*.[29]

Of course, when Paster cites Crooke (or Vitkus cites Richard Knolles' *Generall Historie of the Turkes*), it is generally not to make claims for the artistic excellence of the work in question. But if we agree with Eagleton that '[t]here is no "essence" of literature whatsoever',[30] then criticism itself becomes rela-tively unconcerned with identifying or asserting the artistic merit of given literary works; instead, its principal job is to understand how particular sys-tems of meaning can *confer* merit on particular works. From this standpoint, context is preeminent. And the writings of Crooke and Culpeper, Knolles and Strachey, Hakluyt and Purchas, Camden and Speed, help provide the context in question.

New Attention to Previously 'Neglected' Authors

To claim that there are no qualities intrinsic to literature – let alone 'good' literature – may strike some readers as a nihilistic abdication of critical responsibility. Others, among whom I count myself, would reply that far from denying the existence of literature (or literary merit), this view leads to a relatively realistic understanding of these categories, which emerge not as the product of solitary genius but rather as a function of reading and writing communities that interact with each other in complicated ways over lengthy periods of time. Space still remains for literary evaluation; after all, that is what any literary professional does when she grades a term paper, or writes a book review, or composes a tenure letter. Concomitantly, it is still possible for an author to do good work to the extent that she conforms to – or transforms – the 'horizon of expectation' established for her efforts by a particular community of readers.[31] What is gone (and this is clearly a reaction to the extravagancies of nineteenth-century bardolatry and early twentieth-century formalism) is a sense of the literary work and its author as self-sufficient entities, in control of their own meaning and its proper reception. And by extension, the field of literary studies has witnessed some significant changes to the old cult of literary personality realized most visibly in the study of Shakespeare.

Indeed, if hierarchies of genre can be seen as encoding ideological value-judgments, so too can the specific *kinds of authors* whom literary historians have chosen in the past to celebrate. Thus the canon-changes of the past half century or so have involved broad revisions to an implicitly white, male, educated, Protestant, heterosexual, and propertied standard of authorship endemic to much earlier literary history. In an historical period like the seventeenth century, which predates the more far-reaching effects of British colonialism and imperialism, this has largely meant revising the canon's pervasive maleness, with the consequence that the most visible recent shifts in the roll call of seventeenth-century English literary greats have involved the rehabilitation of previously-neglected women authors.

In short, seventeenth-century literature has become a proving ground for the branch of feminist scholarship Elaine Showalter once denominated 'gynocritics': '[t]he type of feminist criticism . . . concerned with *woman as writer* – . . . with the history, themes, genres, and structures of literature by women'.[32] The past thirty years have witnessed a profusion of new, high-quality critical editions of work by hitherto under-represented early modern women authors. These include Barry Weller and Margaret Ferguson's edition of Elizabeth Cary's *The Tragedy of Mariam* – 'the first original play by a woman to be published in England';[33] Susanne Woods' edition of the poems of Aemilia Lanyer – once luridly but questionably identified as 'Shakespeare's "Dark Lady" ';[34] Josephine Roberts' edition of the poems of Lady Mary Wroth – once luridly but questionably identified as 'the Celia of Jonson's poems';[35] Roberts', Suzanne Gossett's, and Janel Mueller's edition of the same author's monumental prose romance, *The Countesse of Montgomeries Urania*;[36] and numerous other volumes of comparable interest. These editions, in turn, have been supplemented by a range of scholarly studies, from Elaine V. Beilin's *Redeeming Eve: Women Writers of the English Renaissance* (1987) to Maureen Quilligan's *Incest and Agency in Elizabeth's England* (2005), which collectively supply early modern women authors with 'a kinship of continuity' and their own literary-historical backstory.[37]

Feminist revision of the early modern literary canon has been particularly successful in altering the critical landscape at the level of introductory instruction. To return to the example of the *Norton Anthology*: of the fifteen seventeenth-century authors appearing in the seventh edition of the anthology but not represented in the second edition, ten – Aemilia Lanyer, Mary Wroth, Elizabeth Cary, Martha Moulsworth, Rachel Speght, Katherine Philips, Lucy Hutchinson, Lady Anne Halkett, Anna Trapnell, and Margaret Cavendish – are women. In fact, the edition of 1968 admitted *no* women authors *at all* to its coverage of the seventeenth century. With almost one-third of its representation devoted to women (if we measure by head-count rather than, say, by page-count), the seventh edition of 2000 provides its readers with a substantially different vision of this period in early modern English literary history. As for the *Norton Anthology*'s readers, a very large proportion of them consists of second- and third-year undergraduates who encounter the anthology as a textbook for introductory survey courses in English literature. To this extent, feminism has arguably produced the single most far-reaching revision of the early modern literary canon to occur within the past fifty years.

However, there has also been a parallel movement operating on the levels of social rank and religious persuasion. The 1968 *Norton Anthology* enshrines a seventeenth-century literary pantheon full of knights and peers (Sir Thomas Browne; Sir John Suckling; Sir Thomas Overbury; Sir William Davenant; Sir Richard Blackmore; Edward Hyde, Earl of Clarendon; Francis Bacon, Viscount St. Albans); Anglican clergy (Donne, Herrick, Herbert, Corbet, King); scholars and professionals (Browne, Vaughan, Burton, Bacon, Clarendon); and government appointees and recipients of royal patronage (Donne, Jonson, Marvell, Milton, Bacon, Hobbes, Carew, Lovelace, etc.). As fierce as the religious and political antipathies may have been between certain of these figures, one can easily come away from this list more impressed by their similarities – of wealth, of education, of political connection. Nor was this homogenizing impulse confined to undergraduate literature anthologies; as Christopher Hill noted in 1977, the mid-twentieth century had witnessed an influential scholarly effort to 'annex Milton for "orthodoxy" ' by depicting him as 'a traditional authoritarian who can be used to rebuke the sinful modern world'.[38] If one can do this with Milton, one can arguably do it with anybody.

Hill's own work – which insisted that Milton was 'a radical Protestant heretic' who 'shed far more of mediaeval Catholicism than did the Church of England'[39] – proved important in countering this trend. Thanks in part to the efforts of Hill and like-minded scholars, a recent critical anthology like *Milton and the Grounds of Contention* can include, quite comfortably, an essay on Milton and the Socinian heresy, and another dealing with the poet's affinity for 'some of the most outrageous and forward-looking principles of Antitrinitarian rationalism'.[40] As for the *Norton Anthology*, the seventh edition draws new attention to the heterodox impulses of a poet like Milton by placing him alongside the Levellers Lilburne and Winstanley, a Fifth Monarchist like Anna Trapnell, and a Ranter like Abiezer Coppe. Likewise, the inclusion of a laborer like Winstanley and self-appointed prophets like Trapnell and Coppe can broaden the volume's frame of socioeconomic reference.

Beyond such developments, the recent growth of queer studies as an independent discipline has led to a concomitant reappraisal of the seventeenth-century literary canon from the standpoint of sexual orientation. While acknowledging that the concept of homosexuality – like the contemporary queer culture that reacts to that concept's creation and stigmatization – imposes a form of anachronistic distortion upon early modern sexual thought and behavior, scholars have nonetheless traced what we might call a prehistory of gay culture in the literature of early modern England. In some cases, this process has lent unexpected prominence to otherwise minor authors. The poetic reputation of Richard Barnfield, for instance, has been burnished by recent work in queer studies, and while the current boom in Margaret Cavendish's literary stock is largely due to her broader feminist appeal, this has certainly not been hurt by the lesbian overtones of a play like *The Convent of Pleasure*. In a similar vein, scholars like Jonathan Goldberg, Stephen Orgel, Bruce Smith, Gregory Bredbeck, and Richard Rambuss have focused on the alternative sexualities of more solidly canonical poets such as Marlowe, Shakespeare, Jonson, Crashaw, and Milton.[41] If we add this work to the other bodies of scholarship mentioned above, the result is a generation of critics who have rewritten the seventeenth-century literary canon in the image of various social diversities: of gender, of spirituality, of class, and of sexual orientation.

Developments in Bibliographical and Editorial Scholarship

The strategies of canon-revision outlined above – concentration upon the minor works of major authors, interest in traditionally sub-literary genres of writing, and rehabilitation of neglected authors – should be understood to operate in complementary and synergistic fashion. Exploring the minor works of major literary figures, for instance, leads one more or less irresistibly to a consideration of non-belletristic literary genres. Likewise, the serious study of ostensibly inferior genres can lead, by a replication of logic, to the serious study of ostensibly inferior writers. And the study of the otherness of supposedly minor writers can return one yet again to the major figures, whom one can revisit and revise from the standpoint of this alterity. The result is a process of scholarly growth in which one set of changes builds upon others, while simultaneously laying the groundwork for still further development in those other related areas.

Along with these mutually-reinforcing methods for revising the canon, one more deserves mention as well. Developments in bibliographical and editorial scholarship (sometimes grouped under the title of The New Textualism) have wrought fundamental changes in the printed form assumed by some of seventeenth-century England's most established literary classics. Here as elsewhere, the field of Shakespeare studies offers an especially clear example of tendencies that may also be traced in seventeenth-century literary scholarship as a whole. The publication in 1986 of *The Oxford Shakespeare*, edited by Stanley Wells and Gary Taylor, proved to be an important – and predictably controversial – event in the growth of the movement that Leah Marcus has called 'Unediting the Renaissance'.[42] Wells and Taylor set a precedent for the abandonment of single-text eclectic editions in favor of multiple texts representing variant textual sources, and in the case of Shakespeare, this trend has led to startling results. For instance, none of the three texts of *Hamlet* presented in Anne Thompson and Neil Taylor's 2006 Arden 3 edition of that play contains both the hero's final soliloquy and his famous declaration that 'Denmark's a prison'. The reader is left, instead, to sort out for herself the relative merits – and authority – of three separate and competing *Hamlets*.[43]

When it comes to the other major figures of seventeenth-century literature, the effects of The New Textualism are more muted, in part because writers like Jonson and Milton represent a new model of authorship, seriously devoted – as Shakespeare was not – to exercising authorial control over the forms in which a literary work might see print. Yet, despite their relative care to establish definitive, authorized versions of their work, Jonson and Milton, too, have been subject to editorial redefinition and debate of a serious nature. To take the most obvious examples: when Jonson completely rewrote *Every Man In His Humour* (1598) in order to include it in the 1616 folio edition of his works, in the process changing the play's setting, character names, and much else besides, the effect was not to replace one version of the play with another, but rather to impose an editorial situation in which neither version suffices to represent the play in its entirety; likewise, when the theological treatise entitled *De Doctrina Christiana* was first published under Milton's name in 1823, its posthumous attribution provided the starting-point for a fierce debate over its actual authorship. This controversy, raging through the 1990s and into the first decade of the twenty-first century, has led scholars to call for the creation of 'something like a hypertext edition of the treatise' drawn from the work's unique manuscript.[44] In these and other cases, the effect of editorial change, like that of the other changes enumerated in this essay, has been to introduce greater diversity into the canon.

But then, it can surprise no one that recent scholars should take the issue of diversity so seriously. For one thing, they operate in a university environment that is itself increasingly subject to the effects of racial, sexual, religious, cultural, and social difference; for another, their own progressive political commitments often incline them to favor diversity over unity as an ideological principle. Needless to say, this preference places them at odds with the more authoritarian tendencies of much seventeenth-century literature itself, particularly that produced by representatives of the period's dominant political order. But the generation of scholars producing English literary history at present has also grown up with the legacy of Vietnam and Watergate, Contragate, the 2000 United States presidential election, and the Iraq Wars. Many of these scholars find it easy, therefore, to regard the pronouncements of any dominant political order as at best dishonest and at worst self-deluding. As Stephen Greenblatt has summarized this view, 'one of the highest achievements of power is to impose fictions upon the world and one of its supreme pleasures is to enforce the acceptance of fictions that are known to be fictions'.[45]

If recent changes to the canon therefore reflect the dominant ideological sensibility of today's literary profession, one might wonder what changes lie in store for both our literature and our politics. Were I to speculate (and the exercise would be nothing more than informed speculation), I would hazard that environmental questions will prove ever more pressing in the fifty years that lie ahead. I believe these questions, which speak to the finitude of the earth's resources and to issues of equity and prudence in their distribution, will loom ever larger, in both politics and literature, over the coming decades. To this extent green criticism, still in its infancy, may have much to say to us in the years to come.

10 Issues of Sexuality, Gender, and Ethnicity

Robert C. Evans and Eric J. Sterling

Chapter Overview

Recent Trends

Perhaps the most remarkable recent change in the study of seventeenth-century literature has been the growing emphasis on women writers and on issues of gender and race. These developments have helped transform the field. Topics that were once discussed only rarely (if at all) now seem highly important; authors and texts that once seemed marginal or neglected have become the focus of intense attention. Seventeenth-century women writers, in particular, have benefited from this explosion of scholarship. Modern academics who once debated whether women in the 1500s and 1600s had enjoyed a Renaissance have essentially produced such a Renaissance themselves. In scholarship, at least, women of the seventeenth century have probably received more sustained and sympathetic attention in the last fifty years than they ever enjoyed in their own lifetimes.

Along with this growing interest in the lives and writings of women has come a rapid rise in attention paid to various sexual minorities, particularly to persons who felt same-sex erotic desire or engaged in same-sex erotic activity. To call such persons 'homosexuals' or 'gays' would be (in the view of many recent scholars) anachronistic or imprecise. Indeed, some of the most significant scholars in this field have argued that for much of the sixteenth and seventeenth centuries (and, of course, before then) there *were* no 'homosexuals' in England in the recent senses of that word. According to such scholars, there *were* no people who self-consciously defined themselves (or were thought of by others) as members of a coherent, recognized sexual minority with a particular 'sexual orientation'. Instead, there were people who felt (and sometimes wrote about or acted on) same-sex desires, and there were people who engaged in particular sexual acts that are today often associated with a 'gay' minority. Nevertheless, as a matter of convenience, many modern scholars do use the word 'homosexual' as a neutral term to describe same-sex desire and behavior, and that term will also be used in this chapter for the same reason and purposes. The crucial point, for the time being, is that whereas almost no one, fifty years ago, was writing on the topic of seventeenth-century literature by or about homosexuals, today that topic is ubiquitous.

The same is true, although to a lesser extent, of writings by or about members of various ethnic minorities who appear in seventeenth-century British literature. Issues of race and ethnicity have become the focus of plentiful recent scholarship. Although much of this recent work focuses on the ways black persons were treated and/or written about in the early modern period, interest in ethnicity and in cultural minorities of all sorts has also led to a newly intense focus on such groups as Jews, Muslims, Native Americans, and the Irish, as well as on other minorities within the British Isles, such as the Welsh and Scots. In general, the whole trend of recent scholarship in seventeenth-century studies has reflected a new interest in 'minorities' or marginal groups of all kinds, even when those 'minorities' may in fact have constituted a majority of the actual population (as may have been the case with women and was certainly the case with the working poor). Interest in religious minorities (such as Catholics and the members of various Protestant sects, such as the Quakers, Levelers, Diggers, and Family of Love, to name only a few) has also grown, and fascination with other marginal groups (such as prostitutes, cross-dressers, Jesuits, Puritans, and Anabaptists, to mention merely several) has ballooned. Gone are the days when studying seventeenth-century literature meant focusing mainly on aristocrats or the upper classes or on canonical authors and texts. The whole trend of the last half-century has been to examine lives, writings, and groups that had previously been marginalized or ignored, both in their own era and by later scholars. In particular, issues of sexuality, gender, race, and ethnicity – which once tended to be neglected – have now moved close to the front and center of recent scholarship.

Writings by and about Women

Perhaps no other aspect of the study of seventeenth-century British literature has seen more dynamic development than the examination of writings by and about women of the period. Whereas once such writings were mostly unknown and largely ignored, in the past three decades they have received an extraordinary amount of attention. Typical of this new focus on previously neglected writers is Barbara Lewalski's *Writing Women in Jacobean England*, which in fact deals not only with female authors *per se* but with women known mainly as patrons. Lewalski usually begins by providing solid biographical overviews, carefully placing her subjects in their larger historical and cultural contexts and examining the writings they penned or inspired in relation to such issues as 'the power of social and cultural institutions, the ideology of absolutism and patriarchy, the formation of subjectivity, the forms of authorial "self-fashioning," [and] the possibility and manifestation of resistance and subversion'.[2] Even this lengthy list, however, is hardly comprehensive, since Lewalski often treats the writings by or about her subjects by connecting them to the texts (both by other women and by males) that influenced their composition. She also discusses such writings in terms of their structures, genres, and even their rhetorical and artistic effectiveness.

Lewalski opens by admitting that the Jacobean women she has chosen to study – Queen Anne, Princess Elizabeth, Arbella Stuart, the Countess of Bedford, Anne Clifford, Rachel Speght, Elizabeth Cary, Aemilia Lanyer, and Mary Wroth – are not entirely representative, since most were privileged. She calls them a

> group of highly articulate women whose resistance takes various but striking forms: defining an oppositional role vis-à-vis patriarchal institutions; claiming rights, status, and power not usually accorded women; projecting in literary texts a fantasy of overt resistance and rebellion, of dominant or separate female communities, or of feminist politics and values; claiming genres and rewriting literary discourses for women's voices and stories.[3]

Lewalski tries to situate these women in as many different contexts as possible, but particularly refreshing (in a period in which the *literary* study of literary texts has often seemed passé) is her stated intention 'to read the works as responsibly as possible, using techniques of formalist analysis to begin a consideration of them in aesthetic as well as political terms'. Lewalski sensibly cautions that we 'need to know much more about these texts before we can address questions of aesthetics very securely', but she asserts that 'it is already evident that Cary, Lanyer, and especially Wroth are writers of considerable merit'. Some of her best pages are devoted to patient discussions of artistic skill and structural talent, but she also honestly notes aesthetic shortcomings.

Typical of both her forthrightness and her balance, for instance, are her comments on 'The Dream', a poem included in Rachel Speght's *Mortalities Memorandum*:

> the verse is sometimes pedestrian, and the first few stanzas are also marred by awkward poetic diction. But this work is much enlivened by the allegorical fiction, by the dialogue of the speaker with allegorical characters, by the author's emotional engagement with sensitive autobiographical concerns, and especially by the fictional representation of a woman's obstacle-laden path to education.[4]

Likewise, her comments on Aemilia Lanyer's *Salve Deus Rex Judaeorum* are suggestive in their precision and admirable in their candor:

> As poet-narrator, Lanyer treats her material variously, sometimes relating events, sometimes elaborating them in the style of biblical commentary, sometimes meditating upon images or scenes, often apostrophizing participants as if she herself were present with them at these events. She uses rhetorical schemes – especially figures of sound, parallelism, and repetition – with considerable skill; her apostrophes convey strength of feeling; she describes and sometimes dramatizes a scene effectively. And the inset rhetorical speeches such as 'Eves Apologie' are forceful and effective. There are few striking images or metaphors, but Lanyer's allusions are usually appropriate and her language straightforward, taking on at times colloquial directness. Her greatest fault is a tendency to pad lines and stanzas to fill out the metrical pattern.[5]

Few critics were better prepared than Lewalski to compose such a book as *Writing Women in Jacobean England*. It appeared after she had already made substantial contributions to the study of such male writers as Donne and Milton and to such important topics as Renaissance genres and the seventeenth-century Protestant religious lyric. Her book on Jacobean women is thus extremely well informed, and it is also exceptionally clear and free of fashionable jargon.

Clear and well informed in its own way is the 'Introduction' to *Kissing the Rod: An Anthology of Seventeenth-Century Women's Verse*, which offers generous, well-edited, and fully annotated selections from fifty different authors.[6] This was a path-breaking and highly influential collection. Edited by Germaine Greer, Susan Hastings, Jeslyn Medoff, and Melinda Sansone and introduced with typical vigor by Greer, the book is the product of extensive archival research, and it remains one of the best works to consult when starting research on a whole host of seventeenth-century women writers. Greer's feisty 'Introduction' begins by proclaiming the book's purpose: 'to show who the women were who tried to storm the highest bastion of the cultural estab-lishment, the citadel of "sacred poetry". They were all *guerrilleras*, untrained, ill-equipped, isolated and vulnerable'.[7] This may overstate the case a bit, but Greer's 'Introduction' is never dull. It has the added advantage of discussing and reproducing various poems not included in the main anthology, and it also offers a spirited survey of the whole terrain, including both the opportunities and the difficulties of research in the field and the strengths and weaknesses of previous scholarship. Greer solidly outlines the social and cultural contexts her women had to contend with, including the impedi-ments they faced in seeking literacy and education and their practical challenges as wives, mothers, workers, or 'spinsters'. She is especially helpful in discussing the transition from a manuscript culture to a culture of printers and booksellers.

Particularly valuable are the cautions Greer provides about authorship, especially against simply assuming that any work attributed to a woman author must have been written by a female. She is judiciously skeptical of many such claims and shows why it was often advantageous – and profitable – to assert that a woman had written a work that was probably written by a man. Her prudence in this regard makes the attributions she does accept seem all the more reliable, and her tough-mindedness is typical of her whole approach. She isn't reluctant, for instance, to call attention to the frequently poor quality of some of the verse that women (like men) were capable of composing, and she finds it amusing that religious prophetic poems, allegedly inspired by God, were almost always written in the same very sim-ple and pedestrian stanzaic pattern ('Why the Holy Ghost should have favored this form has not been revealed to us').[8] On a more serious note, Greer is especially good at discussing the wide variety of particular genres in which early modern women often composed, including not only religious proph-ecies but also epitaphs on loved ones (often their own sons, daughters, and husbands), celebrations of friends and relatives, advice to children, spiritual diaries, and religious meditations, not to mention lyrics, complaints, comed-ies, tragedies, satires, and prose romances. In roughly thirty pages, Greer manages to sketch a whole century's worth of literary and social develop-ments, covering not only such well-known writers as Aphra Behn and Katherine Philips but also persons virtually unknown before the publication of *Kissing the Rod*. The book itself, moreover, offers concise but substantial and reliable biographical introductions to each of the authors it surveys, and the notes on the texts are shrewd and thorough. Few anthologies have had the kind of lasting impact of *Kissing the Rod*. It remains a nearly indispensable book.

Anthologies of a different sort – collections of critical essays – are also helpful in giving useful overviews of the state of scholarship and of the issues that are both under discussion and up for debate. A monograph by a single author (such as Lewalski's) provides a particular critic's point of view; critical anthologies, by definition, provide the diverse views of many different contributors. Among the numerous such anthologies that might be mentioned, two edited by Anita Pacheco seem particularly worth recommending. The first – *Early Women Writers: 1600–1720* – contains essays by twelve different scholars on five distinct authors (Mary Wroth, Katherine Philips, Margaret Cavendish, Aphra Behn, and Anne Finch). Most of these writers were especially productive in the middle or closing decades of the century, and so Pacheco's collection nicely complements the mainly Jacobean emphasis of Lewalski's book. Especially worthwhile is Pacheco's own 'Introduction', which provides a lucid guide to various important matters.[9]

Pacheco discusses (for instance) the distinctions between the Anglo-American tendency to research writing by actual females and the tendency of French theorists to explore a more abstract 'feminine writing' (whose practitioners might include men), and she assesses how both approaches might be open 'to charges of collusion in patriarchal ideology'.[10] She also explains the different assumptions of 'new historicists' and 'cultural materialists', noting that '[m]aterialist feminists and cultural materialists would argue that cultures are nowhere near as monolithic' as new historicism might suggest – an important point, since an effective monolithic system would prevent or forestall subversion or revolution.[11] Pacheco additionally notes that most of the essays she reprints 'address at some level the question of what happens when a woman tackles a genre or poetic tradition whose conventions have been shaped by men, and a consensus clearly emerges that early women writers did, to varying degrees, appropriate literary conventions for their own ends'.[12] Like both Lewalski and Greer, then, Pacheco and her contributors stress the importance of genre (of writing in different forms or 'kinds' of literature) – an issue which indeed is crucial in approaching practically any seventeenth-century text.

Finally, Pacheco closes her introduction by turning to a topic 'central to materialist-feminist criticism: the relationship between gender and racial oppression'. This matter (Pacheco notes) 'remains a hotly contested issue in feminist theory and criticism, especially for feminists of colour, who argue that any attempt to construct a common history of marginalization [of women] obscures the ways in which European women benefited from and, at times, actively participated in the colonial enterprise, while simultaneously ignoring or misrepresenting the very different histories of oppression and struggle of men and women of colour'.[13] Pacheco's collection closes with a glossary of recent critical terms, a nicely annotated bibliography, and an index that includes not only names but also topics. All these features make her book – which stresses 'theory' much more explicitly than does either Lewalski's volume or *Kissing the Rod* – far more accessible than it might otherwise have been.

Perhaps even more valuable is another book edited by Pacheco: *A Companion to Early Modern Women's Writing*, a large collection of essays on a wide variety of topics and authors. Anyone seeking a single-volume comprehensive critical overview of seventeenth-century women writers will find this one hard to surpass. All the essays are clearly written; jargon is minimal; and both the discussions and the often extensive bibliographies provide a solid sense of relevant scholarship. The book exemplifies recent work in its heavy focus on issues of history, politics, and social conditions; it pays correspondingly less attention to matters of artistry, structure, and rhetorical skill, although it hardly ignores those topics by any means.[14]

Kenneth Charlton's opening essay stresses the fact that most lower-level education in the seventeenth century, especially for girls, took place at home, at church, or in other households where young people were sent to live or where they worked as servants. The royal court was the greatest such household, but as the century wore on, more and more schools that accepted girls began to spring up. (It goes without saying that women could not attend universities.) There was always a strong stress, however, on practical training for women (especially in household skills), and much of the writing intended for females consisted of 'how-to' manuals. Charlton shows that women sometimes helped educate themselves and others, although most educators were inevitably men. Diane Willen, meanwhile, discusses the contradictory and complicated impact of religion on early modern women. She claims that religious influences could sometimes have a more important impact than either gender or class alone, and she also shows how religious commitments – especially in the mid- to late-seventeenth century – helped foster a growing political involvement by women.

Tim Stretton, in discussing women and the law, shows how unexpectedly complicated their rights and powers could be. He also shows the impact of different kinds of laws and legal systems (such as the common law and statutes, ecclesiastical law, customary law, the various kinds of equity), and he discusses how variable the experiences of different kinds and classes of women often were. He argues that by the end of the seventeenth century, women became increasingly aware of the contradictions and inequities they often faced. In an essay following Stretton's, Sara H. Mendelson discusses the working lives of ordinary women, their vulnerability to poverty, their movement into the cities, and their limited opportunities for financial relief. Mendelson also outlines the kinds of work done by women of the middling and upper ranks, noting that aristocratic women were primarily expected to have babies and run large households, while women of the middle ranks often either helped with family businesses, labored as housewives, or sometimes worked in various professions (such as medicine, midwifery, or teaching). Changes during the course of the century in the working lives of the rich and poor were less common (Mendelson concludes) than were developments among women of the middling classes. Finally, in the last of the general essays that introduce Pacheco's second collection, Margaret J. M. Ezell surveys women and writing, providing an overview of recent scholarly developments and then stressing devotional writing, writing done in extreme situations, writing done in and for small groups (or 'coteries'), writing done to advance political or religious causes, writing done to defend women, and writing done (especially in the second half of the century) in order to make money.

In the first of the essays in this collection to deal with seventeenth-century writers, Susanne Woods discusses Aemilia Lanyer's *Salve Deus Rex Judaeorum*. Woods sees the book as the first attempt by an English woman to define herself professionally as a poet. She also discusses the repetition of key words (such as 'grace', 'beauty', and 'virtue'), compares and contrasts the poem with Ben Jonson's 'To Penshurst', and shows Lanyer's awareness of gender and class. In the essay that follows – on Elizabeth Cary's *The Tragedy of Mariam* – Elaine Beilin contrasts Cary's play with various sorts of history plays that preceded it; notes the relatively small number of lines spoken by Mariam herself; and discusses the play's indebtedness to contemporary trends in the writing of history, arguing that the play emphasizes disorder especially as it closes. Meanwhile, in a discussion of Mary Wroth's prose romance *The Countess of Montgomery's Urania*, Naomi J. Miller begins by noting Wroth's work in a variety of genres; discusses the ways *Urania* explores diverse possibilities for women (especially as mothers, lovers of males, and female friends); and examines the differences between *Urania* and other works by Wroth and other works (especially other romances) by other authors.

Gweno Williams, in an essay on Margaret Cavendish's autobiographical *A True Relation . . .* (1656), begins by noting Cavendish's open desire for fame, her self-conscious efforts to achieve it through publication, and her changing attitudes toward *A True Relation*, a work she eventually failed to republish. Williams finds the book a well-written text; emphasizes its distinctive stress on individuality; discusses its complicated relationships with 'truth'; and explores its equally complicated presentation of feminine self-assertion. She connects the book to the Civil War and argues that in her later career, Cavendish was more interested in invented fictions than in supposed veracity. Claims to truth are also an issue in Hilary Hinds' article on Anna Trapnel's radical and religious text *Anna Trapnel's Report and Plea* (1654). Hinds discusses its hostile reception, its distinctive style, and its mixture of autobiographical, polemical, and prophetic utterance. Meanwhile, in an article on Katherine Philips' *Poems* (1667), Elizabeth H. Hageman examines

Philips' methods of self-presentation, compares and contrasts her work with that of various male writers (such as Theophrastus, Martial, Ben Jonson, and of Abraham Cowley), and discusses her poems on other women of her day. Anita Pacheco herself then focuses on Aphra Behn's *The Rover, Part One* (1677) arguing that Behn, although a royalist, uses her play to examine libertine values and elite versions of masculinity in a significantly critical fashion. Likewise, Patricia Springborg sees Mary Astell as offering a critique of contemporary analogies (by such writers as John Locke) comparing the marriage contract to the social contract. Instead of viewing Astell as a proto-feminist, Springborg situates her in her own time as a Tory (i.e., royalist) critic of Whig (i.e., republican) political philosophy.

In the final set of essays in Pacheco's volume, various genres are discussed. Thus, Sheila Ottway provides an overview dealing with autobiography, noting the great growth of autobiographical texts (including ones by women) from 1600 to 1700 as well as the growing number of autobiographies with a secular orientation. More and more women, and from a greater range of social backgrounds, began to present their lives in manuscript and even in print, both in prose and in poetry. Sometimes they wrote diaries; sometimes they offered chronological surveys; often they described their relations with God and with members of their families. Cavendish's *A True Relation* was the first secular prose autobiography to be printed while its author was still alive, while An Collins and Martha Moulsworth were two of various women to compose autobiographical poems. In a chapter on 'Defences of Women', Frances Teague and Rebecca De Haas emphasize the use of polemics as well as catalogues of exemplary females as common ways for such texts to be structured; they also explore the variety of tones and motives exhibited in such defenses (some of which were composed, sometimes seriously and sometimes merely as profit-making ploys, by men). Teague and De Haas note the changes of tone often found in such texts between the early and later parts of the century; later texts tended to be more dignified and sophisticated, partly because they were less likely to be anonymous.

In a chapter on prophesies, Elaine Hobby discusses such 'ecstatic and visionary prophets' as Lady Eleanor Davies, Elinor Channel, Sarah Wight, Anna Trapnel, Katherine Evans, Sarah Cheevers, and others. Hobby contends that the fact that these were women always affected how their visions were received (often in negative ways and often by largely male audiences and authorities). Hobby next notes the proliferation of prophesies by nonconformist women (especially Quakers) after the 1640s. Several hundred such women were active, for instance, between 1640 and 1660, although only about one-fourth of their prophecies survive in print. Prophesying became less common after the Restoration, but Hobby rightly calls attention to the fascinating figure of Anne Wentworth, who briefly became a sensation in the late

1670s. Hobby suggests that prophecy allowed women to claim to speak (and often publish) with God's own sanction – a position that gave such women power but could also make them threats to established authorities.

In an ensuing chapter, Bronwen Price surveys women's poetry, emphasizing such recurring themes as bodily weakness but also noting the changes that occurred in female verse as the century progressed. She connects her poets to the various generic, religious, social, and political developments of the time, touching on an impressive number of writers in a mere twenty pages. Prose fiction is covered in even less space by Paul Salzman, who first emphasizes various examples of the romance genre and then moves on to the fantastic fiction of Margaret Cavendish – fiction that he considers highly inventive and imaginative. Salzman next offers a suggestive discussion of Aphra Behn's *Oroonoko*, which he finds complicated in its depiction of the title character and in its attitude toward slavery, but which he also considers an effective indictment of the hypocrisy of the white Christians it presents. He concludes by noting that the three most important female writers of seventeenth-century prose fiction – Mary Wroth, Margaret Cavendish, and Aphra Behn – were comfortable working in a variety of genres but were especially inventive in prose. Finally, in a concluding chapter on drama, Sophie Tomlinson surveys the work of various women in such various forms as translations, closet dramas (i.e, works intended to be read rather than staged), tragedies, and comedies. Special attention (and rightly so) is paid to Aphra Behn and the women she inspired. Tomlinson stresses Behn's skill at depicting physical comedy, at exploiting the stage, and at presenting erotic emotions and conduct.

In its range of topics and the quality of its contributors, Pacheco's collection is an exemplary book of its kind, but it also exemplifies the usefulness of critical anthologies in general. Almost inevitably such books offer valuable overviews of the common topics, typical methods, points of consensus, and issues under dispute in any given field. And, in a field as lively and as brimming with various voices and perspectives as the study of seventeenth-century English women writers, multi-authored collections are especially helpful.

Writings by and about 'Homosexuals'

Few academic books have been as influential in their own fields of study as Alan Bray's *Homosexuality in Renaissance England*, which was first published in 1982 and then reissued (with an 'Afterword') in 1995. Bray's achievement is all the more impressive since, at the time he wrote the book, he was not an 'academic' in the technical sense at all: he had no full-time job as a professor at a college or university. Rather, he researched and composed the text 'largely in isolation and mostly late at night after a day's work as a British career civil servant'.[15] A few previous books had discussed homosexuality in early modern England before Bray's appeared, but no other book (it seems safe to say) had, and continues to have, the impact his study quickly achieved.

Bray begins by disputing earlier accounts that had argued for a relatively benign attitude toward homosexuality during the English Renaissance. Instead he emphasizes 'the considerable evidence for the deep horror with which homosexuality was widely regarded' during that era.[16] Yet he also contends that there was often a significant disparity between what was widely preached and believed about homosexuality and how people actually often behaved. Same-sex desire and conduct were apparently more widespread than the often virulent condemnations of sodomites, 'buggers', 'ingles', 'catamites', 'ganymedes' (and other such terms) might lead one to suspect. 'Sodomy' was considered less a state of being (a distinct sexual identity) than a set of specific acts to which anyone might succumb. In the early modern period (Bray argues) 'no clear line' tended 'to be drawn between contemporary attitudes to homosexuality and to debauchery as a whole'.[17] Buggery was one of the many sins a person might commit; it was often associated with other acts of licentiousness; and it was often used as a convenient target for attacking people accused of treason, atheism, and other forms of alleged corruption.

Bray is especially effective in calling attention to the caution with which contemporary accounts of homosexual behavior must be interpreted; literary texts (such as satires) and even court records cannot always be taken entirely at face value. Nevertheless, by patiently examining a wide range of evidence, Bray comes to a number of persuasive conclusions about same-sex conduct in the early modern period. It often involved (for instance) relations between people who were fairly well acquainted and who were often living in the same households or institutions, sometimes as masters and servants, sometimes as fellow students, sometimes as students and teachers.[18] Homosexual prostitution especially in large cities such as London was not uncommon, and homosexual conduct was sometimes also linked with the London theaters.[19] People tended to marry later in life than is now the case, and homosexual contact was often a way for people who did not think of themselves as 'homosexuals' (as few people then did) to achieve sexual release without fears of illegitimate pregnancies. Yet despite the fact that homosexual relations were by no means unknown, attitudes in the late 1500s and early 1600s toward 'homosexuality had hardly changed since the thirteenth century; it was in the Renaissance as it was then, a horror, a thing to be unreservedly execrated', so that 'it is difficult to exaggerate the fear and loathing of homosexuality to be read in the literature of the time'.[20] Even many people who probably engaged in homosexual conduct (such as King James VI and I) roundly condemned it. Paradoxically, then, homosexuality was anathemized in many writings of the day, but homosexual relations were more common than such condemnation might lead one to expect. Only rarely was homosexual sex prosecuted. In one especially important passage, Bray contends that so

> long as homosexuality was expressed through established social institutions, in normal times the courts were not concerned with it; and generally this meant patriarchal institutions – the household, the educational system, homosexual prostitution and the like. . . . Despite the contrary impression given by legal theorists, so long as homosexual activity did not disturb the peace or the social order, and in particular so long as it was consistent with patriarchal mores, it was ignored.[21]

'Sodomy' in the abstract was considered a heinous sin and was often associated with witches, devils, treason, and atheism; yet the occasional act of sodomy was mostly overlooked, and few people consciously thought of themselves as 'sodomites' or professed any conscious commitment to sodomy as an ideal or a way of life. There was, Bray says, a clear 'discrepancy between this society's extreme hostility to homosexuality' – a hostility 'which one comes across when homosexuality was being referred to in the abstract' – and this same society's 'reluctance to recognize [homosexuality] in most concrete situations'.[22] Theory and practice (according to Bray) tended to be separated and compartmentalized. One could commit the occasional homosexual act without thinking of oneself as homosexual.

By the end of the seventeenth century, however, things had begun to change – at least according to Bray and various other scholars. By that period, so-called 'molly houses' had begun to flourish, and they had also begun to attract the attention and persecution of authorities. These were places (often associated with taverns) where people who had begun to think of themselves as homosexuals (and who were increasingly seen as such by others) gathered to socialize and even (at least in some cases) to have sex. Bray sees the molly houses as societies within the larger society and thus as the beginnings of a separate homosexual subculture. Distinctions of class began to dissolve in these places, but 'most of all what gave' the molly house 'its independence in society was its elaboration of its own distinctive conventions: ways of dressing, of talking, distinctive gestures and distinctive acts with an understood meaning, its own jargon'. By the late 1690s, then, 'new meanings were now being attached to homosexuality: it was more than a mere sexual act'.[23] The more that homosexuals began to define themselves (and be defined by others) as a distinct minority, the more they were harshly persecuted, and the more they were harshly persecuted, the more they began to think of themselves as a distinct minority:

There was now a continuing culture to be fixed on and an extension of the area in which homosexuality could be expressed and therefore recognised; clothes, gestures, language, particular buildings and particular public places – all could be identified as having specifically homosexual connotations. In contrast, the socially diffused homosexuality of the early seventeenth century was far less obtrusive, and violent condemnations of it rarely had any significance outside of a world of symbol and myth.[24]

'Molly houses' became places where homosexuals were sometimes persecuted but could also increasingly bond. 'What had once been thought of as a potential in all sinful human nature', Bray writes, 'had become the particular vice of a certain kind of people, with their own distinctive way of life'.[25] Bray connects this change to a general movement, during the seventeenth century, toward nonconformist subcultures of all sorts (especially in matters of religion), and he relates both kinds of change to a general abandonment of the ideal of unity in society and philosophy as a whole. By 1700, individuality of thought and behavior had become much more widely accepted than it had been in 1600, and so in 1726, when one homosexual was being prosecuted for his behavior, he defended himself by saying, 'I think there is no crime in making what use I please of my own body'.[26] Who, Bray asks, could imagine anyone making such a defense a century earlier?

In the 1995 'Afterword' to his original 1982 study, Bray notes the support and challenges his book had in the meantime evoked, including arguments alleging that homosexual desire and behavior were even more widely accepted throughout the century than he had at first suggested. What is most striking about recent studies of homosexuality in early modern England, however, is how much Bray – in a short book that is nonetheless full of clearly presented data and cogent arguments – has set the terms of subsequent discussion.

One of the many later studies clearly influenced by Bray is Bruce R. Smith's 1991 study titled *Homosexual Desire in Shakespeare's England: A Cultural Poetics*. As its title suggests, Smith's book tends to concentrate on the late sixteenth and early seventeenth centuries, but its implications for study of homosexuality in early modern England in general are profound. In particular, Smith argues that homosexual desire was often more positively presented in the art and literature of the period than Bray had suggested, and he especially emphasizes how presentations often differed from one genre of writing to another. He contends, for instance, that the four basic 'kinds of discourse' about homosexuality in this period ('moral, legal, medical, and poetic') 'in fact address different subjects entirely. Moral, legal, and medical discourse are concerned with sexual *acts*; only poetic discourse can address homosexual *desire*'. Smith claims to have 'isolated six separate myths [i.e, kinds of stories]

of homosexual desire, each of which involves a different combination of characters and plot, a different set of ideas about sodomy, a different way of
enacting homosexual desire in imagination'.[27] This fundamental assumption –
that homosexuality could be presented quite differently in different kinds of
writing – is perhaps Smith's most valuable contribution; certainly it helps
caution us against reading various discourses about homosexuality without
paying attention to matters of genre. Thus, Smith treats stories 'of male
friendship in chapter 2, pastoral fantasies in chapter 3, romance narratives
in chapter 4, and verse satires in chapter 5', concluding with a long and
suggestive discussion of Shakespeare's sonnets.[28] Much of his evidence comes
from sixteenth-century and/or Shakespearean texts (and thus lies outside
the scope of the present handbook), but what emerges from his valuable
study is a clear sense of the importance of genre and of literary precedents
to the study of homosexuality in any literary text, and what also emerges is a
generally more positive account than Bray offered of how homosexuality
could be viewed in writings of the early modern period.

More relevant to the present handbook is Paul Hammond's monograph
of 2002 titled *Figuring Sex between Men from Shakespeare to Rochester*, which
discusses not only the authors mentioned in its title but also such other
seventeenth-century figures or issues as James I, the Civil War, Titus Oates,
King William III, and Andrew Marvell. Hammond opens by arguing that

> *circa* 1600, one finds poetry explicitly articulating homoerotic desire, along
> with plays in which homoerotic possibilities are teasingly explored. What
> seems to us now to be a vein of homoeroticism often colours the expression
> of male friendship. And yet this was also a period in which sexual relations
> between men were fiercely condemned by the law and the church. By
> contrast, *circa* 1700 it is hard to find any literature which celebrates the male
> body homoerotically, while at the same time there is now a self-confident,
> self-defining subculture, with its own meeting places (the 'molly houses')
> and its own language; meanwhile, one encounters an anxious insistence on
> the lack of eroticism of male friendships, and denunciations of 'sodomy'
> from groups such as the Societies for Reformation of Manners.[29]

During the course of his clearly written book, Hammond makes a number of
arguments that are specifically relevant to the literature of the seventeenth
century. He suggests, for instance, that '[w]riters wishing to voice love
between men' during this period 'often develop strategies (such as allusions
to the Greeks) which allow such desire to be identified, while also inviting
readers to construe it as something other than sexual – as masculine friendship,
as religious devotion. Open texts result, which offer the reader various possibilities, space for the imagination'. On the other hand, 'writers condemning

such desires as diabolical sodomy may insist upon punitive definitions, turning the complexities of real human beings into caricatures, into monsters'. Thus, in his chapter on allegations of homosexuality leveled against various political figures, Hammond shows 'how the actual lives of historical individuals become mythologized, as their sexuality generates resources for figuring them as destroyers of the symbolic order and the values of godly, Protestant England'. Meanwhile, in his chapter on Andrew Marvell, Hammond uses various 'sexually charged caricatures' of Marvell 'as the starting point for a reading of the ambiguous elements in Marvell's own lyric poetry, highlighting moments when homoerotic motifs complicate the texture of ostensibly heterosexual poems'. Finally, in his chapter on John Wilmot, Earl of Rochester, Hammond suggests 'that for all the homosexual bravado which we encounter from time to time' in Rochester's poetry, 'there is no real homoeroticism here, in the sense of felt desire for the male body'.[30] Like much other recent scholarship on early modern homosexuality, Hammond is as much interested in politics as in literature, assuming – as do many others – that 'literature' is inevitably written and read in ways that involve issues of power. Hammond's book is also typical of recent scholarship in its heavy (and valuable) historical emphasis.

As a final example (in this all-too-brief survey) of some of the splendid recent work being done on homosexuality in seventeenth-century literature, one could hardly do better than to cite Denise A. Walen's study from 2005 titled *Constructions of Female Homoeroticism in Early Modern Drama*. Walen is one of a growing number of scholars who have begun to focus on 'lesbianism' in literature of the period, although (once again) that modern term must be used with caution. Walen begins by noting that initially 'the consensus among scholars' was that few early modern 'texts of any kind, including drama, presented female homoeroticism', and she also reports that at first literary critics 'failed to identify a significant cultural discourse surrounding desire between women'. Walen, however, through patient and painstaking research, has discovered 'more than seventy plays' from the late sixteenth and early seventeenth centuries that 'include both minor, passing references to female-female sexual activity or erotic interests and long, involved plot situations that complicate the narrative action'. She shows convincingly that playwrights 'placed female characters in erotic situations with other female characters in: (1) playful scenarios of mistaken identity, (2) in anxious moments of erotic intrigue, (3) in predatory situations, and (4) in enthusiastic, utopian representations of romantic love'.[31] Her book argues that although 'female homoeroticism was primarily suspect and threatening' to many people during this era,

> playwrights found wonderfully inventive ways to construct the desire and introduce it as not only tolerable but also pleasurable. The desire was

always dangerous but, at least in drama, playwrights found ways to circumvent social fears and expectations; hence the need to couch constructions of female homoeroticism in subtextual strategies. They succeeded partly because they presented constructs of homoerotic desire – or affinity/friendship/homosociality, eroticism in general – rather than sexual experiences. Homoeroticism, especially a romanticized view of female companionship, was rendered acceptable while homosexuality would have been, and in the plays was, condemned or rejected. In general, the more sexually explicit the desire that one female character consciously directs toward another female character, the more implicit the condemnation directed at the character and her apparently deviant desire. However, overt declarations of romantic love, sexually untainted, represent the most socially acceptable forms of female homoeroticism in these plays.[32]

Walen's book, which is written and organized with impressive clarity, would be valuable if it did nothing else than excavate and summarize the various plays it surveys; her study, like much of the other recent work done on same-sex desire in early modern England, suggests that there are many more intriguing discoveries yet to be made and much more probing criticism and analysis yet to be undertaken.

Writings by and about Members of Ethnic and Racial Minorities

Ethnic and racial minorities of various kinds have been the focus of much recent study of seventeenth-century literature, but especially intense attention has been paid to blacks. Typical of such work is Anthony Gerard Barthelemy's 1987 monograph *Black Face, Maligned Race: The Representation of Blacks in English Drama from Shakespeare to Southerne.*[33] Barthelemy begins by discussing the historical associations that have often been made between blackness and evil in western culture and the long-lasting prejudices that associated black people with bestiality, sin, and sexual promiscuity. He discusses the various meanings the word 'Moor' had developed by the 1600s, and then he examines the desire of the 'Black-mores' in Ben Jonson's 1605 *Masque of Blackness* to be freed from their symbolically unattractive color. Although such a transformation could be achieved relatively easily in a work of fiction, Barthelemy notes that in the real world, blacks could never be washed white. He then studies the negative ways in which blacks were usually depicted in London's Mayors' Pageants. Blacks were portrayed in almost twenty such civic shows between 1585 and 1692, and the later pageants tended to support colonization and slavery. Meanwhile, in his next chapter, he reports that between 1589 and 1695, the vast majority of black characters presented in stage plays were linked with evil and/or with sexual license, including a significant number of black females. A few virtuous black characters were sometimes presented on stage (Shakespeare's Othello being the obvious example), but even those characters often conformed to, and thus seemed to confirm, various negative stereotypes. Black heroes (such as the title character of Thomas Southerne's 1695 play *Oroonoko*) were few and far between, and even they were often presented ambiguously. The overall picture that emerges from Barthelemy's book, therefore, is dark in more ways than one.

By the 1990s, interest in issues of 'race' in early modern writing was not only growing rapidly but was becoming increasingly interdisciplinary. In 1994, for instance, Margo Hendricks and Patricia Parker edited an important collection of essays combining an interest in 'race' with an interest in gender and exploring the relevance of both categories to literature, history, anthropology, medicine, religion, sociology, and other fields.[34] The book focuses on women's writing and female authorship during the early modern and Restoration periods. The essayists also cover feminist criticism, 'race' (a word that the editors place in quotation marks to indicate that it is a constructed category), empires, and colonialism, among various other topics.

Jean Howard, for instance, links sexuality, gender, and race to English nationalism and nationalistic discourse in her essay 'An English Lass Amid the Moors: Gender, Race, Sexuality, and National Identity in Heywood's *The Fair Maid of the West*'. Howard demonstrates how gender and sexuality, as well as class and racial differences, help influence Renaissance England's sense of nationhood. Meanwhile, Dympna Callaghan's chapter covers Elizabeth Cary's underrated closet drama *The Tragedie of Mariam, Faire Queene of Jewry*, the first play written by an Englishwoman (1603 or 1604). Callaghan believes that feminist critics have privileged explorations of gender at the expense of 'race'. She places quotation marks around the word because otherwise the term could be considered racist because it would marginalize the subject as 'the other'. Callaghan attributes the scant attention to the play not to any lack of aesthetic value, but rather to the fact that it has been judged by patriarchal biases. She argues that revising the traditional canon necessitates upsetting the cultural hierarchy that evaluates literary works, a hierarchy rooted in prejudices concerning gender and 'race'. Callaghan asserts that the omission of the study of 'race' in a text leads to a flawed study of gender because the two categories are often intertwined. In Cary's play, the plot, set in Palestine, is racialized because of the Jewish characters; Jews were demonized and marginalized in the Renaissance England in which the author wrote; they were hated, considered Christ killers.

Other essays in the collection edited by Hendricks and Parker cover seventeenth-century works such as Shakespeare's *Othello* (1604) and Lady Mary Wroth's *The Countess of Montgomerie's Urania* (1621), both of which feature Moorish characters. The book also contains essays on Restoration literature, such as articles on Aphra Behn's novel *Oroonoko* and her play *The Widow Ranter*. Margaret W. Ferguson writes about the intersections of race, class, and gender in Behn's novel and also focuses on Behn's personal life, particularly on her education and social class. Margo Hendricks writes of the idealization of American Indians in Behn's tragicomedy *The Widow Ranter*. Hendricks notes that Behn's work dramatizes Nathaniel Bacon's 1676 rebellion against Virginian authority in which he raised an army of indentured servants, including African slaves, against the American Indians in Virginia. Hendricks is intrigued by Bacon's rebellion and by Behn's alterations of the historical situation, changes that highlight issues of racialism and ethnic identity. All in all, the essays in the Hendricks and Parker collection focus on the relationship between gender, race, and early modern culture, creating an interdisciplinary dialogue about the relevance of feminism and race to groups that were often marginalized and disenfranchised in seventeenth-century English society.

Also combining an interest in 'race' with an interest in sexuality is Kim F. Hall's influential study titled *Things of Darkness: Economies of Race and Gender in Early Modern England*, published in 1995.[35] Hall argues that scholarship on Renaissance English literature should not interpret literary references to blackness and race from a white, Eurocentric perspective, but rather from a perspective that recognizes and accepts distinctions between people of different races. Hall contends that literary critics tend to ignore issues of race and thus explicate imagery, concepts, and language from a white, European viewpoint. Like other recent critics who focus on blackness in Renaissance literature, she links 'race' to gender and to the particular language chosen by the author in question. Hall shows that blacks in the early modern period were considered racial curiosities that created cultural and racial anxieties and prejudices, as demonstrated, for instance, in George Best's description of a racial intermarriage in England, published in Richard Hakluyt's *Principal Navigations* (1589). A white Englishwoman engaged in a mixed marriage with a black Ethiopian man in England, and together the two had a child with black skin, which Best attributes to an infection (as if blackness were a disease) that the Northern (English) climate could not prevent. When reading about Africans, the early modern Englishman (according to Hall) often considered them as mere anecdotes and symbols of blackness. For one hundred years (for example) the Sackville family named one of their servants John Morocco, thus transforming several individuals into a mere type.

Hall discusses Ben Jonson's *Masque of Blackness* (1605) and *Masque of Beauty* (1608) as they pertain to blackness and Jacobean nationalism. The former masque involves a discourse on race, gender differences, nationalism, and imperialism. Audience member Dudley Carleton disapproved of the females (including Queen Anne) performing in blackface and claimed that their clothes looked like those of courtesans and that the painted women themselves looked like ugly Moors, a comment which suggests racial anxiety because he connects their blackness with illicit behavior and sexual appetite.

Mary Wroth helped to stage Jonson's *Masque of Blackness* and, according to Hall, was deeply engaged in the discourse of racial and gender differences, as is demonstrated in *The Countess of Montgomerie's Urania*. Hall believes that the relationship in Wroth's book between European females and 'the other' (women of other ethnic groups) is significant, such as when Urania's white maid wrongly believes that she sees Allimarlus kissing a 'BlackMoor'. The maid's anger and thirst for revenge suggest not only jealousy, but also racial anxiety and nationalism. Hall notes that black women in seventeenth-century English literature usually serve one of two bifurcated roles – maid or prostitute – as in John Marston's *The Wonder of Women* (1606).

Hall's work is an important book on blackness and gender in early modern literature, and its influence is noteworthy because it has often been quoted by subsequent books on the subject. Hall, in fact, is one of a number of significant critics whose work appears in a noteworthy collection of essays edited by Joyce Green MacDonald in 1997: *Race, Ethnicity, and Power in the Renaissance*.[36] Rebecca Ann Bach's essay, for instance (titled 'Bearbaiting, Dominion, and Colonialism'), links the early modern practice of bearbaiting to dehumanization and colonialism, and ultimately to theater. Bach discusses bearbaiting by drawing on Clifford Geertz's seminal anthropological essay 'Deep Play: Notes on the Balinese Cockfight', arguing that the inhumane treatment of animals in bearbaiting and cockfighting was important in early modern England because it sometimes led to the kinds of arguments for colonialism and imperialism found, for example, in Edmund Spenser's 'View of the Present State of Ireland' or, in Bach's example, Edward Waterhouse's 1622 tract *A Declaration of the State of the Colonies in VIRGINIA*, which advocated the massacre of Indians after they had attacked English colonists. Bach links bearbaiting to seventeenth-century English theater, particularly since theater manager Philip Henslowe (who led the Lord Admiral's Men and ran the Rose Theatre) and renowned actor Edward Alleyn, two prominent leaders of Renaissance theater, applied for and received licenses in 1604 for bearbaiting, which was performed onstage. Bearbaiting and theater both involve treating subjects as spectacles.

In another article in MacDonald's collection, Daryl W. Palmer writes about the racial identity of the Jew, just as Bach wrote about the racial identity of the Indians. Palmer links racial identity to buying, selling, and commercial trade, not just with Jews, but also Turks. English adventurers, such as Sebastian Cabot and Richard Hakluyt, were able to explore other cultures by trading with them, which often led to misconceptions and prejudices. Palmer mentions that Robert Wilson's play *The Three Ladies of London*, which deals with usury and the Jewish merchant Gerontus, profoundly influenced early modern plays about ethnicity and racial identity. Like other essayists in this collection, Kim F. Hall, in ' "Troubling Doubles:" Apes, Africans, and Blackface in *Mr. Moore's Revels*', links British explorers and their encounters with the natives of other cultures to racial identity in Renaissance English drama. She notes that Sir Thomas Herbert voyaged to the Cape of Good Hope, where he encountered Africans, whom he considered uncivilized – 'Troglodytes' – because, he claimed, they spoke like apes. Hall connects the racist descriptions of explorers such as Herbert to racially charged English drama, including such works as the antimasque *Mr. Moore's Revels* (1636) in which six characters appear in blackface and in which four actors dressed as apes steal coats; William Cartwright's *The Royal Slave* (1638); and Richard Brome's *The English Moore* (1639). The latter two texts include instances of characters employing blackface disguise and, like the aforementioned antimasque, contain obvious puns on the word 'Moor'. (The other chapters in MacDonald's book focus on Shakespearean drama rather than on works by his contemporaries and thus are not treated here.)

In another work exhibiting the recent interest in issues of race and ethnicity, Mary Floyd-Wilson discusses Englishness in relation to such matters as history, geography, nationhood, and 'geohumoralism'.[37] Floyd-Wilson argues, for instance, that Desdemona denies Emilia's charge that Othello is jealous because Desdemona believes that the climate and heat from his African culture have deprived him of the physical 'humor' that causes jealousy. Floyd-Wilson asserts that humoralism, which was often used in the early modern period to explain a person's comportment and social disposition, derives from climactic theories, such as Desdemona's above, that related behavior to color, ethnicity, geographic region, and climate. Of all seventeenth-century writers, Ben Jonson, Floyd-Wilson believes, most exhibits this kind of humoralism. Jonsonian works that deal with humors and ethnology include *Every Man Out of His Humour* (1600), *Cynthia's Revels* (1601), and *The Masque of Blackness* (1604). Floyd-Wilson believes that *The Masque of Blackness* is relevant to James I's efforts to control his subjects and get them to behave in an orderly manner. James wanted to join Scotland to England, but many English persons feared that the union could be problematic because the Scots might subvert the civilized and moderate comportment of the English. Jonson's masque (Floyd-Wilson believes) used blackness symbolically in ways that were designed to allay such fears. In general, Floyd-Wilson argues that such authors as Jonson, Christopher Marlowe, and William Shakespeare unconsciously contributed to attitudes toward British visions of self that helped promote the growth of the slave trade and English colonization of other nations.

Also typical of recent scholarship concerned with issues of 'race' and ethnicity is Virginia Mason Vaughan's book of 2005 titled *Performing Blackness on English Stages, 1500–1800*.[38] Vaughan deftly traces the history of white actors wearing blackface – and the theme of blackness – on the early modern English stage. She analyzes how blackface and the manner in which it was interpreted by the exclusively white audiences evolved in relation to cultural and political events during the era. Vaughan's well-researched study discusses both well-known Renaissance texts and little-known dramas that, although often ignored by previous scholars, provide valuable insights into racial identity and subjectivity in early modern theater.

Vaughan examines, for instance, Ben Jonson and Inigo Jones' 1605 court masque entertainment, *The Masque of Blackness*. The masque juxtaposes Moorish royalty with the white characters (who represented purity). This examination of Moorish royalty is complicated by the fact that Queen Anne insisted that she and her ladies in waiting dress as Moors, including the black face paint. Vaughan considers it unusual for someone at court, a queen no less, to request specifically that she appear as a Moor. Instead of merely employing a vizard to disguise herself as a Moor, Anne and her ladies wore paint, meaning that the transformation at the end of the masque to whiteness could not be enacted abruptly; instead, the text indicates that the transfiguration to whiteness would take a year. The play, Vaughan suggests, was not well received by courtiers, who found the spectacle disturbing and subversive, partly because they failed initially to identify the Moorish queen as Anne.

Vaughan also discusses the Moors in John Webster's *The White Devil* (1612), Mulinassar and Zanche. She contends that the blacks add exoticism and eroticism to the play and that they create a 'double consciousness', because the audience knows that underneath the Moorish black exterior exists a white European actor. Vaughan believes that unconsciously the audience, watching a white actor playing a black role, worried about racial pollution. Also, Vaughan examines Thomas Southerne's *Oroonoko* (1695), a dramatic adaptation of Aphra Behn's novel, which focuses on the noble black titular character who fights against slavery because he realizes that his children with Imoinda will become slaves. It is noteworthy that in the play, Southerne alters the character Imoinda from Behn's novel, making her white, which creates dramatic tension in the play and could remind audiences of the marriage between Othello and Desdemona in Shakespeare's famous drama.

Vaughan's book also focuses on bedtricks in non-canonical works such as John Fletcher's *Monsieur Thomas* (1614–1617), and Philip Massinger's *The Parliament of Love* (1624). She believes that bedtricks are significant because they include mistaken and confused identity, which sometimes leads white men to find themselves in bed with female Moors. Vaughan follows Wendy

Doniger in suggesting that bedtricks allow playwrights to bring together people with white and black skin in scenes that, while humorous, also would have created racial tensions in their original audiences. Vaughan's book also contains chapters on *Othello* (1603) and avenging villains; the book provides exhaustive coverage of issues of race and blackness in early modern theater, and it is one of the very best examples of recent scholarship on race and ethnicity in the literature of this period.

Although much of this recent scholarship has dealt extensively – as Vaughan's book does – with blacks and blackness, a number of significant studies have dealt with other ethnic groups, including Indians, Irish, Scots, Turks, and even Russians. Typical of this recent concern in early modern scholarship with cultural, ethnic, and racial minorities is James Shapiro's important book *Shakespeare and the Jews*. Shapiro's study illuminates English attitudes toward Jews from Shakespeare's time until the eighteenth century and supports its assertions with information from a wealth of sources, including diaries, sermons, travel narratives, dramas, and political commentaries.

Shapiro acknowledges that few Jews lived in Shakespeare's England but asserts that the English were, nonetheless, obsessed with Jews and perpetuated myths, such as assertions that Jews possessed a unique kind of sexuality and that Jewish men even menstruated. Shapiro also discusses the legend that Jews surreptitiously kidnapped and circumcised Christians and then used their blood (an idea accepted by John Donne and found in his sermons). The English (Shapiro contends) often classified themselves by what they were not (by contrasting themselves with aliens such as Jews); in their attempts to identify themselves positively, they tended to exaggerate and fictionalize 'the other'.

This, of course, is the very same process that tends to occur whenever one group – whether racial, ethnic, religious, sexual, or otherwise – wants to assert its distinctness (and often its alleged superiority), and it is precisely this process that has been the focus of so much recent attention from scholars of early modern literature.

11 Mapping the Current Critical Landscape: Seventeenth-Century English Literature

Albert C. Labriola

<table>
<tr><td colspan="2" align="center">**Chapter Overview**</td></tr>
<tr><td>The New Historicism</td><td>207</td></tr>
<tr><td>Feminist Criticism</td><td>214</td></tr>
<tr><td>Gay and Lesbian Studies</td><td>216</td></tr>
<tr><td>Ecocriticism</td><td>218</td></tr>
<tr><td>Conclusion</td><td>219</td></tr>
</table>

Recent trends in critical commentary have reshaped our understanding of the literary 'canon' – works deemed 'classics' because they survived the so-called test of time, served as landmarks along the continuum of literary history, demarcated the respective literary epochs, and regularly appeared in anthologies. Enshrined and validated by such perceptions, canonical works traditionally elicited three major kinds of critical commentary in the twentieth century: biographical criticism, historical study, and the New Criticism.

The first kind of commentary resulted in literary biographies. On the one hand, commentators used the life of an author as a means to explicate his or her works; on the other, commentators interpreted the works to learn more about the life of the author. Either way, the resulting interpretations partially illuminated the interaction of an author's life and works, but much of the commentary was speculative.

The second kind of commentary, which involved historical study, interpreted a literary work by referring to certain contexts often, but not always, from a previous era. Typically, the contexts were literary, such as the conventions that appear and reappear in sonnets, elegies, dream-visions, epics, dramas, odes, novels, and the like. In such cases, literary conventions and their adaptation in an author's works promoted comparative study with classical and medieval analogues. In addition to elaborating on literary conventions of a particular genre, traditional historical study often cited transcendent ideas, philosophical contexts, rhetorical traditions, and the like that distinguish the intellectual milieu of a particular epoch. An example of a transcendent idea is the Great Chain of Being, whose corollaries are plenitude, continuity, and gradation. Such an overarching idea informed the worldview of certain epochs, including the Middle Ages and the Renaissance. Accordingly, a character in medieval and Renaissance literature that became inordinately ambitious violated the so-called natural hierarchical order or the Great Chain of Being, which was perceived as ordained by God. The resulting misdeeds generated instability and upheaval in society. Numerous works of literature both instructed and delighted readers by providing examples of ambitious overreachers, ranging from Marlowe's Tamburlaine to Milton's Satan. Sometimes historical study was called humanistic criticism when the emphasis was on great ideas and philosophy, such as Platonism and Neoplatonism, issuing from works of classical antiquity and the Middle Ages, works that were cited as landmarks in an unfolding tradition.

The third kind of commentary, New Criticism, disengaged literary works from all contexts – biographical, historical, intellectual – in order to pursue analysis based on artistic features. This formalist approach practiced in Britain and the USA tended to focus on canonical authors whose works were valued for aesthetic excellence. New Critics, like I.A. Richards, John Crowe Ransom, Allen Tate, Robert Penn Warren, and Cleanth Brooks, used terms and concepts like theme, imagery, symbolism, paradox, irony, and ambiguity to accommodate seeming inconsistencies or dissonances in a work of art to an enriched and harmonious interpretation of the aesthetic whole.

While the methods of critical commentary cited above held sway from the end of the nineteenth and through most of the twentieth centuries, several reactions ensued. The most important and influential reaction is the New Historicism, the principal mode of present-day analysis of seventeenth-century English literature.

The New Historicism

The tenets of the New Historicism include the following: enlarging the canon by adding authors whose works were overlooked, leveling the hierarchy of authorship so that canonical writers no longer enjoy privileged status, collapsing distinctions between literary and non-literary texts, examining diverse reading materials to which the literate public and literary authors had access, mitigating or erasing the importance of aesthetic formalism and artistic features such as literary conventions, studying and comparing various texts from all classes of society, and broadening historical contexts to include such matters as polemical works, politics, law, medicine, economics, religion, travelogues, journals, and material means of production, such as the printing, licensing, censorship, and dissemination of texts.

In the vanguard of the New Historicism is Stephen Greenblatt's *Renaissance Self-Fashioning: From More to Shakespeare* (1980).[1] Initiated by reference to late sixteenth- and early seventeenth-century texts, the New Historicism has spread to other areas of English literary history and to American studies. In Britain, the closest counterpart of the New Historicism is Cultural Materialism. While Greenblatt is credited with initiating the New Historicism, he would be the first to acknowledge that others contributed to the development of the critical method. A major contributor was Michel Foucault, whose *Discipline and Punish* (1979), a translation of *Surveiller et Punir* (1975), analyzed the implications of Jeremy Bentham's *Panopticon; or The Inspection-House* (1791).[2] For Bentham, the panopticon was the ideal prison, which was shaped like a cylinder with cells at the outside walls. At the center of the cylinder was a guard tower from which a light shined into all of the cells. The surveillance tower, whether occupied or not, and the shining light disciplined prisoners, who felt that they were being watched continuously. This kind of induced self-discipline prompted Foucault to view the architectural panopticon as a metaphor for structures of power ingrained in institutions of all kinds, in codes of conduct, and in discourse. Greatly influenced by Foucault, the New Historicists dwell on historical circumstances and writings of all kinds contemporaneous with, not previous to, the literature being analyzed, thereby adopting a synchronic, not a diachronic, approach to their investigations. The New Historicists therefore discern how and why a culture engenders and preserves hierarchical order or classes in various spheres of activity: social, religious, political, economic, and the like. While examining texts of all kinds that ostensibly support power and authority, the New Historicism focuses on the so-called sites of conflict or contestation that are manifested between the dominant structures of power and the challenges to their hegemony. The challenges may be expressed but disguised in the ambiguous language of various texts or in dramatizations onstage of episodes and speeches that subvert the hegemony of royalty or nobility.

A prominent example of the New Historicism includes Greenblatt's *Shakespearean Negotiations: The Circulation of Social Energy in Renaissance England* (1988), in which the author discusses several plays: *Henry IV* and *Henry V*, *Twelfth Night*, *King Lear*, and *The Tempest*.[3] Greenblatt juxtaposes these dramas with practices and texts contemporaneous with Shakespeare, notably colonial propaganda, martial codes of conduct, cross-dressing, the ritual of exorcism, and the like. He uses, for example, Thomas Harriot's *A Brief and True Report of the New Found Land of Virginia* (1588) to highlight resemblances, on the one hand, between the colonists' use of Christianity and of 'invisible bullets' to engender awe in the Indians and, on the other hand, the monarchy's deployment of charisma and of its powerful impact on subjects, whether in dramas like *Henry V* or offstage in the political sphere. From Harriot's account, Greenblatt also cites tensions between attempts at containment and expressions of subversion, not only between the colonists and the Indians but also in the so-called cultural negotiations and transactions in England itself. This dynamic or 'social energy' involves processes whereby objects, rituals, and practices are appropriated, displaced, modified, or exchanged. From this anthropological perspective, culture becomes a medium in which numerous social determinants interact, all affecting literature and our understanding of its meaning and significance. From this vantage point, moreover, literature as such is neither intensely scrutinized in the manner of New Criticism nor explicated by reference to a transcendent or overarching idea of a particular philosophical milieu, a method of traditional historical study or humanistic criticism. Rather, the New Historicists interact with literature tangentially and almost always politically, but not comprehensively or intensively. Rarely, in short, is there sustained analysis of literature.

British studies of Shakespeare may be correlated with, but distinguished from, Greenblatt's. A foremost example is an influential multi-author collection, *Political Shakespeare: New Essays in Cultural Materialism* (1985).[4] The volume, co-edited by Jonathan Dollimore and Alan Sinfield, acknowledges in at least two overt ways its indebtedness to Raymond Williams: (1) by using his term 'cultural materialism' in the subtitle and (2) by including his epilogue that praises the new generation of cultural critics, including the contributors to the multi-author collection. Dollimore and Sinfield adapt and apply to Renaissance texts the principles of materialism that Raymond Williams derived, in large measure, from Marxism. Accordingly, Dollimore, more than Greenblatt, advocates that the autonomous individual is free to act within, and without, the confines of a culture, such action thereby effecting change in society. Interpreting Shakespeare's dramas as enactments of subversion and containment, Dollimore advocates social justice and the present-day redress of grievances of people who are exploited because of their race, class, and gender. For Dollimore, in other words, challenges to structures of power recounted in literature and enacted in drama rehearse the manner by which reform may and should occur in the social and political environment of the present era. Including an essay by Greenblatt in *Political Shakespeare* enables the coeditors to contrast the socially activist Cultural Materialism with the New Historicist emphasis on the illusive aspects of identity, on self-representation, and on the performative roles that we adopt in a culture, which is governed, however, by social and political realities that override or inhibit our true freedom of action.

A more recent example of the New Historicism is Louis A. Montrose's *The Subject of Elizabeth: Authority, Gender, and Representation* (2006).[5] Some of the chapters of this book revise and enlarge previously published essays, but there are substantive additions. Montrose thoroughly investigates the paradox of a woman, Elizabeth I, who held authority and power in a patriarchal culture. He interrelates texts, portraits, and spectacles that promoted the queen's reign as the zenith of the Tudor dynasty and that permitted Elizabeth I to be represented as male and female. The former representation emerged when she identified with her father, Henry VIII, whereas the latter issued from her courtiers and corsairs, like Sir Walter Raleigh and Sir Francis Drake, who composed poems, travel narratives, and the like that compared the paradisal topography of the Americas to the queen's body. And by citing John Knox's *The First Blast of the Trumpet Against the Monstruous Regiment of Women* (1558), which deplores rule by women, Montrose examines the political culture of Elizabethan England, including speeches in the House of Commons, for a spectrum of views on a female sovereign and a sovereign female. The texts that he analyzes are manifold, including some that are literary, most notably Spenser's *The Faerie Queene*. The kaleidoscopic view of Elizabeth that informs texts across all levels of society, from courtiers to commoners, indicates that the queen was variously projected and perceived as Amazonian, maternal, conjugal, virginal, amatory, and filial.

Like Shakespeare and Spenser, Ben Jonson has been reinterpreted according to the tenets of the New Historicism. In *Ben Jonson and the Poetics of Patronage* (1989), Robert C. Evans engages chiefly the poems, though there is some attention to masques and plays.[6] Evans situates Jonson's poetry in the context of the patronage system of the Elizabethan and Jacobean eras. While this context is explored to the fullest, Evans, unlike most of the New Historicists, focuses intensively on the language of the poems. Detecting Jonson's keen urge to compete with rivals for patronage from King James, Robert Cecil, Sir Thomas Egerton, Bishop John Williams, and others, Evans blends historical study of the patronage system with close analysis of Jonson's skillful use of language, the fluctuating tonal range of the poems, the use of irony, the depth of ambiguity, and the creation of *personae* that disclose or disguise Jonson's own self. Though New Historicist in its orientation, primarily because it emphasizes the power inherent in the patronage system, this study simultaneously enriches understanding not only of Jonson's style, which has been downplayed in the past as 'plain', but also of the substance of Jonson's poems, which provide psychological insights into an author who depends on patronage.

Extending his New Historicist approach to Jonson's masques and dramas, Evans in *Jonson and the Contexts of His Time* (1994) focuses on historical topicalities and personages that impact on patronage.[7] *Volpone*, for instance, reflects a series of admonitions to Thomas Sutton, a prosperous businessman, to use his money prudently. From Jonson's viewpoint, patronage supporting authors, of course, is one such worthy and worthwhile outlet for one's resources. In *The Devil Is an Ass*, Evans detects a complex network of relationships involving royalty and nobility in Jonson's era. In sum, Evans' two books teem with facts and informed speculation concerning Jonson's personal relationships, on which count alone our biographical understanding of the poet and dramatist has been significantly enlarged and new avenues of investigation charted for our study of other authors.

But most important in the two foregoing studies of Jonson is evidence of the permutation that the New Historicism is undergoing, for the critical method, though distinguished by certain underlying tenets (cited above), is often reinvented because of the intellectual curiosity and interests of a scholar. Sufficiently flexible, the tenets of the New Historicism enable and encourage scholars to focus on particularities not merely to provide tenuous or tendentious justification for a commentator's predilections but to construct and enhance an argument for which evidence redoubles still and multiplies. In Evans' case the New Historicist attention to structures of power when redirected to a study of the patronage system enables us to understand that interpersonal relationships as well as governmental activities are informed by politics.

New Historicist interest in John Donne has also resulted in innovative scholarship. Most revolutionary is Arthur F. Marotti's *John Donne, Coterie Poet* (1986), which stresses determinants in the socio cultural system of patronage for a so-called manuscript poet like Donne.[8] That is, except for a very few poems published in his lifetime, Donne wrote for a coterie audience, whether for the Inns of Court, where presumably his early love poetry was circulated in manuscript and perhaps read aloud, or he composed works for prospective patrons or patronesses, such as Lucy, Countess of Bedford. Donne's fit audiences though few were presumably attuned intellectually to his rich, at times allusively dense, poetry. More sophisticated than I have suggested, Marotti's study verges at times on biographical criticism, not unlike Evans' studies of Jonson. Their biographical criticism inclines more to psychological analysis of Jonson and Donne, emphasizing the dependence of the authors on patronage and the attendant effects on their mind, art, and interpersonal relationships. As such, Evans and Marotti manifest an eclecticism resulting from the careful and insightful admixture of more than one critical method while eschewing a relentless thesis-driven analysis whose outcome is predetermined, reductive, and simplistic.

Another book by Marotti on Donne and his contemporaries, including Philip Sidney, Jonson, George Herbert, John Skelton, and several others, though New Historicist in its viewpoint, is different in its interpretive emphasis. In *Manuscript, Print, and the English Renaissance Lyric* (1995), Marotti dwells on the material means and conditions of publishing and disseminating poems in the late sixteenth and early seventeenth centuries, chiefly at the juncture when a manuscript culture gave way to print.[9] He highlights the transition from the one means of publication to the other, analyzing the period of time when the two means overlapped and interacted. In addition, Marotti contrasts the changing concepts of authorship, of reception, and of literature itself at the very cusp when publication by manuscript yielded to print. For instance, he discusses the social settings (such as universities, the court, Inns of Court, and noble families) in which the Renaissance lyric flourished. When disseminated by manuscript, these poems may have undergone changes beyond the state in which the author composed them. For if readers or listeners in a particular coterie revised the text by modifying verses and words, then it may be impossible to recover the so-called authoritative reading, the one most closely approximating an author's final intention. In traditional textual scholarship, determining the authoritative reading was the goal. By adapting the New Historicism to investigate the composition, circulation, and revision not only of manuscripts but also of printed works, Marotti acknowledges how sociocultural determinants affect the construction of texts in a manuscript culture, more so than in the print culture that supplanted it. When the provenance of a manuscript of Donne's love lyrics is linked to a particular coterie, then the textual variants of a poem may be attributable to revisions by an identifiable group.

The era in the seventeenth century that draws most of the New Historicist commentary includes the nearly 20-year span of the English Revolution, the Commonwealth, and the Protectorate. Preceding the New Historicism but profoundly affecting it, Christopher Hill's *Milton and the English Revolution* (1977) disengages Milton's writings from the erudite, often elitist, frame of reference in which they are traditionally studied.[10] These traditional contexts include, but are not limited to, classical sources and analogues of the poems, as well as medieval and Renaissance contexts, such as Christian theology, Italian epics, Renaissance encyclopedias, commentaries on the Judaeo-Christian scriptures, and the like.

Distinguishing himself from previous literary historians and commentators on Milton, Hill, a cultural historian with a Marxist bias, explicates Milton's prose tracts and the three great poems – *Paradise Lost*, *Paradise Regained*, and *Samson Agonistes* – against the underground culture of mid-seventeenth century England. This culture was distinguished by a splinter coalition of radicals – political, religious, and religio-political – like the Diggers, Ranters,

Levelers, Seekers, Muggletonians, Fifth Monarchists, and others. Hill situates Milton in 'dialogue' (as he phrases it) with the radical underground. Precisely what Hill means by 'dialogue' is uncertain because he is very circumspect in making claims. He may mean that Milton read some of the pamphlets of these radical groups whose views may have instructed him or harmonized with his own. He does not contend that Milton personally interacted with the radicals. Nevertheless, Hill, without recourse to earlier history, cites analogues of Milton's political and religious views in mid-seventeenth-century pamphlets. In doing so, Hill highlights the radical underground as a third player in the religio-political struggles of the 1640s. Until Hill succeeded in this endeavor, the two principal players in those struggles were the Laudian Church of England and middle-class Puritanism. Interpreting Milton's three great poems in a radical milieu, Hill becomes more suggestive and associative than definite in his interpretations of characters such as Satan, God, the Son (of *Paradise Lost* and *Paradise Regained*), and Samson. Satan is variously perceived, almost kaleidoscopically, as one interpretation after another emerges when Hill compares Milton's epic poem to diverse radical texts and ideas. Without a clear-cut interpretive emphasis, Hill's study is less valuable as literary interpretation and more important for uncovering the radical culture that literary historians overlooked in analyzing Milton's works.

But what became a tenet of the New Historicism – examining texts of all kinds contemporaneous with an author's writings – is clearly manifested in Hill's work. Following Hill's initiative, the New Historicists reexamined the radical underground to propose more definite interpretations of characters in Milton's poems and to pursue more refined literary analysis. These outcomes are achieved by intertextual analysis between the harsh, shrill, and ideologically radical texts, on the one hand, and Milton's subtle, allusive, and sophisticated literary accommodation of religio-political ideas, on the other. Exemplifying this kind of intertextual analysis are two, among several, recent studies: David Loewenstein's *Representing Revolution in Milton and His Contemporaries: Religion, Politics, and Polemics in Radical Puritanism* (2001) and Sharon Achinstein's *Literature and Dissent in Milton's England* (2003).[11] In the writings of radical dissenters, Loewenstein, for instance, identifies two concepts of sainthood: the one rejects worldly temptations; the other is a militant heroism enacted in the vengeance that one wreaks against God's enemies. The Son of *Paradise Regained* exemplifies the former, whereas the protagonist of *Samson Agonistes* embodies the latter. Both works by Milton were published together in one volume (1671), thereby suggesting that they may be complementary and contrasting in their embodiments of radical heroic sainthood.

Achinstein dwells on the origins and manifestations of dissent in seventeenth-century England, stressing how and why religio-political nonconformity challenged royalism and eventually the personal and absolutist rule of Charles I. Among other things, dissenters, in their hymns, their eulogies of deceased leaders, and their interpretations of Scripture, challenged hierarchical structures in government and in the Church of England. Like Loewenstein, Achinstein heightens our attention to dissenters and even elevates them in our admiration, so that they are not the laughable enthusiasts who sometimes became subversive and revolutionary in their rhetoric, tone, and actions. She, like Loewenstein, situates Milton's three great poems in the context of mid-century dissent, striving to clarify how religio-political controversies inform *Paradise Lost, Paradise Regained*, and *Samson Agonistes*. Adapted to foremost expressions of literary art in that era – an epic, a brief epic, and a dramatic poem – dissent informs, for instance, Abdiel's resistance to Satan's rulership over the angels. And in the interaction of Adam and Eve, Achinstein cites the former's dissent when Eve proposes to work alone in the Garden of Eden. Soon afterwards, Adam accedes to Eve's proposal because he acknowledges her liberty of conscience and his opposition to physical coercion, two principles that dissenters advocated.

In sum, the New Historicism has created an innovative paradigm for reinterpreting, if not reconceiving, literary history. One might argue, in fact, that the term 'literary history' is outdated, but literary analysis is not. Some New Historicists continue to examine literary texts intensively after having re-created more comprehensive contexts in which to do so. Despite their impulse toward leveling the hierarchy of authorship, ironically the New Historicists continue to develop, test, and adapt their methodology while applying it to canonical authors, including Spenser, Shakespeare, Jonson, Donne, and Milton.

Feminist Criticism

Feminist criticism or feminist literary theory, of course, antedates the New Historicism. But the New Historicism impacted on feminism, which in many instances has been retitled feminist cultural analysis, especially when applied to seventeenth-century English literature. The thrust of such analysis is to recognize women as a sociological group and to identify the tensions and conflicts that they experienced among themselves or between themselves and the patriarchal culture in domestic life, religion, politics, the marketplace, and authorship. A spate of studies on these topics has redefined our understanding of women in the tumultuous 1640s and 1650s in England. Though nonconformists or dissenters in religion and politics were affirming their individual rights and freedom of conscience, they did not include women in this struggle. Nevertheless, in this era when traditions and structures of power in a culture were being challenged, women were emboldened to speak and write on their own behalf. Accordingly, researchers have since delved into works of all kinds by women: books, pamphlets, letters, and diaries. These writings are devotional or religious, religio-political, or secular. Accordingly, women's writings in seventeenth-century England, bibliographies of their works and of commentaries on them, and biographies have appeared in print and online at numerous websites.

Brought to the foreground are poets such as Lady Mary Wroth, Katherine Philips, Aemilia Lanyer, Aphra Behn, Lucy Hutchinson, and Margaret Cavendish, Duchess of Newcastle, along with many others. Accordingly, Katharine Gillespie in *Domesticity and Dissent in the Seventeenth Century* (2004) and Hilary Hinds in *God's Englishwomen: Seventeenth-century Sectarian Writing and Feminist Criticism* (1996) focus on seventeenth-century English women who advocated religious freedom for dissenters.[12] Among others, Katherine Chidley, Anna Trapnel, Elizabeth Poole, and Anne Wentworth sought toleration for women to preach and to prophesy. The spiritual autobiographies and prophetic writings by Quaker, Baptist, and Fifth Monarchist women greatly enlarge the context in which to understand mid-seventeenth-century religious controversies. By reinterpreting the Bible, moreover, these thinkers also revaluated womanhood in relation to the dominant patriarchal culture. Their ideas, however, extended beyond women's rights to include separation of church and state and the role of public speech, including women's voices therein. As such, these women thinkers explored ideas more typically associated with political philosophers, such as Locke and Hobbes.

Antonia Fraser's *The Weaker Vessel: Woman's Lot in Seventeenth-Century England* (1984) also investigates the status of women during the English Civil War by focusing on marriage and childbirth, divorce, infant and maternal mortality, the role of widowhood, and the like.[13] The book ranges across many levels of society to encompass the entire spectrum of womankind: governesses, milkmaids, fishwives, nuns, courtesans, nobility, witches, widows, and so forth. Furthermore, Hilda L. Smith's *Reason's Disciples: Seventeenth-Century English Feminists* (1982) comprehensively researches how, when, and why women intervened in the controversies of the era.[14] Focusing on Margaret Cavendish, Smith contends that this noble woman was informed by female and feminist subjectivity, self-consciously so. Although Cavendish did contradict herself – objecting to the oppression of women while acceding to the cultural perception that women were inferior to men – the very fact that such discussion was occurring becomes crucial to our understanding of the controversies in seventeenth-century England. In effect, the women's movement, when added to the Laudian Church of England, middle-class Puritanism, and the radical underground, becomes the fourth player in the tumultuous milieu of religion and politics.

To exemplify the impact of feminist cultural analysis, one may draw attention to Lucy Hutchinson, whose husband, Colonel John Hutchinson, was one of the Puritans who signed the order to execute Charles I. For many reasons Lucy Hutchinson has been elevated to prominence. Her poem *Order and Disorder* is the first epic by an Englishwoman, but only five cantos were published in her lifetime and the other twenty did not appear until 2001. A biblical poem interspersed with meditations, observations of the natural world, discussions of the role of women, and views on justice, *Order and Disorder* merits comparative study with Milton's *Paradise Lost*. Furthermore, Hutchinson composed the first English translation of Lucretius' *The Nature of the Universe*, as well as a political biography of her husband. Similarly, the writings of other women are being recovered, edited, and published; and scholarly commentaries are being written. Such primary writings will add immeasurably to the seventeenth-century texts that the New Historicists tend to use for comparative study with the works of canonical authors. And by reframing our perception of mid-seventeenth-century England to take into account the myriad of women's writings, scholarly commentaries will redress an imbalance in our previous and present understanding of that epoch. In the foreseeable future, this trend in feminist cultural analysis should continue unabated.

Gay and Lesbian Studies

Despite the dominance of the New Historicism and Feminist Cultural Analysis, other modes of critical interpretation, sometimes related to them, continue to flourish, though their impact is not as widespread. Fewer scholars, in other words, are pursuing psychoanalytic criticism, reader-response criticism, studies in narratology, postcolonial criticism, and queer theory. The synergy among the scholars who adopt any one of the foregoing critical perspectives is not as all-encompassing and intense as the interaction among the New Historicists, on the one hand, and among the Feminists, on the other. Nevertheless, each of these critical perspectives has a following, among whom there are notable commentators.

This point may be illustrated by referring to one of the foregoing critical perspectives, notably queer theory, which includes both gay and lesbian studies. Two of the most prominent present-day critics are Jonathan Goldberg and Richard Rambuss, who follow in the wake of Alan Bray, John Boswell, Bruce Smith, and Eve Sedgwick, all pioneers in gay and lesbian studies. Much as feminists challenge masculinity as the cultural norm, so also commentators who practice gay and lesbian studies interrogate another cultural norm, namely heterosexuality. If women constitute a sociological group, then gays and lesbians have their social identity. By asserting that a 'gay' social and individual identity should not be perceived as a violation of the so-called normative criteria for relationships, queer theorists thereby challenge the cultural stereotypes whereby 'gay' and 'straight' are charged with negative and positive views, respectively.

Like the New Historicists' reliance on Foucault, queer theorists also cite his work, most notably *Histoire de la sexualité* or *The History of Sexuality* (1976–1984), in which he broadly defines sodomy as a sexual act not intended to result in procreation whether performed inside or outside a marital relationship.[15] Using Foucault as a point of departure, Jonathan Goldberg in *Sodometries: Renaissance Texts, Modern Sexualities* (1992) investigates homoeroticism and homosexuality in literature and culture in Early Modern England.[16] Ranging far and wide across writings of various kinds, but including canonical authors like Shakespeare, Marlowe, and Spenser, Goldberg strives to dismantle the traditional perception that same-sex eroticism is unnatural and deviant, if not sinful because of scriptural injunction against it. By citing intimacy as the *sine qua non* of idealized male friendship and of sodomy, Goldberg collapses distinctions between the former and the latter, both of which, he argues, are more aptly encompassed by the concept of sodomitical ambiguity. Whether biographically examining the letters of Edmund Spenser and Gabriel Harvey or literarily interpreting, say, Gaveston, the character in Marlowe's *Edward II*, Goldberg heightens awareness of the prevalence of same-sex eroticism. Soon after completing his monograph, Goldberg edited the multi-author collection, *Queering the Renaissance* (1994), which includes some essays by women on lesbian eroticism in seventeenth-century England.[17] Having received lesser attention than male homoeroticism, lesbianism is being brought to the foreground in many recent studies.

In *Closet Devotions* (1998), Richard Rambuss, another well-known queer theorist, interrelates seventeenth-century sensuality and spirituality.[18] The terms 'queer erotics' and 'sacred eroticism' describe this interplay of desire and devotion. Emphasizing the religious poetry of Donne, Herbert, Crashaw, and their contemporaries, Rambuss focuses on the body of Christ as it was rendered in the visual and verbal arts of the seventeenth century, a sacred body open to desire, indecorousness, and penetration. Also examining Puritan writings, Rambuss identifies the tone and texture of the erotics of spiritual devotion, which he contends are evident not merely from a present-day perspective but in the historical moment of composition. Focusing on the language that describes the pleasures of heaven, the master-servant relationship, and the correlatives of physical sensation and spiritual ecstasy, Rambuss drives home the view that the devotee and the Lord, not to mention the poet and Christ, interact homosocially and homoerotically in the privacy of the prayer closet.

Another book, *King James & Letters of Homoerotic Desire* (1999) by David M. Bergeron, extends analysis of homoeroticism to the Jacobean court.[19] In disclosing the private life of James I, these letters recount his relations with three courtiers: Esmé Stuart, Duke of Lennox; Robert Carr, Earl of Somerset; and George Villiers, Duke of Buckingham. The intimacy of the king's letters testifies to his desires as he interacts successively with the three men. The epistolary evidence, however, is unbalanced, for the exchange of letters between the king and the duke of Lennox is relatively slight. Only three letters from the courtier and one from the king are extant. But one of Esmé's last letters supplies evidence of total commitment to the king, who had ended the relationship in order to develop a liaison elsewhere. Moreover, on his deathbed Esmé made the request to have his heart removed, embalmed, and presented to the king. He wished, in short, to bestow his heart where it belonged, namely with the king. The most preponderant evidence of intimacy involves the liaison of James and Buckingham, both of whom share graphic details in their letters. The latter, in fact, refers to himself as the king's 'slave' and 'dog'. Bergeron, however, enriches his study with historical research into letter-writing, including amorous letters. The span of historical research ranges from St. Paul's epistles through the Jacobean era, including study of letter-writing manuals, such as Angel Day's *The English Secretary* (1599).

Ecocriticism

At present, the newest form of commentary, and presumably a wave of the future, is ecocriticism. This critical approach is evolving in several directions, so that commentators may pursue any one line of inquiry, or several simultaneously. Focusing on depredations of the environment, ecocritics assimilate ethical models into their analysis of literature, particularly works that stress humankind's interaction with the habitat. Sometimes accommodated also to social and cultural history, ecocriticism expresses profound concern for the biosphere, which is contaminated by industrial waste, paved over with concrete and asphalt, tainted by fertilizers and chemicals, and inhabited by human beings who are knowledgeable of applied technology but who do not think or act wisely. Ecocritics base their interpretations on ethical values that come into play especially when ecosystems are affected by social, economic, scientific, and political upheavals. Indeed, ecocritics challenge interests of any and all kinds that do or would jeopardize the biosphere and its peoples.

When such principles inform a critical method, literary analysis becomes fixed on the concept of 'place' and humankind's symbiotic or deleterious interaction with the environment. More than anyone, Diane K. McColley, in *Milton's Eve* (1983) and *A Gust for Paradise: Milton and the Arts of Eden* (1993), initiated the movement toward ecocriticism in Milton studies.[20] In the title of the more recent book, 'Gust' carries its etymological significance of 'taste' or even 'keen delight'. In this book, moreover, the trend toward (what I will call) 'Green Milton' is impelled to the forefront of analysis. Issuing from this trend is Ken Hiltner's *Milton and Ecology* (2003).[21] Using ecocriticism to interpret three of Milton's major works – *Comus, Paradise Lost,* and *Paradise Regained* – Hiltner provides the first systematic analysis of 'Green Milton' by referring to classical, Judaic, and Christian texts, including Scripture, that all deal with the concept of place. Against this frame of reference, he tracks certain ecological upheavals, focusing, of course, on sixteenth- and seventeenth-century England, when deforestation and mining were occurring. In that era, literary authors were nostalgic for the pristine landscape, using the pastoral mode to celebrate the innocence of the past. Integrated into Hiltner's critical perspective, however, is a keen awareness of debates that were taking place in mid-seventeenth-century England concerning the use and despoliation of land and trees. After the manner of the New Historicists, Hiltner cites these debates and texts, as well as legislation resulting from them. Milton, he contends, appropriated and adapted such topicalities into *Paradise Lost*. When the fallen angels excavate minerals from the terrain of hell, they are likened to miners who, in Milton's era, scarred the landscape to unearth coal, thereafter proceeding elsewhere to pursue the same despoliation. Stressing the mythic and scriptural overtones of a pristine environment as the ideal natural habitat for humankind, Hiltner focuses on the 'uprooting' of Adam and Eve and their expulsion from Eden as a traumatic dislocation into a postlapsarian condition. His study, moreover, is informed by traditional historical analysis, by the New Historicist emphasis on seventeenth-century texts (in Hiltner's case, texts that express either the heightened consciousness to protect the environment or the rapaciousness to pillage it), and by philosophical ideas concerning humankind's rapport with the environment.

Conclusion

The foregoing account emphasizes the more predominant present-day approaches to seventeenth-century literary studies. Though the New Historicism prevailed in the last two decades of the twentieth century, it still remains influential though its impact is somewhat attenuated. Having been assimilated into other critical approaches, such as feminism, gay and lesbian studies, and ecocriticism, the New Historicism is still a discernible strand in most critical commentaries. Perhaps its most durable contribution is to focus attention on non-literary texts as a means of more richly understanding so-called literary texts. Soon after it was originated, the New Historicism appeared to be reductive, simplistic, and even predictable in its conclusions. For in its early form, this critical methodology dwelled on concepts of power, hierarchy, and the oppression or victimization of marginalized, subordinate, and disadvantaged people. Perhaps the popularity of the New Historicism derives from ideological alignment with present-day liberalism and the endeavor to discern manifestations of revolution or traces of resistance and subversion against the structures of power in a society. Feminism, queer studies, and ecocriticism are likewise informed by liberalism. Through such critical lenses, the past may be harmonized with present-day interests involving various sociological groups. Under such circumstances, texts are interpreted so that commentators do discern antecedents of our own predilections, a practice that folds the present into the past, or vice versa. By such interpretive means, commentators may establish a trajectory across centuries for an ongoing struggle against oppressive forces of all kinds. Indeed, this revolutionary discontent enacts the archetypal struggle for recognition, equal opportunity, and the freedom to dissent. Much more than in the past, when critical endeavors sought chiefly to chart literary history, to understand literary works aesthetically, and to interpret them in an intellectual or philosophical milieu, recent trends in critical commentary often forego the 'literary' in order to focus on socio political elements in texts of all kinds.

Glossary of Critical and Theoretical Terminology

Laura Schechter

Allegory: A narrative in which the characters and other elements of the plot work reasonably within the narrative itself but in which they also contribute to a second (sometimes more meaningful) narrative. Two types of allegory generally can be found: historical allegory, in which a narrative's characters and other elements simultaneously function as actual historical figures or activities, as in John Dryden's *Absalom and Achitophel*; and the allegory of ideas, in which characters signify values, traits, or emotions and the narrative emphasizes these elements, as in Edmund Spenser's *The Faerie Queene*. Both types of allegory can be successfully utilized in a single text.

Allusion: A form of indirect reference, often to a commonly known source, such as the Bible. Seventeenth-century writers often allude to earlier classical or Judaeo-Christian texts to enrich the significance of their own works.

Carpe Diem: Latin for 'seize the day', *carpe diem* is a popular device in early modern work, particularly in lyric poetry from the era such as Robert Herrick's 'To the Virgins, to Make Much of Time'. The speaker in a *carpe diem* poem is frequently an older man who speaks to hesitating virgins, urging the young women to enjoy their youth, for life and beauty are both impermanent and death is irrevocable.

Cavalier: Derived from the same root as *chevalier* and *caballeros* (French for 'knight' and Spanish for 'horseman'), 'Cavalier' by the 1640s became a term used to describe someone who was loyal to King Charles I, or whose work celebrated or reflected nostalgically on court values. Cavalier work is often lighthearted in tone and may treat topics such as beauty, the senses, conviviality, or the *carpe diem* motif. Authors frequently labeled as Cavalier include Thomas Carew, Robert Herrick, and Richard Lovelace, while certain texts by Henry Vaughan and Andrew Marvell are also classified as such.

Connotation: The meanings suggested by words rather than the ones openly and definitively stated; the opposite of 'denotation'. Literary works often imply meanings rather than spelling them out unequivocally.

Epic: A long poem that follows a narrative sequence on a grave and historically or theologically important matter, the epic generally follows a plot that emphasizes the thoughts and actions of a central heroic character. It also characteristically begins by plunging *in medias res* (into the middle of things), or into the thick of the action, with the technical 'beginning' of the narrative revealed later in the text. The epic's setting is vast in scope and the action frequently relies on interactions between mortal and divine agents. Classical epics include Homer's *Iliad* and *Odyssey*, while John Milton's *Paradise Lost* is the most important early modern English text that could be classified as such.

Epic Simile: Characteristic of classical **epics** and works that imitate these earlier narratives, the epic simile is found when one thing is compared to another in an extended manner, such that the second thing is described far beyond the needs of the comparison itself. The epic simile is used to elevate the subject matter at hand.

Epigram: A short poem or piece of prose that often relies on barbed humor or wit.

Folio: A printing term that describes a sheet of paper that is folded once, thus creating two leaves and four usable sides for each sheet.

Iambic Meter: A common rhythm found in poetry that consists of iambic 'feet', each foot containing an unstressed syllable followed by a stressed syllable. Five such feet constitute an iambic 'pentameter' line.

Interregnum: A period of time that sees a break in continuous political rule. The English Interregnum spans 1649–1660, the time between the execution of King Charles I and the Restoration of the monarchy under King Charles II, and a time in which England was governed by Oliver Cromwell (most notably, although his son, Richard Cromwell, also briefly acted as Lord Protector), first as a Commonwealth and then as a Protectorate.

Irony: An unexpected twist or reversal, either in words, conduct, or situation. Irony is a favorite technique of seventeenth-century writers, who often convey meanings indirectly or by implication. Thus, if an ugly man is praised as handsome, the praise is ironic; if a Christian character behaves in un-Christian ways, his behavior is ironic.

Libertine: A figure (and characteristic quality) often associated with the court of King Charles II; the libertine is also a precursor to the eighteenth-century 'rake'. The libertine eschews traditionally moral behavior, social conventions and religious dogma, arguing that such conduct and values are merely superficial, often hypocritical niceties. The lifestyle and written work of John Wilmot, Second Earl of Rochester, epitomize the libertine attitude, and the libertine tradition is often associated with hedonism as a comparable way of life.

Masque: A subgenre of drama that was specific to court life and could involve both paid, professional actors and unpaid, amateur nobility, although nobility always performed the central roles. Masques were often highly **allegorical**, and they were written and performed to celebrate the monarch. Expensive to produce, masques relied on lavish sets and costumes. They were generally performed once at great cost and included several hours' worth of dancing and reveling, always including members of the audience for portions of the spectacle.

Metaphor: A literary technique and form of figurative language in which, for aesthetic effect, one thing or idea is said to be another. A simile compares two things by using the words 'like' or 'as', whereas a metaphor omits those words when making a comparison.

Metaphysical: Works of poetry that address questions of being in the world in a manner that encompasses more than a physical or material sense of existence. Metaphysical poets such as George Chapman, John Donne, George Herbert,

Andrew Marvell, and Henry Vaughan chose topics that were either secular or religious, and their work often includes wit, paradox, and the **metaphysical conceit**. Critics of metaphysical work have accused the poets of being deliberately difficult and of relying on arcane knowledge in their work.

Metaphysical Conceit: An extended metaphor found in metaphysical poetry that compares two disparate things to create a heightened effect.

Neoclassic: The period roughly extending from the Restoration in 1660 until the publication of such works as Blake's *Songs of Innocence* in 1789. Neoclassical authors frequently praise and emulate classical authors, often resisting drastic stylistic or formal change in the process. Neoclassical works were created through intense, lengthy study, and they often stressed the importance of recognizing the realistic abilities of humans and promoting improvement through deliberate, measured practice. Pride and hubris are often attacked, and innate genius is treated as uncommon (but to be celebrated when it does occur).

Paradox: A term or idea that seems to contradict itself or that seems to fly in the face of common opinion but that makes sense in one way or another. Christianity, for instance, is a highly paradoxical religion: its central figure is a god who is also a human; he was the product of a virgin birth; his deliberately humiliating death was the moment of his greatest triumph; and his death resulted in eternal life for those who believe in him. Paradox, like irony, is a device highly favored in seventeenth-century texts.

Pun: A play on words, so that a single word conveys two or more meanings. Thus the word 'vain' may mean both 'futile' and 'egotistical,' and both meanings may be relevant in the same context. Seventeenth-century writers were often fond of punning since the technique allowed them to cram multiple meanings into the same word or phrase.

Restoration: Referring specifically to the restoration of the throne in 1660, when King Charles II was invited to return from exile and assume rule of England, this aesthetic and literary period is often thought of as lasting until the beginning of the eighteenth century. Restoration culture was often marked by the wit, **satire**, and hedonism of Charles II's court, and it often reacted strongly against the Puritan ethic of modesty, temperance, and decorum that could be found in so many earlier seventeenth-century texts. With the reopening of the public theatres in 1660 (and the appearance of professional female actors on English stages for the first time), authors such as William Congreve, John Dryden, and William Wycherley were able to take part in a renaissance of drama, particularly of comedy.

Satire: A literary technique that has the aim of producing varying degrees of contempt for a chosen subject of ridicule. Satire most frequently takes the form of Horatian satire (a witty and gentle ribbing of human foibles and of moments of hypocrisy or weakness) or Juvenalian satire (a moralizing reaction to human vice or action which expects readers to feel disgust for the treated subject), although other forms can also be also utilized (Menippean satire, for example, which relies on dialogues rather than a single speaker).

Sonnet: A poem of fourteen lines that is usually composed mostly in **iambic** pentameter and that is typically lyric in nature. Two main forms exist: the Italian or the Petrarchan sonnet, made famous by the poet Petrarch, consists of two conceptual units, one of eight lines (the 'octet') and one of six (the 'sestet'), and contains a rhyme scheme of ABBAABBA CDCCDC (with some variation allowed in the latter section); and the English or Shakespearean sonnet, which was of course named after William Shakespeare (but was practiced by many others), and which contains three conceptual quatrains and a rhyming couplet and follows a rhyme scheme of ABAB CDCD EFEF GG.

Appendix: Teaching, Curriculum, and Learning

Julie Sutherland

This Chapter is available online at
www.continuumbooks.com/resources/9780826498502

Notes on Contributors

James S. Baumlin is a Professor of English at Missouri State University. He has published widely in fields of criticism, the history of rhetoric, and English Renaissance poetry.

Brian Blackley is an Assistant Professor of English at North Carolina State University and Assistant Head of the department. He is also the Managing Editor of the *John Donne Journal*. He teaches courses on literature of the sixteenth and seventeenth centuries and on Shakespeare and has published on John Donne, Edmund Spenser, and William Basse.

Bruce Boehrer is Bertram H. Davis Professor of early modern English literature at Florida State University. Most recently, he is the author of *Animal Characters: Nonhuman Beings in European Literature 1400–1700* (University of Pennsylvania Press, forthcoming 2010) and editor of *A Cultural History of Animals in the Renaissance* (Berg, 2007).

Nancy Mohrlock Bunker is an Assistant Professor of English at Macon State College in Georgia, where she teaches writing and specializes in Renaissance literature. She is published in *Explorations in Renaissance Culture* and in a forthcoming *Composing Ourselves* volume for composition students. A regular reviewer for *Seventeenth Century News*, she is also a contributor to the *Annotated Bibliography of English Studies* Renaissance and Early Modern team. Her current research concentrates on the links among dramatic comedy, artistic representation, and legal application in the works of Shakespeare and Thomas Middleton.

Lara M. Crowley is an Assistant Professor of English literature at Texas Tech University. Her articles on Renaissance literature and textual studies have appeared or are forthcoming in *English Literary Renaissance, English Manuscript Studies, 1100–1700, John Donne Journal*, and *Modern Philology*. She received an Andrew W. Mellon fellowship to study literary manuscripts in England in 2006–2007, and she composed an essay on archival research for the forthcoming *Handbook of John Donne* (Oxford University Press). Currently, she serves as Assistant Editor for *The Variorum Edition of the Poetry of John Donne: Songs and Sonnets* (Indiana University Press) and the John Donne Letters Project (Oxford University

Press), the first scholarly edition of his letters. Her current book project is tentatively entitled 'Interpreting Manuscripts: John Donne's Poetry and Prose in Seventeenth-Century England'.

Robert C. Evans earned his Ph.D. from Princeton University in 1984. In 1982 he began teaching at Auburn University Montgomery, where he has been named Distinguished Research Professor, Distinguished Teaching Professor, and University Alumni Professor. External awards include fellowships from the ACLS, the APS, the NEH, the UCLA Center for Medieval and Renaissance Studies, and from the Folger, Huntington, and Newberry Libraries. He is the author or editor of more than twenty books (about half of them dealing with seventeenth-century topics or figures) and the author of numerous essays. An editor of the *Ben Jonson Journal*, he is also a contributing editor of the *Donne Variorum* edition.

Richard Harp is the Director of Graduate Studies in English at the University of Nevada, Las Vegas. He is founding co-editor of *The Ben Jonson Journal* (Edinburgh University Press) and editor of the Norton Critical Edition of Ben Jonson's *Plays and Masques*. Most recently he has contributed critical essays on *Hamlet*, *Pride and Prejudice*, *The Picture of Dorian Gray*, and *The Scarlet Letter* to the Ignatius Critical Editions series.

James Hirsh is a Professor of English at Georgia State University. He is the author of *The Structure of Shakespearean Scenes* (Yale University Press, 1981) and *Shakespeare and the History of Soliloquies* (Fairleigh Dickinson University Press, 2003), the latter of which won the South Atlantic Modern Language Association 2004 Book Award. His articles have appeared in *Shakespeare Quarterly*, *Papers on Language and Literature*, *Papers of the Bibliographical Society of America*, *Ben Jonson Journal*, *Essays in Theatre*, *Modern Language Quarterly*, and other journals. He participated in two debates published in *PMLA*.

Albert C. Labriola was, until his untimely death in March 2009, Professor of English and Distinguished University Professor at Duquesne University. He was editor of *Milton Studies* (University of Pittsburgh Press), of the monograph series *Medieval & Renaissance Literary Studies* (Duquesne University Press), of the volume on the *Songs and Sonnets* in *The Variorum Edition of the Poetry of John Donne* (Indiana University Press), and of *A Variorum Commentary on the Poems of John Milton* (Duquesne University Press).

Laura Schechter is a Ph.D. Candidate in English at the University of Alberta. Her dissertation focuses on the Amazon woman as early modern political metaphor for Elizabeth I specifically, and female rule more broadly. She also enjoys early modern travel and exploration literature, poetry, translation studies, and texts that are written by or deal chiefly with women.

Deborah Cosier Solomon is a beginning Ph.D. student at Florida State University. She is the author of published or forthcoming work on Ambrose Bierce, Kate Chopin, E.E. Cummings, Brian Friel, Henry James, Ben Jonson, Anne Vaughan

Lock, Arthur Miller, Frank O'Connor, John Steinbeck, and Virginia Woolf. She earned her B.A. and Master's degrees at Auburn University Montgomery.

Eric J. Sterling is Distinguished Research Professor of English at Auburn University Montgomery, where he has taught since 1994. He earned his Ph.D. in English, with a minor in theatre, from Indiana University in 1992. He has published *The Movement Towards Subversion: The English History Play from Skelton to Shakespeare* (1995) and articles on literature by Ben Jonson, Martha Moulsworth, Edmund Spenser, William Shakespeare, George Gascoigne, Thomas Deloney, Sir Thomas More, Henry Mackenzie, and others. His most recent book is on Arthur Miller's *Death of a Salesman* (Rodopi, 2008).

Matthew Steggle is a Reader in English at Sheffield Hallam University. His teaching and research interests lie in early modern literature and in digital humanities. His books include *Richard Brome: Place and Politics on the Caroline Stage* (2004) and *Laughing and Weeping in Early Modern Theatres* (2007).

Julie Sutherland, Ph.D. (Durham) teaches part time at the University of British Columbia (Canada). She has published on several early modern plays and has contributed articles on the Renaissance to a number of reference books and encyclopedias. Concurrently she works as Director of Public Relations at Pacific Theatre, a professional company in Vancouver. Current research projects deal with Shakespeare and film and with Women in Canadian productions of Shakespeare.

Jonathan Wright is an Associate Professor of English at Faulkner University. As a Hudson Strode Fellow in the University of Alabama's program in Renaissance Studies, he completed a dissertation in 2006 on self-destructive drinking in Shakespeare. His publications include work on Ambrose Bierce, Kate Chopin, Joseph Conrad, Ben Jonson, Martha Moulsworth, Frank O'Connor, George Cavendish, and John Day, the latter two as part of *Tudor England: An Encyclopedia* (edited by Arthur F. Kinney and David W. Swain).

Notes

Chapter 1

1 Thomas N. Corns, *A History of Seventeenth-Century English Literature*, Oxford: Blackwell, 2007, p. 105.

2 Hugh Jenkins, *Feigned Commonwealths: The Country-House Poem and the Fashioning of the Ideal Community*, Pittsburgh: Duquesne University Press, 1998, pp. 161, 163.

3 Elaine V. Beilin, *Redeeming Eve: Women Writers of the English Renaissance*, Princeton: Princeton University Press, 1987, p. 179.

4 Susanne Woods, *Lanyer: A Renaissance Woman Poet*, New York: Oxford University Press, 1999, p. 118.

5 John Vanbrugh, 'Preface', *The Relapse, The Provok'd Wife, The Confederacy, A Journey to London, The Country House*, Oxford: Oxford University Press, 2004, p. 3.

6 Virginia Woolf, *A Room of One's Own*, Orlando: Harvest, 2005, pp. 63, 65.

7 Judith Milhous, 'Polewheele, E.', in *Oxford Dictionary of National Biography*, 61 vols, H.C.G. Matthew and Brian Harrison (eds), Oxford: Oxford University Press, 2004, 44:741.

8 Rebecca Mertens, 'Unmanned with Thy Words: Regendering Tragedy in Manley and Trotter', in *Broken Boundaries: Women & Feminism in Restoration Drama*, Katherine M. Quinsey (ed.), Lexington: University of Kentucky Press, 1996, p. 32.2.

Chapter 2

1 See especially the chronology by Rebecca Lemon in *The Cambridge History of Early Modern Literature*, David Loewenstein and Janel Mueller (eds), Cambridge: Cambridge University Press, 2002; the timeline in Barry Coward, *The Stuart Age*, 3rd edn, Harlow: Pearson Education, 2003; and the chronologies and notes on individual authors in the following volumes: Richard W. Bevis, *English Drama: Restoration and Eighteenth Century, 1660–1789*, London: Longman, 1988; Alexander Leggatt, *English Drama: Shakespeare to the Restoration, 1590–1660*, London: Longman, 1988; George Parfitt, *English Poetry of the Seventeenth Century*, 2nd edn, London: Longman, 1992; and Roger Pooley, *English Prose of the Seventeenth Century, 1590–1700*, London: Longman, 1992. In addition, see the chronologies in *The Oxford Illustrated History of Tudor and Stuart Britain*, John Morrill (ed.), Oxford: Oxford University Press, 1996 and in *The Oxford Illustrated History of Britain*, Kenneth O. Morgan (ed.), Oxford: Oxford University Press, 1984.

Chapter 3

1 James I, *The True Law of Free Monarchies and Basilikon Doron*, Daniel Fischlin and Mark Fortier (eds), Toronto: Centre for Reformation and Renaissance Studies, 1996, p. 72.

2   Samuel Rawson Gardiner, *History of England from the Accession of James I to the Outbreak of the Civil War, 1603–1642*, London: Longmans, 1883, I, p. 54.

3   James Harvey Robinson, *Readings in European History*, Boston: Ginn and Co., 1906, II, p. 223.

4   John H. Leith, (ed.), *Creeds of the Churches: A Reader in Christian Doctrine, from the Bible to the Present*, 3rd edn, Atlanta, GA: John Knox Press, 1982, p. 198.

5   David Nicol Smith (ed.), *Characters from the Histories and Memoirs of the Seventeenth Century*, Oxford: Oxford University Press, 1967, pp. 140, 143.

6   Bishop Gilbert Burnet in Smith (ed.), *Characters*, p. 254.

Chapter 4

1   Virginia Woolf, *A Room of One's Own*, New York: Harcourt, Brace, and Company, 1929, p. 69.

2   Some scholars suggest that other plays contain evidence of collaboration; particularly that Fletcher had a hand in writing *King Henry VIII*.

3   *Shakespeare, Ben Jonson, Beaumont and Fletcher: Notes and Lectures*, Liverpool: Edward Howell, 1874, p. 81.

4   *The Letters of John Wilmot, Earl of Rochester*, Jeremy Treglown (ed.), Chicago: University of Chicago Press; Oxford: Blackwell, 1980, p. 232.

5   Robin Skelton, *The Cavalier Poets*, New York: Oxford University Press, 1970, p. 9.

6   See *The Variorum Edition of the Poetry of John Donne*, general editor Gary A. Stringer, Bloomington: Indiana University Press, 1995–.

7   'The Dedication', *Satires of Decimus Junius Juvenalis*, John Dryden (trans.), London, 1693, p. iii.

8   *The Lives of the English Poets*, Vol. 1, Dublin, 1780–1781, pp. 19–21.

Chapter 5

1   John Donne, 'The Flea', cited from Margaret Ferguson, Mary Jo Salter, and Jon Stallworthy (eds), *The Norton Anthology of Poetry*, 4th edn, New York: Norton, 1996, 279.

2   Webster, *The Duchess of Malfi*, 1.1.420–448, cited from Webster, *The Duchess of Malfi and Other Plays*, Rene Weis (ed.), Oxford: Oxford World's Classics, 1996.

3   Jennifer Panek, *Widows and Suitors in Early Modern English Comedy*, Cambridge: Cambridge University Press, 2004.

4   On all of these issues, see Ian Gadd, 'The Use and Misuse of Early English Books Online', *Literature Compass* (forthcoming).

5   For an excellent introduction to performance criticism, see Martin White, *Renaissance Drama in Action*, London: Routledge, 1998.

6   See Ann Rosalind Jones and Peter Stallybrass, *Renaissance Clothing and the Materials of Memory*, Cambridge: Cambridge University Press, 2000, 210–11.

7   John Milton, *Paradise Lost* (ed.) Alistair Fowler, 2nd edn., London: Longman, 1998, X.272–305.

8   William Wycherley, *The Country Wife*, 4.2.139–166, cited from William Wycherley, *The Country Wife and Other Plays*, Peter Dixon (ed.), Oxford: Oxford World's Classics, 1996.

Chapter 6

1   Stanley E. Fish, *Surprised by Sin: The Reader in Paradise Lost*, Berkeley: University of California Press, 1971; *Self-Consuming Artifacts: The Experience of Seventeenth-Century Literature*, 1972, rpt. Pittsburgh: Duquesne University Press, 1998.

2   Stanley E. Fish, *Self-Consuming Artifacts*, p. 1.

3   Quoted by Fish, *Self-Consuming Artifacts*, p. 43.

4 Quoted by Fish, *Self-Consuming Artifacts*, p. 45.

5 Fish, *Self-Consuming Artifacts*, p. 53.

6 Quoted by Fish, *Self-Consuming Artifacts*, p. 102.

7 Quoted by Fish, *Self-Consuming Artifacts*, pp. 114–15.

8 Fish, *Self-Consuming Artifacts*, p. 155.

9 Fish, *Self-Consuming Artifacts*, p. 154.

10 Fish, *Self-Consuming Artifacts*, p. 212.

11 Fish, *Self-Consuming Artifacts*, p. 245.

12 Fish, *Self-Consuming Artifacts*, p. 250.

13 Fish, *Self-Consuming Artifacts*, pp. 269 and 270.

14 Fish, *Self-Consuming Artifacts*, p. 351.

15 Fish, *Self-Consuming Artifacts*, pp. 336 and 337.

16 Fish, *Self-Consuming Artifacts*, p. 363.

17 Fish, *Self-Consuming Artifacts*, p. 357.

18 Fish, *Self-Consuming Artifacts*, p. 371.

19 Fish, *Self-Consuming Artifacts*, p. 63.

20 Fish, *Self-Consuming Artifacts*, p. 400.

21 Barbara Kiefer Lewalski, *Protestant Poetics and the Seventeenth-Century Religious Lyric*, Princeton University Press, 1979, p. ix.

22 Lewalski, *Protestant Poetics*, p. 13.

23 Lewalski, *Protestant Poetics*, p. 20.

24 Lewalski, *Protestant Poetics*, p. 25.

25 Lewalski, *Protestant Poetics*, p. 26.

26 Lewalski, *Protestant Poetics*, p. 26.

27 Lewalski, *Protestant Poetics*, p. 39.

28 Lewalski, *Protestant Poetics*, p. 42.

29 Lewalski, *Protestant Poetics*, p. 58.

30 Lewalski, *Protestant Poetics*, p. 104.

31 Quoted in Lewalski, *Protestant Poetics*, p. 107.

32 Lewalski, *Protestant Poetics*, p. 108.

33 Lewalski, *Protestant Poetics*, p. 110.

34 Lewalski, *Protestant Poetics*, p. 131.

35 Lewalski, *Protestant Poetics*, p. 139.

36 Louis L. Martz, *The Poetry of Meditation: A Study in English Religious Literature of the Seventeenth Century*, New Haven, CT: Yale University Press, 1954.

37 Lewalski, *Protestant Poetics*, p. 148.

38 Lewalski, *Protestant Poetics*, p. 150.

39 Quoted in Lewalski, *Protestant Poetics*, p. 210.

40 Lewalski, *Protestant Poetics*, p. 212.

41 Lewalski, *Protestant Poetics*, p. 219.

42 Quoted in Lewalski, *Protestant Poetics*, p. 221.

43 Lewalski, *Protestant Poetics*, p. 281.

44 Lewalski, *Protestant Poetics*, p. 286.

45 Lewalski, *Protestant Poetics*, p. 317.

46 Lewalski, *Protestant Poetics*, p. 340.

47 Lewalski, *Protestant Poetics*, p. 353.

48 Lewalski, *Protestant Poetics*, p. 357.

49 Lewalski, *Protestant Poetics*, p. 389.

50 Quoted in Lewalski, *Protestant Poetics*, p. 404.

51 Lewalski, *Protestant Poetics*, p. 390.

52 E.M.W. Tillyard, *The Elizabethan World Picture*, 1943, rpt. London: Chatto & Windus, 1948.

53 Jonathan Dollimore, *Radical Tragedy: Religion, Ideology, and Power in the Drama of Shakespeare and His Contemporaries*, 2nd edn, Durham, NC: Duke University Press, 1993.
54 Dollimore, p. 25.
55 Dollimore, p. 44.
56 Dollimore, p. 40.
57 Thomas Middleton, *The Revenger's Tragedy*, (ed.) R.A. Foakes, Manchester: Manchester University Press, 1996.
58 Dollimore, p. 4.
59 Dollimore, p. 155.
60 Quoted by Dollimore, p. 154.
61 Dollimore, p. 176.
62 Dollimore, p. 179.
63 Dollimore, p. 109.
64 Dollimore, p. 110.
65 Dollimore, p. 189.
66 Dollimore, p. 189.
67 Dollimore, p. 190.
68 Dollimore, p. 191.
69 Dollimore, p. 201.
70 Dollimore, p. 209.
71 Dollimore, p. 221.
72 Dollimore, p. 222.
73 Dollimore, p. 220.
74 Dollimore, p. 231.
75 Dollimore, p. 234.
76 Dollimore, p. 231.
77 Dollimore, p. xxi.
78 Leah Marcus, *The Politics of Mirth: Jonson, Herrick, Milton, and the Defense of Old Holiday Pastimes*, Chicago: University of Chicago Press, 1986.
79 Marcus, p. 31.
80 Marcus, p. 31.
81 Marcus, p. 49.
82 Marcus, p. 66.
83 Marcus, p. 70.
84 Marcus, p. 74.
85 Marcus, p. 133.
86 Marcus, p. 142.
87 Marcus, p. 187.
88 Marcus, p. 188.
89 Marcus, p. 199.
90 Marcus, p. 226.
91 Marcus, p. 237.
92 Marcus, p. 241.
93 Marcus, p. 261.
94 J. Hillis Miller, 'Deconstructing the Deconstructors', *Diacritics*, 5, 1975, pp. 24–31.

Chapter 7

1 John Milton, 'The Printer to the Reader', in *Paradise Lost: A Poem in Twelve Books*, Merritt Y. Hughes (ed.), Indianapolis, IN: Hackett, 2003, p. 4.
2 Gail Kern Paster, *The Idea of the City in the Age of Shakespeare*, Athens, GA: University of Georgia Press, 1985, pp. 6–7.

3 Brian Gibbons, *Jacobean City Comedy*, 2nd edn, London: Methuen, 1980, pp. 1, 5.

4 See Theodore Leinwand, *The City Staged: Jacobean Comedy 1603–1613*, Madison, WI: University of Wisconsin Press, 1986.

5 See Marta Straznicky (ed.), *Privacy, Playreading, and Women's Closet Drama 1550–1700*, Cambridge: Cambridge University Press, 2004. Straznicky's collection offers historical analysis of early modern women's closet plays and argues for the genre as politically more radical than commercial drama.

6 See Maurice Charney, *Comedy High and Low: An Introduction to the Experience of Comedy*, New York: Oxford University Press, 1978. This thorough volume surveys comic language, types and forms of comedy, aspects of the comic hero, and comedy in theory and practice.

7 Aristotle, *Poetics*, 1449a32f, cf 1448a2–5, 16–18, 1448b24–6, 1449a34f.

8 Philippe Ernest Legrand, *The New Greek Comedy*, James Loeb (trans.), London: William Heinemann, 1917, p. 68. This is a seminal discussion of classical comedy and its forms.

9 See Robert Henke, *Performance and Literature in the Commedia dell'arte*, New York: Cambridge University Press, 2002. In this work, the history and criticism of commedia dell'arte are explored in relation to sixteenth-century Italian theatre and its effect on later drama.

10 For a Marxist reading of the genre, see Hugh Jenkins, *Feigned Commonwealths: The Country-House Poem and the Fashioning of the Ideal Community*, Pittsburgh, PA: Duquesne University Press, 1998.

11 Sir Philip Sidney, *The Defence of Poesie*, in *English Renaissance Literary Criticism*, Brian Vickers (ed.), Clarendon: Oxford University Press, 1999, p. 361.

12 John Milton, *Complete Poems and Major Prose*, Merritt Y. Hughes (ed.), New York: Macmillan, 1957, p. 120.

13 For the political background behind Milton's pastoral, see David Norbrook, *Poetry and Politics in the English Renaissance*, London: Routledge, 1984. For the poem's literary and prophetic themes, see Joseph A. Wittreich, Jr., *Visionary Poetics: Milton's Tradition and His Legacy*, San Marino, CA: Huntington Library Press, 1979.

14 Popularly titled *Sermones* or 'Conversations', the Horatian satires are thus familiar and colloquial in style, as opposed to the 'mixed' declamatory style of Juvenalian satire.

15 Leo Braudy, 'Dryden, Marvell, and the Design of Political Poetry', in *Enchanted Ground: Reimagining John Dryden*, Jayne Lewis and Maximillian E. Novak (eds), Toronto: University of Toronto Press, 2004, pp. 52–69; see esp. p. 54.

16 Alvin B. Kernan, *Cankered Muse: Satire in the English Renaissance*, New Haven: Yale University Press, 1959, remains a seminal discussion.

17 For a brief general discussion, see Heather Dubrow, *Genre*, London: Methuen, 1982. Dubrow's critical works explore the complex intersections among genre, gender, and the cultural-historical production of literature. Also, see her *A Happier Eden: The Politics of Marriage in the Stuart Epithalamium*, Ithaca: Cornell University Press, 1990 and *Echoes of Desire: English Petrarchism and its Counterdiscourses*, Ithaca: Cornell University Press, 1995. For an historical application see Barbara K. Lewalski, *Donne's Anniversaries and the Poetry of Praise: The Creation of a Symbolic Mode*, Princeton: Princeton University Press, 1973. See also John T. Shawcross, *Intentionality and the New Traditionalism*, University Park, PA: Pennsylvania State University Press, 1991. Prolific critic, editor, and biographer, Shawcross is best-known for his historical scholarship on the life, works, texts, contexts (classical and Judeo-Christian), and literary influences of John Milton. Shawcross's scholarship remains committed to genre as a regulating principle of reading.

18 Ignatius Loyola, *The Spiritual Exercises*, Elder Mullan (trans.), New York: J.P. Kennedy and Sons, 1914, p. 39.

19 The seminal discussion of Ignatian meditation is Louis Martz, *The Poetry of Meditation*, New Haven: Yale University Press, 1954.

20 Barbara Lewalski, *Paradise Lost and the Rhetoric of Literary Forms*, Princeton: Princeton University Press, 1985. See also Richard S. Peterson's seminal discussion, *Imitation and Praise in the Poetry of Ben Jonson*, New Haven: Yale University Press, 1981.

21 Douglas Bruster, *Drama and the Market in the Age of Shakespeare*, Cambridge: Cambridge University Press, 1992, p. 17.

22 Mary Beth Rose, *The Expense of Spirit: Love and Sexuality in Renaissance Drama*, Ithaca, NY: Cornell University Press, 1988, pp. 224, 226.

23 Kevin Sharpe and Steven Zwicker (eds), *Reading, Society, and Politics in Early Modern England*, Cambridge: Cambridge University Press, 2003. This collection of essays addresses the gendering of women as readers, the development of newspapers in seventeenth-century Britain, and the politicizing of print.

24 See Lena Cowen Orlin, *Private Matters and Public Culture in Post Reformation England*, Ithaca, NY: Cornell University Press, 1994.

25 See David M. Bevington and Peter Holbrook (eds), *The Politics of the Stuart Masque*, Cambridge: Cambridge University Press, 1998. This collection includes Bevington's essay on *The Tempest* and the Jacobean court masque and Holbrook's discussion of the masque and James' policies of peace; other essays (by Tom Bishop, Leah Marcus and Stephen Orgel among others) address the genre's traditions, structures, and relation to London city ceremonies.

26 See, in Bevington and Holbrook, Barbara Lewalski's essay 'Milton's *Comus* and the Politics of Masquing', pp. 296–320.

27 For a useful discussion, see Elizabeth Skerpan, *Rhetoric of Politics in the English Revolution*, 1642–1660, Columbia: University of Missouri Press, 1992. See also Thomas Kranidas, *Milton and the Rhetoric of Zeal*, Pittsburgh: Duquesne University Press, 2005.

28 For a seminal discussion, see William Kerrigan, *Prophetic Milton*, Charlottesville: University Press of Virginia, 1974. See also Thomas Kranidas, *Milton and the Rhetoric of Zeal*, Pittsburgh: Duquesne University Press, 2005 for explication of Milton's prose.

29 Barbara Lewalski, *Protestant Poetics and the Seventeenth-Century Religious Lyric*, Princeton: Princeton University Press, 1979.

30 John Donne, *The Sermons of John Donne*, 10 vols, George R. Potter and Evelyn M. Simpson (eds), Berkeley: University of California Press, 1953–1961, Vol. 6, p. 56.

31 Lewalski, *Protestant Poetics*, pp. 16–27.

32 Brian Corman (in *Genre and Generic Change in English Comedy 1660–1710*, Toronto: Toronto University Press, 1993) examines the changing faces of comedy and the lasting effects on theatre history.

33 See Harold Weber, *The Restoration Rake-Hero: Transformation in Sexual Understanding in Seventeenth-Century England*, Madison, WI: University of Wisconsin Press, 1986.

34 David Hirst, *Comedy of Manners*, London: Methuen, 1979, provides a thorough subgenre examination.

35 Robert D. Hume, *The Development of English Drama in the Late Seventeenth Century*, Oxford: Oxford University Press, 1976. See also Hume's *The Rakish Stage: Studies in English Drama 1660–1800*, Carbondale, IL: Southern Illinois University Press, 1983, for an outline and examination of the role Restoration drama plays in theatre history.

36 J. Douglas Canfield, *Heroes and States: On the Ideology of Restoration Tragedy*, Lexington, KY: The University Press of Kentucky, 2000.

37 See also Eileen Jorge Allman, *Jacobean Revenge Tragedy and the Politics of Virtue*, Newark, DE: University of Delaware Press, 1999.

38 For an examination of the roots of the novel in early romance and characteristic novel types with their classical sources, see Niklas Holzberg, *The Ancient Novel: An Introduction*, London: Routledge, 1994. See also an important collection that examines relationships among prose forms, passion, and perceptions of sexuality: Constance Caroline Relihan and Goran V. Stanivukovic (eds), *Prose Fiction and Early Modern Sexuality 1570–1640*, New York: Palgrave Macmillan, 2004.

39 Aristotle. *Poetics*, 1449b24–29.

40 See Richard W.F. Kroll, *Restoration Drama and the 'Circle of Commerce': Tragicomedy, Politics, and Trade in the Seventeenth Century*, Cambridge: Cambridge University Press, 2007.

41 Baldesar Castiglione, *The Book of the Courtier*, Charles S. Singleton (trans.), Garden City, NY: Anchor, 1959, p. 32.

42 Alexander Pope, 'Essay on Criticism' (1711), l. 298. See Pope's *Selected Poetry*, Pat Rogers (ed.), Oxford: Oxford University Press, 1998, p. 8.

43 Jasper Mayne, 'On Dr. Donne's Death', in *Donne: Poetical Works*, 2 vols, Herbert John Clifford Grierson (ed.), Oxford: Clarendon Press, 1933. Vol. 1, p. 382.

44 Samuel Johnson, 'Cowley', in *Lives of the English Poets*, 3 vols, G. Birkbeck Hill (ed.), Oxford: Clarendon Press, 1905, Vol. 1, p. 20.

Chapter 8

1 M.H. Abrams, *The Mirror and the Lamp: Romantic Theory and the Critical Tradition*, Oxford: Oxford University Press, 1953, pp. 3–29. For a much fuller discussion of the 'Abrams Scheme', see Robert C. Evans, 'Literary Theory and Literary Criticism: What's the Use?' in Robert C. Evans, Anne C. Little, and Barbara Wiedemann (eds), *Short Fiction: A Critical Companion*, West Cornwall, CT: Locust Hill Press, 1997, pp. xv–lxxvi.

2 The original version of this chapter, which did include lengthy explanations of each theory, was nearly twice as long as the present version and thus had to be significantly cut. For fuller accounts of the various theories, see practically any standard textbook, such as Wilfred L. Guerin, et al. (eds), *A Handbook of Critical Approaches to Literature*, 5th edn, Oxford: Oxford University Press, 2005 or Lois Tyson, *Critical Theory Today: A User-Friendly Guide*, 2nd edn, New York: Routledge, 2006. For my own account of various theories, see the title mentioned in Note 1 (above).

3 See Terence Dawson and Robert Scott Dupree (eds), *Seventeenth-Century English Poetry: The Annotated Anthology*, New York: Harvester Wheatsheaf, 1994, pp. 104–06 for a good text with full explanatory notes.

Chapter 9

1 Alex Preminger and T.V.F. Brogan (eds), *The New Princeton Encyclopedia of Poetry and Poetics*, Princeton: Princeton University Press, 1993, p. 166.

2 *Oxford English Dictionary*, s.v. 'Canon' [1], 4.

3 George Orwell, *Essays*, New York: Alfred A. Knopf, 2002, p. 1187.

4 'The Norton Anthology of English Literature', http://www.norton.com/college/titles/english/nael7/

5 Tom Ashbrook, 'The Norton Anthology of English Literature', WBUR and National Public Radio, January 19, 2006.

6 The second edition of the *Norton* also includes brief excerpts from Dryden's criticism in its coverage of the seventeenth century, whereas the 2000 edition does not. However, since both the second and the seventh editions represent Dryden

extensively in their coverage of the eighteenth century, I do not count him among the authors excluded by the latter.

7 T.S. Eliot, *Selected Essays 1917–1932*, New York: Harcourt, Brace, and Company, 1932, p. 82.

8 William Hazlitt, *The Collected Works of William Hazlitt*, 12 vols, A.R. Waller and Arnold Glover (eds), London: J.M. Dent, 1902–1904, Vol. I, p. 221.

9 See Stella Revard, *Milton and the Tangles of Neaera's Hair: The Making of the 1645 'Poems'*, Columbia: University of Missouri Press, 1997, pp. 8–63, 205–63, and Stephen Guy-Bray, *Homoerotic Space: The Poetics of Loss in Renaissance Literature*, Toronto: University of Toronto Press, 2002, pp. 117–32. Also see Gary Bouchard, *Colin's Campus: Cambridge Life and the English Eclogue*, Selinsgrove: Susquehanna University Press, 2000; Gordon Campbell, 'Imitation in "Epitaphium Damonis" ', *Milton Studies*, 19, 1984, pp. 165–77; Bruce Boehrer, 'The Rejection of Pastoral in Milton's "Elegia Prima" ', *Modern Philology*, 99.2, November, 2001, pp. 181–200; and Bruce Boehrer, 'Animal Love in Milton: The Case of the "Epitaphium Damonis" ', *ELH*, 70, 2003, pp. 787–811.

10 M.H. Abrams, et al. (eds), *The Norton Anthology of English Literature*, 2 vols, New York: Norton, 1968, Vol. I, p. 993.

11 Keith W. Stavely, *The Politics of Milton's Prose Style*, New Haven: Yale University Press, 1975; Thomas Corns, *The Development of Milton's Prose Style*, Oxford: Clarendon Press, 1982; Michael Lieb and John T. Shawcross (eds), *Achievements of the Left Hand: Essays on the Prose of John Milton*, Amherst: University of Massachusetts Press, 1974.

12 For instance, see Larry S. Champion, *Ben Jonson's 'Dotages': A Reconsideration of the Late Plays*, Lexington: University of Kentucky Press, 1967; Anne Barton, *Ben Jonson: Dramatist*, Cambridge, UK: Cambridge University Press, 1984, pp. 235–52 and 258–99; and James Bednarz, *Shakespeare and the Poets' War*, New York: Columbia University Press, 2001.

13 Stephen Orgel, *The Jonsonian Masque*, Cambridge, US: Harvard University Press, 1965.

14 Stephen Orgel and Roy Strong (eds), *The Theatre of the Stuart Court*, Berkeley: University of California Press, 1973; Joseph Loewenstein, *Responsive Readings: Versions of Echo in Pastoral, Epic, and the Jonsonian Masque*, New Haven: Yale University Press, 1984; Dale B.J. Randall, *Jonson's Gypsies Unmasked: Background and Theme of 'The Gypsies Metamorphos'd'*, Durham: Duke University Press, 1975. Among other work in this vein, see also Orgel, *The Illusion of Power: Political Theater in the English Renaissance*, Berkeley: University of California Press, 1975 and Lesley Mickel, *Ben Jonson's Antimasques: A History of Growth and Decline*, Aldershot: Ashgate, 1999.

15 Richard Peterson's *Imitation and Praise in the Poetry of Ben Jonson*, New Haven: Yale University Press, 1981, reads the poet's non-dramatic verse through the lens of his commonplace book; for his engagement with Latin translation, see especially Katharine Eisaman Maus, *Ben Jonson and the Roman Frame of Mind*, Princeton: Princeton University Press, 1984; for his marginalia, see James A. Riddell and Stanley Stewart, *Jonson's Spenser: Evidence and Historical Criticism*, Pittsburgh: Duquesne University Press, 1995, and also Robert C. Evans, *Habits of Mind: Evidence and Effects of Ben Jonson's Reading*, Lewisburg: Bucknell University Press, 1995.

16 David Colclough, 'Introduction: Donne's Professional Lives', in *Donne's Professional Lives*, David Colclough (ed.), Cambridge: D.S. Brewer, 2003, p. 2.

17 John Carey, *John Donne: Life, Mind, and Art*, London: Faber and Faber, 1981, p. xiii.

18 Terry Eagleton, *Literary Theory: An Introduction*, 2nd edn, Oxford: Blackwell, 1996, p. 1.

19 Eagleton, p. 8.

20 Eagleton, p. 14.

21 For the tradition of the *rota Virgilii*, see *The 'Parisiana Poetria' of John of Garland*, Traugott Lawler (ed.), New Haven: Yale University Press, 1974, pp. 39–41 and 87; for Milton's remark, see *The Reason of Church-Government Urg'd Against Prelaty* in Roy Flannagan (ed.), *The Riverside Milton*, Boston: Houghton Mifflin, 1998, p. 922.

22 Peter Blayney, 'The Alleged Popularity of Playbooks', *Shakespeare Quarterly*, 56.1, Spring, 2005, pp. 33–50; see p. 47.

23 Frank Whigham, 'The Rhetoric of Elizabethan Suitors' Letters', *PMLA*, 96.5, October, 1981, pp. 864–82; see pp. 864–65.

24 David Bergeron, *Textual Patronage in English Drama, 1570–1640*, Aldershot: Ashgate, 2006, p. 16.

25 Richard Helgerson, *Forms of Nationhood: The Elizabethan Writing of England*, Chicago: University of Chicago Press, 1992, p. 1.

26 Helgerson, p. 147.

27 For the quoted phrase, see Stephen Greenblatt, *Marvelous Possessions: The Wonder of the New World*, Oxford: Clarendon, 1991, p. 25.

28 For the narratives, see Daniel J. Vitkus (ed.), *Piracy, Slavery, and Redemption: Barbary Captivity Narratives from Early Modern England*, intr. by Nabil Matar, New York: Columbia University Press, 2001, passim. For *Othello*'s relation to these tales, see Vitkus, *Turning Turk: English Theater and the Multicultural Mediterranean, 1570–1630*, New York: Palgrave, 2003, pp. 77–106.

29 See Gail Kern Paster, *The Body Embarrassed: Drama and the Disciplines of Shame in Early Modern England*, Ithaca: Cornell University Press, 1993, pp. 88–90 and 143–62.

30 Eagleton, p. 8.

31 For discussion of the quoted phrase, see Hans Robert Jauss, *Toward an Aesthetic of Reception*, Timothy Bahti (trans.), Minneapolis: University of Minnesota Press, 1982, pp. 23–24.

32 Elaine Showalter, 'Toward a Feminist Poetics', in *The New Feminist Criticism: Essays on Women, Literature and Theory*, Elaine Showalter (ed.), New York: Pantheon, 1985, p. 128.

33 Barry Weller and Margaret A. Ferguson, 'Introduction', in *The Tragedy of Mariam, the Fair Queen of Jewry*, Barry Weller and Margaret A. Ferguson (eds), Berkeley: University of California Press, 1994, p. 1.

34 Susanne Woods, 'Introduction', *The Poems of Aemilia Lanyer*, Susanne Woods (ed.), New York: Oxford University Press, 1993, p. xix, n. 14.

35 Josephine A. Roberts, 'Introduction', *The Poems of Lady Mary Wroth*, Josephine A. Roberts (ed.), Baton Rouge: Louisiana State University Press, 1983, p. 16.

36 Josephine A. Roberts, Suzanne Gossett, and Janel Mueller (eds), *The Second Part of the Countess of Montgomery's Urania*, by Lady Mary Wroth, Tempe: Renaissance English Text Society, 1999.

37 See Elaine V. Beilin, *Redeeming Eve: Women Writers of the English Renaissance*, Princeton: Princeton University Press, 1987 and Maureen Quilligan, *Incest and Agency in Elizabeth's England*, Philadelphia: University of Pennsylvania Press, 2005 (for the quoted phrase, see p. 23).

38 Christopher Hill, *Milton and the English Revolution*, Harmondsworth: Penguin, 1979, p. 3.

39 Hill, p. 3.

40 John Rogers, 'Milton's Circumcision', in Mark R. Kelley, Michael Lieb, and John Shawcross (eds), *Milton and the Grounds of Contention*, Pittsburgh: Duquesne University Press, 2003, pp. 188–213 (for the quoted phrase, see p. 192).

41 See, for instance, Jonathan Goldberg, *Sodometries: Renaissance Texts, Modern Sexualities*, Stanford: Stanford University Press, 1992, passim; Stephen Orgel, *Impersonations: The Performance of Gender in Shakespeare's England*, Cambridge, UK: Cambridge University Press, 1996, passim; Bruce Smith, *Homosexual Desire in Shakespeare's England*, Chicago: University of Chicago Press, 1991, pp. 182–86; Gregory Bredbeck, *Sodomy and Interpretation: Marlowe to Milton*, Ithaca: Cornell University Press, 1991, pp. 213–29; and Richard Rambuss, *Closet Devotions*, Durham: Duke University Press, 1998, pp. 26–38.

42 Gary Taylor and Stanley Wells (eds), *William Shakespeare: The Complete Works*, Oxford: Clarendon Press, 1986; Leah Marcus, *Unediting the Renaissance: Shakespeare, Marlowe, and Milton*, London: Routledge, 1996.

43 Neil Taylor and Anne Thompson (eds), *Hamlet*, by William Shakespeare, London: Arden, 2006.

44 Roy Flannagan (ed.), *The Riverside Milton*, Boston: Houghton Mifflin, 1998, p. 1156.

45 Stephen Greenblatt, *Renaissance Self-Fashioning: From More to Shakespeare*, Chicago: University of Chicago Press, 1980, p. 141.

Chapter 10

1 Robert Evans is responsible for the writing of the first three sections of this chapter and for the first item covered in the fourth section; Eric Sterling is responsible for the rest of section four (the section on race and ethnicity).

2 Barbara Kiefer Lewalski, *Writing Women in Jacobean England*, Cambridge, MA: Harvard University Press, 1993, p. 2.

3 Lewalski, p. 4.

4 Lewalski, p. 171.

5 Lewalski, p. 227.

6 Germaine Greer, Susan Hastings, Jeslyn Medoff, and Melinda Sansone (eds), *Kissing the Rod: An Anthology of Seventeenth-Century Women's Verse*, London: Virago Press, 1988.

7 Greer, et al., p. 1.

8 Greer, et al., p. 14.

9 Anita Pacheco (ed.), *Early Women Writers: 1600–1720*, London: Longman, 1998, p. v.

10 Pacheco (ed.), *Early Women Writers: 1600–1720*, p. 4.

11 Pacheco (ed.), *Early Women Writers: 1600–1720*, p. 7.

12 Pacheco (ed.), *Early Women Writers: 1600–1720*, p. 14.

13 Pacheco (ed.), *Early Women Writers: 1600–1720*, p. 19.

14 Anita Pacheco (ed.), *A Companion to Early Modern Women's Writing*, Oxford: Blackwell, 2002.

15 Alan Bray, *Homosexuality in Renaissance England*, New York: Columbia University Press, 1995, p. 115.

16 Bray, p. 7.

17 Bray, p. 31.

18 Bray, pp. 43–53.

19 Bray, pp. 53–57.

20 Bray, pp. 61–62.

21 Bray, p. 74.

22 Bray, p. 77.

23 Bray, pp. 86, 88.

24 Bray, p. 92.

25 Bray, p. 104.

26 Quoted in Bray, p. 114.

27 Bruce R. Smith, *Homosexual Desire in Shakespeare's England: A Cultural Poetics*, Chicago: University of Chicago Press, 1991, pp. 17 and 20.

28 Smith, p. 24.

29 Paul Hammond, *Figuring Sex between Men from Shakespeare to Rochester*, Oxford: Clarendon Press, 2002, p. 1.

30 Hammond, pp. 2–3.

31 Denise A. Walen, *Constructions of Female Homoeroticism in Early Modern Drama*, New York: Palgrave Macmillan, 2005, pp. 1–2.

32 Walen, pp. 3–4.

33 Anthony Gerard Barthelemy, *Black Face, Maligned Race: The Representation of Blacks in English Drama from Shakespeare to Southerne*, Baton Rouge, LA: Louisiana State University Press, 1987.

34 Margo Hendricks and Patricia Parker (eds), *Women, 'Race', & Writing in the Early Modern Period*, London: Routledge, 1994.

35 Kim F. Hall, *Things of Darkness: Economies of Race and Gender in Early Modern England*, Ithaca and London: Cornell University Press, 1995.

36 Joyce Green MacDonald (ed.), *Race, Ethnicity, and Power in the Renaissance*, Madison, NJ: Fairleigh Dickinson University Press; London: Associated University Presses, 1997.

37 Mary Floyd-Wilson, *English Ethnicity and Race in Early Modern Drama*, Cambridge: Cambridge University Press, 2003.

38 Virginia Mason Vaughan, *Performing Blackness on English Stages, 1500–1800*, Cambridge: Cambridge University Press, 2005.

Chapter 11

1 Stephen Greenblatt, *Renaissance Self-Fashioning: From More to Shakespeare*, Chicago: University of Chicago Press, 1980.

2 Michel Foucault, *Discipline and Punish: The Birth of the Prison*, Alan Sheridan (trans.), New York: Vintage, 1979.

3 Stephen Greenblatt, *Shakespearean Negotiations: The Circulation of Social Energy in Renaissance England*, Berkeley: University of California Press, 1988.

4 Jonathan Dollimore and Alan Sinfield (eds), *Political Shakespeare: New Essays in Cultural Materialism*, 2nd edn, Ithaca, NY: Cornell University Press, 1994.

5 Louis A. Montrose, *The Subject of Elizabeth: Authority, Gender, and Representation*, Chicago: University of Chicago Press, 2006.

6 Robert C. Evans, *Ben Jonson and the Poetics of Patronage*, Lewisburg, PA: Bucknell University Press, 1989.

7 Robert C. Evans, *Jonson and the Contexts of His Time*, Lewisburg, PA: Bucknell University Press, 1994.

8 Arthur F. Marotti, *John Donne, Coterie Poet*, Madison: University of Wisconsin Press, 1986.

9 Arthur Marotti, *Manuscript, Print, and the English Renaissance Lyric*, Ithaca, NY: Cornell University Press, 1995.

10 Christopher Hill, *Milton and the English Revolution*, London: Faber, 1977.

11 David Loewenstein, *Representing Revolution in Milton and His Contemporaries: Religion, Politics, and Polemics in Radical Puritanism*, Cambridge: Cambridge University Press, 2001; Sharon Achinstein, *Literature and Dissent in Milton's England*, Cambridge: Cambridge University Press, 2003.

12 Katharine Gillespie, *Domesticity and Dissent in the Seventeenth Century: English Women Writers and the Public Sphere*, Cambridge: Cambridge University Press, 2004; Hilary Hinds, *God's Englishwomen: Seventeenth-Century Radical Sectarian Writing and Feminist Criticism*, Manchester: Manchester University Press, 1996.

13 Antonia Fraser, *The Weaker Vessel: Woman's Lot in Seventeenth-Century England*, New York: Knopf, 1984.
14 Hilda L. Smith, *Reason's Disciples: Seventeenth-Century English Feminists*, Urbana: University of Illinois Press, 1982.
15 Michel Foucault, *The History of Sexuality*, 3 vols, Robert Hurley (trans.), London: Penguin: 1990–1992.
16 Jonathan Goldberg, *Sodometries: Renaissance Texts, Modern Sexualities*, Stanford, CA: Stanford University Press, 1992.
17 Jonathan Goldberg (ed.), *Queering the Renaissance*, Durham, NC: Duke University Press, 1994.
18 Richard Rambuss, *Closet Devotions*, Durham, NC: Duke University Press, 1998.
19 David M. Bergeron, *King James & Letters of Homoerotic Desire*, Iowa City: University of Iowa Press, 1999.
20 Dianne K. McColley, *Milton's Eve*, Urbana: University of Illinois Press, 1983; McColley, *A Gust for Paradise: Milton and the Arts of Eden*, Urbana: University of Illinois Press, 1993.
21 Ken Hiltner, *Milton and Ecology*, Cambridge: Cambridge University Press, 2003.

Annotated Bibliography

Jonathan Wright

General Studies

These studies offer diverse overviews, often by various authors, of the whole period. The volumes edited by Cheney focus on individual literary works; the books by Corns, King, and Loewenstein and Mueller are comprehensive; the anthology by Dawson and Dupree contains full introductions and detailed notes. The books by Hebron, Rivers, and Donker and Muldrow complement one another nicely.

Cheney, Patrick, Andrew Hadfield, and Garrett A. Sullivan, Jr., (eds), *Early Modern English Drama: A Critical Companion*, New York: Oxford University Press, 2006.
—— , *Early Modern English Poetry: A Critical Companion*, New York: Oxford University Press, 2007.
Corns, Thomas N., *A History of Seventeenth-Century English Literature*, Malden, MA: Blackwell, 2007.
Dawson, Terence and Robert S. Dupree (eds), *Seventeenth-Century English Poetry: The Annotated Anthology*, Hemel Hempstead: Harvester Wheatsheaf, 1994.
Donker, Marjorie and George M. Muldrow, *Dictionary of Literary-Rhetorical Conventions of the English Renaissance*, Westport, CT: Greenwood, 1982.
Hebron, Malcolm, *Key Concepts in Renaissance Literature*, London: Palgrave Macmillan, 2008.
King, Bruce, *Seventeenth-Century English Literature*, London: Macmillan, 1982.
Loewenstein, David and Janel Mueller (eds), *The Cambridge History of Early Modern English Literature*, New York: Cambridge University Press, 2002.
Parry, Graham, *The Seventeenth Century: The Intellectual and Cultural Context of English Literature, 1603–1700*, New York: Longman, 1989.
Rivers, Isabel, *Classical and Christian Ideas in English Renaissance Poetry*, 2nd edn, London: Routledge, 1994.
Waddington, Raymond B. and C.A. Patrides (eds), *The Age of Milton: Backgrounds to Seventeenth-Century Literature*, Manchester: Manchester University Press, 1980.

Political and Social Contexts

Bray's brief text is a classic. Coward's work is extremely helpful. Each of the other books listed here deals with key concepts in recent study of the period.

Amussen, Susan Dwyer, *An Ordered Society: Gender and Class in Early Modern England*, New York: Columbia University Press, 1993.
Barbour, Reid, *Literature and Religious Culture in Seventeenth-Century England*, Cambridge: Cambridge University Press, 2002.

Bray, Alan, *Homosexuality in Renaissance England*, 2nd edn, New York: Columbia University Press, 1995.

Brown, Cedric C. (ed.), *Patronage, Politics, and Literary Traditions in England, 1558–1658*, Detroit: Wayne State University Press, 1993.

Coward, Barry, *The Stuart Age: A History of England, 1603–1714*, 3rd edn, New York: Longman, 2003.

Keeble, N.H. (ed.), *The Cambridge Companion to Writing of the English Revolution*, Cambridge: Cambridge University Press, 2001.

Loewenstein, David, *Representing Revolution in Milton and His Contemporaries: Religion, Politics, and Polemics in Radical Puritanism*, New York: Cambridge University Press, 2001.

Love, Harold, *The Culture and Commerce of Texts: Scribal Publication in Seventeenth-Century England*, Amherst, MA: University of Massachusetts Press, 1998.

Marotti, Arthur F. (ed.), *Catholicism and Anti-Catholicism in Early Modern English Texts*, New York: St. Martin's Press, 1999.

Marotti, Arthur F., *Manuscript, Print, and the English Renaissance Lyric*, Ithaca, NY: Cornell University Press, 1995.

Norbrook, David, *Writing the English Republic: Poetry, Rhetoric, and Politics, 1627–1660*, New York: Cambridge University Press, 1999.

Patterson, Annabel M., *Censorship and Interpretation: The Conditions of Writing and Reading in Early Modern England*, Madison, WI: University of Wisconsin Press, 1984.

Literature, Culture, and Power

Tillyard's brief book presents a traditional view that has been attacked by more recent scholars. Many of the works listed here (Goldberg's in particular) reflect recent debates about the so-called 'new historicism'. The books edited by Summers and Pebworth and by Sharpe and Zwicker offer multiple perspectives.

Goldberg, Jonathan, *James I and the Politics of Literature: Jonson, Shakespeare, Donne, and Their Contemporaries*, Baltimore: Johns Hopkins University Press, 1983.

Marcus, Leah S., *The Politics of Mirth: Jonson, Herrick, Milton, Marvell, and the Defense of Old Holiday Pastimes*, Chicago: University of Chicago Press, 1986.

Norbrook, David, *Poetry and Politics in the English Renaissance*, Revised edn, New York: Oxford University Press, 2002.

Parry, Graham, *The Golden Age Restor'd: The Culture of the Stuart Court, 1603–1642*, New York: St. Martin's Press, 1981.

Sharpe, Kevin and Steven N. Zwicker (eds), *The Politics of Discourse: The Literature and History of Seventeenth-Century England*, Berkeley: University of California Press, 1987.

Shuger, Debora Kuller, *Habits of Thought in the English Renaissance: Religion, Politics, and the Dominant Culture*, Berkeley: University of California Press, 1990.

Smith, Nigel, *Literature and Revolution in England, 1640–1660*, New Haven, CT: Yale University Press, 1994.

Summers, Claude J. and Ted-Larry Pebworth (eds), *Classic and Cavalier: Essays* on *Jonson and the Sons of Ben*, Pittsburgh, PA: University of Pittsburgh Press, 1982.

——, *'The Muses Common-Weale': Poetry and Politics in the Seventeenth Century*, Columbia, MO: University of Missouri Press, 1988.

Tillyard, E.M.W., *The Elizabethan World Picture*, London: Chatto & Windus, 1943.

Zwicker, Steven N., *Lines of Authority: Politics and English Literary Culture, 1649–1689*, Ithaca, NY: Cornell University Press, 1993.

Generic and Stylistic Concerns

Of the books listed below, the several 'Cambridge Companions' make particularly good starting places. The works by Butler, Colie, Fish, Lewalski, and Weber have been especially influential. Miner's three books cover the poetry of the whole period.

Anderson, Thomas Page, *Performing Early Modern Trauma from Shakespeare to Milton*, Aldershot: Ashgate, 2006.

Bailey, Amanda, *Flaunting: Style and the Subversive Male Body in Renaissance England*, Toronto: University of Toronto Press, 2007.

Bovilsky, Lara, *Barbarous Play: Race on the English Renaissance Stage*, Minneapolis: Minnesota University Press, 2008.

Braunmuller, A.R. and Michael Hattaway (eds), *The Cambridge Companion to English Renaissance Drama*, Cambridge: Cambridge University Press, 2003.

Butler, Martin, *The Stuart Court Masque and Political Culture*, Cambridge: Cambridge University Press, 2009.

Clark, Ira, *Professional Playwrights: Massinger, Ford, Shirley, and Brome*, Lexington: University Press of Kentucky, 1992.

Clark, Sandra, *Renaissance Drama*, Cambridge: Polity, 2007.

Colie, Rosalie L., *The Resources of Kind: Genre-Theory in the Renaissance*, Barbara K. Lewalski (ed.), Berkeley: University of California Press, 1973.

Corns, Thomas N. (ed.), *The Cambridge Companion to English Poetry, Donne to Marvell*, New York: Cambridge University Press, 1993.

Cunnar, Eugene R. and Jeffrey Johnson (eds), *Discovering and (Re)covering the Seventeeth-Century Religious Lyric*, Pittsburgh, PA: Duquesne University Press, 2001.

Delany, Paul, *British Autobiography in the Seventeenth Century*, London: Routledge, 1969.

Fish, Stanley E., *Self-Consuming Artifacts: The Experience of Seventeenth-Century Literature*, Pittsburgh, PA: Duquesne University Press, 1994.

—— (ed.), *Seventeenth-Century Prose: Modern Essays in Criticism*, New York: Oxford University Press, 1971.

Gibbons, Brian, *Jacobean City Comedy*, 2nd edn, Cambridge, MA: Harvard University Press, 1980.

Greenblatt, Stephen J., John D. Cox, and David Scott Kastan, *A New History of Early English Drama*, New York: Columbia University Press, 1998.

Guibbory, Achsah, *The Map of Time: Seventeenth-Century English Literature and Ideas of Pattern in History*, Urbana: University of Illinois Press, 1986.

Harvey, Elizabeth D. and Katherine Eisaman Maus (eds), *Soliciting Interpretation: Literary Theory and Seventeenth-Century English Poetry*, Chicago: University of Chicago Press, 1990.

Henslowe, Philip, *Henslowe's Diary*, R.A. Foakes (ed.), 2nd edn, Cambridge: Cambridge University Press, 2002.

Hutner, Heidi, *Colonial Women: Race and Culture in Stuart Drama*, Oxford: Oxford University Press, 2001.

Ioppolo, Grace, *Dramatists and Their Manuscripts in the Age of Shakespeare, Jonson, Middleton, and Heywood: Authorship, Authority, and the Playhouse*, London: Routledge, 2006.

Kastan, David Scott, *Staging the Renaissance: Reinterpretations of Elizabethan and Jacobean Drama*, New York: Routledge, 1991.

Kezar, Dennis (ed.), *Solon and Thespis: Law and Theater in the English Renaissance*, Notre Dame: Notre Dame University Press, 2007.

Kinney, Arthur F. (ed.), *A Companion to Renaissance Drama*, Oxford: Blackwell, 2004.

Lewalski, Barbara Kiefer, *Protestant Poetics and the Seventeenth-Century Religious Lyric*, Princeton, NJ: Princeton University Press, 1979.

Miner, Earl, *The Cavalier Mode from Jonson to Cotton*, Princeton, NJ: Princeton University Press, 1971.

——, *The Metaphysical Mode from Donne to Cowley*, Princeton, NJ: Princeton University Press, 1969.

——, *The Restoration Mode from Milton to Dryden*, Princeton, NJ: Princeton University Press, 1974.

Mullaney, Steven, *The Place of the Stage: License, Play, and Power in Renaissance England*, Ann Arbor: University of Michigan Press, 1995.

Parfitt, George, *English Poetry of the Seventeenth Century*, 2nd edn, New York: Longman, 1992.

Raber, Karen, *Dramatic Difference: Gender, Class, and Genre in the Early Modern Closet Drama*, Newark: University of Delaware Press; London: Associated University Presses, 2001.

Skantze, P.A., *Stillness in Motion in the Seventeenth-Century Theatre*, London: Routledge, 2003.

Straznicky, Marta, *Privacy, Playreading, and Women's Closet Drama, 1550–1700*, Cambridge: Cambridge University Press, 2004.

Styan, J.L., *The English Stage: A History of Drama and Performance*, Cambridge: Cambridge University Press, 1996.

Vickers, Brian (ed.), *English Renaissance Literary Criticism*, New York: Oxford University Press, 1999.

Webber, Joan, *The Eloquent 'I': Style and Self in Seventeenth-Century Prose*, Madison, WI: University of Wisconsin Press, 1968.

Women as Writers and as Subjects of Writing

The anthology by Greer, et al. has been highly influential. Lewalski's book is very substantial. Wilcox's volume offers an especially helpful overview, while the companion edited by Pacheco is quite comprehensive.

Ferguson, Margaret, Maureen Quilligan, and Nancy J. Vickers (eds), *Rewriting the Renaissance: The Discourses of Sexual Difference in Early Modern Europe*, Chicago: University of Chicago Press, 1986.

Graham, Elspeth, et al. (eds), *Her Own Life: Autobiographical Writings by Seventeenth-Century Englishwomen*, New York: Routledge, 1989.

Greer, Germaine, et al. (eds), *Kissing the Rod: An Anthology of Seventeenth-Century Women's Verse*, New York: Farrar, 1988.

Hobby, Elaine, *Virtue of Necessity: English Women's Writing, 1649–88*, Ann Arbor, MI: University of Michigan Press, 1989.

Lewalski, Barbara Kiefer, *Writing Women in Jacobean England*, Cambridge, MA: Harvard University Press, 1993.

Pacheco, Anita (ed.), *A Companion to Early Modern Women's Writing*, Malden, MA: Blackwell, 2002.

Smith, Hilda L. and Susan Cardinale (comps), *Women and the Literature of the Seventeenth Century: An Annotated Bibliography Based on Wing's Short-Title Catalogue*, New York: Greenwood Press, 1990.

Summers, Claude J. and Ted-Larry Pebworth (eds), *Representing Women in Renaissance England*, Columbia, MO: University of Missouri Press, 1997.

Walker, Kim, *Women Writers of the English Renaissance*, Boston: Twayne, 1996.

Wilcox, Helen (ed.), *Women and Literature in Britain, 1500–1700*, New York: Cambridge University Press, 1996.

Studies of Individual Authors

The selections listed below have been made with several purposes in view. One such purpose has been to provide students with an idea of good starting places; for this purpose, the Twayne volumes are usually reliable. Another purpose has been to suggest the variety of opinions and perspectives provoked by major writers; for this purpose, the edited volumes (especially the various 'Companions') are helpful. Finally, another major purpose has been to indicate which scholars or monographs have been especially influential, either by eliciting agreement or by stimulating debate.

Francis Bacon

Peltonen, Markku (ed.), *The Cambridge Companion to Bacon*, New York: Cambridge University Press, 1996.

Vickers, Brian, *Francis Bacon and Renaissance Prose*, Cambridge: Cambridge University Press, 1968.

Francis Beaumont

Bliss, Lee, *Francis Beaumont*, Boston: Twayne, 1987.

Finkelpearl, Philip J., *Court and Country Politics in the Plays of Beaumont and Fletcher*, Princeton, NJ: Princeton University Press, 1990.

Richard Brome

Brome, Catherine M., *Richard Brome*, Boston: Twayne, 1978.
Steggle, Matthew, *Richard Brome: Place and Politics on the Caroline Stage*, Manchester: Manchester University Press, 2004.

Sir Thomas Browne

Patrides, C.A. (ed.), *Approaches to Sir Thomas Browne: The Ann Arbor Tercentenary Lectures and Essays*, Columbia, MO: University of Missouri Press, 1982.
Post, Jonathan F.S., *Sir Thomas Browne*, Boston: MA: Twayne, 1987.

Robert Burton

Gowland, Angus, *The Worlds of Renaissance Melancholy*, Cambridge: Cambridge University Press, 2006.
O'Connell, Michael, *Robert Burton*, Boston: Twayne, 1986.

Thomas Carew

Sadler, Lynn, *Thomas Carew*, Boston: Twayne, 1979.
Selig, Edward I., *The Flourishing Wreath: A Study of Thomas Carew's Poetry*, New Haven, CT: Yale University Press, 1958.

Elizabeth Cary

Wolfe, Heather (ed.), *The Literary Career and Legacy of Elizabeth Cary, 1613–1680*, New York: Palgrave Macmillan, 2007.

Margaret Cavendish

Clucas, Stephen (ed.), *A Princely Brave Woman: Essays on Margaret Cavendish, Duchess of Newcastle*, Burlington, VT: Ashgate, 2003.
Cottegnies, Line and Nancy Weitz (eds), *Authorial Conquests: Essays on Genre in the Writings of Margaret Cavendish*, Cranbury, NJ: Associated University Presses, 2003.
Jones, Kathleen, *A Glorious Fame: The Life of Margaret Cavendish, Duchess of Newcastle, 1623–73*, London: Bloomsbury, 1988.
Rees, Emma L.E., *Margaret Cavendish: Gender, Genre, Exile*, New York: Manchester University Press, 2003.

George Chapman

Braumuller, A.R., *Natural Fictions: George Chapman's Major Tragedies*, Newark, DE: University of Delaware Press, 1992.

Spivack, Charlotte, *George Chapman*, Boston: Twayne, 1967.

Abraham Cowley

Hinman, Robert B., *Abraham Cowley's World of Order*, Cambridge, MA: Harvard University Press, 1960.
Trotter, David, *The Poetry of Abraham Cowley*, London: Macmillan, 1979.

Richard Crashaw

Healy, Thomas F., *Richard Crashaw*, Leiden: E.J. Brill, 1986.
Parrish, Paul A., *Richard Crashaw*, Boston: Twayne, 1980.
Roberts, John R. (ed.), *New Perspectives on the Life and Art of Richard Crashaw*, Columbia, MO: University of Missouri Press, 1990.
Warren, Austin, *Richard Crashaw: A Study in Baroque Sensibility*, Ann Arbor, MI: University of Michigan Press, 1957.

William Davenant

Bordinat, Philip and Sophia B. Blaydes, *Sir William Davenant*, Boston: Twayne, 1981.
Edmond, Mary, *Rare Sir William Davenant: Poet Laureate, Playwright, Civil War General, Restoration Theatre Manager*, Manchester: Manchester University Press, 1987.

Thomas Dekker

Gasper, Julia, *The Dragon and the Dove: The Plays of Thomas Dekker*, Oxford: Clarendon Press, 1990.
Price, George R., *Thomas Dekker*, Boston: Twayne, 1969.

John Donne

Carey, John, *John Donne: Life, Mind and Art*, London: Faber and Faber, 1990.
Guibbory, Achsah (ed.), *The Cambridge Companion to John Donne*, New York: Cambridge University Press, 2006.
Hurley, Ann Hollinshead, *John Donne's Poetry and Early Modern Visual Culture*, Selinsgrove, PA: Susquehanna University Press, 2005.
Marotti, Arthur F. (ed.), *Critical Essays on John Donne*, New York: Macmillan, 1994.
—— , *John Donne: Coterie Poet*, Madison, WI: University of Wisconsin Press, 1986.
Smith, A.J. (ed.), *John Donne: The Critical Heritage*, Boston: Routledge, 1995.
—— , *John Donne: Essays in Celebration*, London: Methuen, 1972.
Stubbs, John. *John Donne: The Reformed Soul*, New York: Norton, 2007.
Summers, Claude J. and Ted-Larry Pebworth (eds), *The Eagle and the Dove: Reassessing John Donne*, Columbia, MO: University of Missouri Press, 1986.

Targoff, Ramie, *John Donne: Body and Soul*, Chicago: University of Chicago Press, 2008.

John Fletcher

McMullan, Gordon, *The Politics of Unease in the Plays of John Fletcher*, Amherst, MA: University of Massachusetts Press, 1994.
Squier, Charles L., *John Fletcher*, Boston: Twayne, 1986.

John Ford

Neill, Michael (ed.), *John Ford: Critical Re-visions*, Cambridge: Cambridge University Press, 1988.

George Herbert

Fish, Stanley, *The Living Temple: George Herbert and Catechizing*, Berkeley: University of California Press, 1978.
Patrides, C.A. (ed.), *George Herbert: The Critical Heritage*, Boston: Routledge, 1983.
Schoenfeldt, Michael C., *Prayer and Power: George Herbert and Renaissance Courtship*, Chicago: University of Chicago Press, 1991.
Stewart, Stanley, *George Herbert*, Boston: Twayne, 1986.
Summers, Claude J. and Ted-Larry Pebworth (eds), *'Bright Shootes of Everlasting-nesse': The Seventeenth-Century Religious Lyric*, Columbia, MO: University of Missouri Press, 1987.
—— *'Too Rich to Clothe the Sunne': Essays on George Herbert*, Pittsburgh, PA: University of Pittsburgh Press, 1980.
Summers, Joseph H., *George Herbert: His Religion and His Art*, Cambridge, MA: Harvard University Press, 1968.
Tuve, Rosemond, *A Reading of George Herbert*, London: Faber and Faber, 1952.
Vendler, Helen, *The Poetry of George Herbert*, Cambridge, MA: Harvard University Press, 1975.

Robert Herrick

Coiro, Ann Baynes, *Robert Herrick's Hesperides and the Epigram Book Tradition*, Baltimore: The Johns Hopkins University Press, 1988.
Deming, Robert H., *Ceremony and Art: Robert Herrick's Poetry*, The Hague: Mouton, 1974.
Rollin, Roger B. and J. Max Patrick (eds) *'Trust to Good Verses': Herrick Tercentenary Essays*, Pittsburgh, PA: University of Pittsburgh Press, 1978.

Thomas Heywood

Baines, Barbara J., *Thomas Heywood*, Boston: Twayne, 1984.

Boas, Frederick S., *Thomas Heywood*, New York: Phaeton Press, 1975.

Ben Jonson

Barton, Anne, *Ben Jonson, Dramatist*, New York: Cambridge University Press, 1984.
Evans, Robert C., *Ben Jonson and the Poetics of Patronage*, Lewisburg, PA: Bucknell University Press, 1989.
Harp, Richard and Stanley Stewart (eds), *The Cambridge Companion to Ben Jonson*, New York: Cambridge University Press, 2000.
Helgerson, Richard, *Self-Crowned Laureates: Spenser, Jonson, Milton, and the Literary System*, Berkeley: University of California Press, 1983.
Hirsh, James (ed.), *New Perspectives on Ben Jonson*, Madison, NJ: Fairleigh Dickinson University Press, 1997.
McEvoy, Sean, *Ben Jonson, Renaissance Dramatist*, Edinburgh: Edinburgh University Press, 2008.
Orgel, Stephen and Roy Strong, *Inigo Jones: The Theatre of the Stuart Court*, 2 vols, Berkeley: University of California Press, 1973.
Riggs, David, *Ben Jonson: A Life*, Cambridge, MA: Harvard University Press, 1989.
Slights, William W.E., *Ben Jonson and the Art of Secrecy*, Toronto: Toronto University Press, 1994.
Watson, Robert N., *Ben Jonson's Parodic Strategy: Literary Imperialism in the Comedies*, Cambridge, MA: Harvard University Press, 1987.

Aemilia Lanyer

Grossman, Marshall (ed.), *Aemilia Lanyer: Gender, Genre, and the Canon*, Lexington, KY: University Press of Kentucky, 1998.
Woods, Susanne, *Lanyer: A Renaissance Woman Poet*, Oxford: Oxford University Press, 1999.

Richard Lovelace

Summers, Claude J. and Ted-Larry Pebworth (eds), *Classic and Cavalier: Essays on Jonson and the Sons of Ben*, Pittsburgh, PA: University of Pittsburgh Press, 1982.
—— (eds), *The Wit of Seventeenth-Century Poetry*, Columbia, MO: University of Missouri Press, 1995.
Weidhorn, Manfred, *Richard Lovelace*, Boston: Twayne, 1970.

John Marston

Cathcart, Charles, *Marston, Rivalry, Rapprochement, and Jonson*, Burlington, VT: Ashgate, 2008.
Ingram, R.W., *John Marston*, Boston: Twayne, 1978.
Wharton, T.F. (ed.), *The Drama of John Marston: Critical Re-Visions*, Cambridge: Cambridge University Press, 2000.

Andrew Marvell

Brett, R.L. (ed.), *Andrew Marvell: Essays on the Tercentenary of His Death*, New York: Oxford University Press, 1979.

Colie, Rosalie L. *'My Ecchoing Song': Andrew Marvell's Poetry of Criticism*, Princeton, NJ: Princeton University Press, 1970.

Donno, Elizabeth Story (ed.), *Andrew Marvell: The Critical Heritage*, Boston: Routledge, 1978.

Friedenreich, Kenneth (ed.), *Tercentenary Essays in Honor of Andrew Marvell*, Hamden, CT: Archon Books, 1977.

Healy, Thomas (ed.), *Andrew Marvell*, New York: Longman, 1998.

Patrides, C.A. (ed.), *Approaches to Marvell: The York Tercentenary Lectures*, Boston: Routledge, 1978.

Patterson, Annabel M., *Marvell and the Civic Crown*, Princeton, NJ: Princeton University Press, 1978.

—— , *Marvell: The Writer in Public Life*, New York: Longman, 1999.

Philip Massinger

Adler, Dorris, *Philip Massinger*, Boston: Twayne, 1987.

Garrett, Martin (ed.), *Philip Massinger: The Critical Heritage*, London: Routledge, 1991.

Howard, Douglas (ed.), *Philip Massinger: A Critical Reassessment*, Cambridge: Cambridge University Press, 1985.

Thomas Middleton

Heinemann, Margot, *Puritanism and Theatre: Thomas Middleton and Opposition Drama under the Early Stuarts*, Cambridge: Cambridge University Press, 1980.

Rowe, George E., *Thomas Middleton & the New Comedy Tradition*, Lincoln: University of Nebraska Press, 1979.

Steen, Sara Jayne, *Ambrosia in an Earthern Vessel: Three Centuries of Audience and Reader Response to the Works of Thomas Middleton*, New York: AMS Press, 1993.

John Milton

Danielson, Dennis (ed.), *The Cambridge Companion to Milton*, 2nd edn, New York: Cambridge University Press, 1999.

Empson, William, *Milton's God*, Westport, CT: Greenwood Press, 1978.

Fish, Stanley, *How Milton Works*, Cambridge, MA: Harvard University Press, 2001.

—— , *Surprised by Sin: The Reader in Paradise Lost*, 2nd edn, Cambridge, MA: Harvard University Press, 1998.

Hughes, Merritt Y. (ed.), *A Variorum Commentary on the Poems of John Milton*, 2 vols, New York: Columbia University Press, 1970.

Hunter, William B., Jr. (ed.), *A Milton Encyclopedia*, 9 vols, Lewisburg, PA: Bucknell University Press, 1978–1983.

Kelley, Mark R. and Joseph Wittreich, *Altering Eyes: New Perspectives on Samson Agonistes*, Cranbury, NJ: Associated University Presses, 2002.

Lewalski, Barbara Kiefer, *The Life of John Milton: A Critical Biography*, Malden, MA: Blackwell Publishers, 2000.

—— , *Milton's Brief Epic: The Genre, Meaning, and Art of Paradise Regained*, Providence, RI: Brown University Press, 1966.

—— , *Paradise Lost and the Rhetoric of Literary Forms*, Princeton, NJ: Princeton University Press, 1985.

Lewis, C.S., *A Preface to Paradise Lost*, Revised edn, London: Oxford University Press, 1960.

Lieb, Michael and John T. Shawcross (eds), *Achievements of the Left Hand: Essays on the Prose of John Milton*, Amherst, MA: University of Massachusetts Press, 1974.

Loewenstein, David, *Representing Revolution in Milton and His Contemporaries: Religion, Politics, and Polemics in Radical Puritanism*, New York: Cambridge University Press, 2001.

Martz, Louis L., *Milton: Poet of Exile*, New Haven, CT: Yale University Press, 1986.

McColley, Diane Kelsey, *Milton's Eve*, Urbana, IL: University of Illinois Press, 1983.

Nyquist, Mary and Margaret W. Ferguson (eds), *Re-membering Milton: Essays on the Texts and Traditions*, New York: Methuen, 1988.

Patrides, C.A., *An Annotated Critical Bibliography of John Milton*, New York: St. Martin's Press, 1987.

Patrides, C.A. (ed.), *Milton's Lycidas: The Tradition and the Poem*, Columbia, MO: University of Missouri Press, 1983.

Patterson, Annabel (ed.), *John Milton*, New York: Longman, 1992.

Rajan, Balachandra and Elizabeth Sauer (eds), *Milton and the Imperial Vision*, Pittsburgh, PA: Duquesne University Press, 1999.

Revard, Stella P., *Milton and the Tangles of Neaera's Hair: The Making of the 1645 Poems*, Columbia, MO: University of Missouri Press, 1997.

Shawcross, John T. (ed.), *Milton: The Critical Heritage*, London: Routledge, 1970.

—— , *Milton, 1732–1801: The Critical Heritage*, Boston: Routledge, 1972.

Walker, Julia M. (ed.), *Milton and the Idea of Woman*, Urbana, IL: University of Illinois Press, 1988.

James Shirley

Forsythe, Robert S., *The Relations of Shirley's Plays to the Elizabethan Drama*, Rpt. from Columbia University Studies in English and Comparative Literature, New York: B. Blom, 1965.

Lucow, Ben, *James Shirley*, Boston: Twayne, 1981.

John Suckling

Squier, Charles L., *Sir John Suckling*, Boston: Twayne, 1978.

Cyril Tourneur

Schuman, Samuel, *Cyril Tourneur*, Boston: Twayne, 1977.

Thomas Traherne

Blevins, Jacob (ed.), *Re-Reading Thomas Traherne: New Critical Essays*, Tempe, AZ: Arizona Center for Medieval and Renaissance Studies, 2007.
Day, Malcolm M., *Thomas Traherne*, Boston: Twayne, 1982.
Stewart, Stanley, *The Expanded Voice: The Art of Thomas Traherne*, San Marino, CA: Huntington Library, 1970.

Henry Vaughan

Post, Jonathan F.S., *Henry Vaughan: The Unfolding Vision*, Princeton, NJ: Princeton University Press, 1982.
Rudrum, Alan (ed.), *Essential Articles for the Study of Henry Vaughan*, Hamden, CT: Archon Books, 1987.

Edmund Waller

Chambers, A.B., *Andrew Marvell and Edmund Waller: Seventeenth-Century Praise and Restoration Satire*, University Park, PA: Pennsylvania State University Press, 1991.
Gilbert, Jack G., *Edmund Waller*, Boston: Twayne, 1979.

Izaak Walton

Martin, Jessica, *Walton's Lives: Conformist Commemorations and the Rise of Biography*, New York: Oxford University Press, 2001.
Stanwood, P.G., *Izaak Walton*, New York: Twayne, 1998.

John Webster

Bliss, Lee, *The World's Perspective: John Webster and the Jacobean Drama*, Brighton, Sussex: Harvester Press, 1983.
Forker, Charles R., *The Skull Beneath the Skin: The Achievement of John Webster*, Carbondale, IL: Southern Illinois University Press, 1986.
Moore, Don D. (ed.), *Webster: The Critical Heritage*, Boston: Routledge, 1981.
Ranald, Margaret Loftus, *John Webster*, Boston: Twayne, 1989.

Mary Wroth

Miller, Naomi J., *Changing the Subject: Mary Wroth and Figurations of Gender in Early Modern England*, Lexington, KY: University Press of Kentucky, 1996.

Miller, Naomi J. and Gary Waller (eds), *Reading Mary Wroth: Representing Alternatives in Early Modern England*, Knoxville, TN: University of Tennessee Press, 1991.

Waller, Gary, *The Sidney Family Romance: Mary Wroth, William Herbert, and the Early Modern Construction of Gender*, Detroit: Wayne State University Press, 1993.

The Restoration

The books by McDowell and Williamson are fine examples of the recent emphasis on women writers of this period. Zwicker is a major scholar, and his book has all the virtues typically found in the 'Cambridge Companions'.

McDowell, Paula, *The Women of Grub Street: Press, Politics, and Gender in the London Literary Marketplace, 1678–1730*, New York: Clarendon Press, 1998.

Rosenfeld, Nancy, *Human Satan in Seventeenth-Century English Literature: From Milton to Rochester*, Aldershot: Ashgate, 2008.

Sitter, John, *Arguments of Augustan Wit*, New York: Cambridge University Press, 1991.

Stauffer, Donald A., *English Biography before 1700*, New York: Russell and Russell, 1930.

Williamson, Marilyn L., *Raising Their Voices: British Women Writers, 1650–1750*, Detroit: Wayne State University Press, 1990.

Zwicker, Steven N. (ed.), *The Cambridge Companion to English Literature 1650–1740*, Cambridge: Cambridge University Press, 1998.

Restoration Drama

Holland and Hume are major scholars; Hughes' volume is especially relevant to the focus of the present book. For varied perspectives, students should especially seek out edited volumes, especially the 'Cambridge Companions'.

Brown, Laura, *English Dramatic Form, 1660–1760: An Essay in Generic History*, New Haven: Yale University Press, 1981.

Canfield, J. Douglas, *Heroes & States: On the Ideology of Restoration Tragedy*, Lexington: University of Kentucky Press, 2000.

Fisk, Deborah Payne (ed.), *The Cambridge Companion to English Restoration Theatre*, Cambridge: Cambridge University Press, 2000.

Fujimura, Thomas H., *The Restoration Comedy of Wit*, Princeton, NJ: Princeton University Press, 1952.

Holland, Norman Norwood, *The First Modern Comedies: The Significance of Etherege, Wycherley, and Congreve*, Cambridge, MA: Harvard University Press, 1959.

Howe, Elizabeth, *The First English Actresses: Women and Drama, 1660–1700*, Cambridge: Cambridge University Press, 1992.

Hughes, Derek, *English Drama, 1660–1700*, New York: Oxford University Press, 1996.

Hume, Robert D., *The Development of English Drama in the Late Seventeenth-Century*, Oxford: Clarendon Press, 1976.

Kroll, Richard W.F., *Restoration Drama and 'The Circle of Commerce': Tragicomedy, Politics, and Trade in the Seventeenth Century*, Cambridge: Cambridge University Press, 2007.

Lowenthal, Cynthia, *Performing Identities on the Restoration Stage*, Carbondale: Southern Illinois University Press, 2003.

Mardsen, Jean I., *Fatal Desire: Women, Sexuality, and the English Stage, 1660–1720*, Ithaca: Cornell University Press, 2006.

Markley, Robert, *Two-edg'd Weapons: Style and Ideology in the Comedies of Etherege, Wycherley, and Congreve*, Oxford: Clarendon, 1988.

Milhous, Judith and Robert D. Hume, *Producible Interpretation: Eight English Plays, 1675–1707*, Carbondale: Southern Illinois University Press, 1985.

Orr, Bridget, *Empire on the English Stage, 1660–1714*, Cambridge: Cambridge University Press, 2001.

Owen, Susan J. (ed.), *A Companion to Restoration Drama*, Oxford: Blackwell, 2001.

—— , *Perspectives on Restoration Drama*, Manchester: Manchester University Press, 2002.

—— , *Restoration Theatre and Crisis*, Oxford: Clarendon, 1996.

Quinsey, Katherine M. (ed.), *Broken Boundaries: Women & Feminism in Restoration Drama*, Lexington: University of Kentucky Press, 1996.

—— , *Restoration Comedy in Performance*, Cambridge: Cambridge University Press, 1986.

Young, Douglas M., *The Feminist Voices in Restoration Comedy: The Virtuous Women in the Play-Worlds of Etherege, Wycherley, and Congreve*, Lanham, MD: University Press of America, 1997.

Studies of Individual Authors

As noted above, the Twayne volumes are usually student-friendly and reliable. Volumes in the 'Critical Heritage' series provide solid overviews of the development of writers' reputations. Volumes in the 'Reference Guide' series offer helpfully annotated bibliographies.

Aphra Behn

Hughes, Derek, *The Theatre of Aphra Behn*, New York: Palgrave, 2001.

O'Donnell, Mary Ann, *Aphra Behn: An Annotated Bibliography of Primary and Secondary Sources*, 2nd edn, Burlington, VT: Ashgate, 2004.

Spencer, Jane, *Aphra Behn's Afterlife*, New York: Oxford University Press, 2000.

John Bunyan

Hill, Christopher, *A Tinker and a Poor Man: John Bunyan and His Church, 1628–1688*, New York: A. Knopf, 1989.

Keeble, N.H. (ed.), *John Bunyan – Conventicle and Parnassus: Tercentenary Essays*, New York: Oxford University Press, 1988.

Samuel Butler

Wasserman, George, *Samuel 'Hudibras' Butler*, Updated edn, Boston: Twayne, 1989.

William Congreve

Hoffman, Arthur W., *Congreve's Comedies*, Victoria, BC: University of Victoria, 1993.

Lindsay, Alexander, *William Congreve: The Critical Heritage*, London: Routledge, 1989.

Love, Harold, *Congreve*, Oxford: Blackwell, 1974.

Novak, Maximillian E., *William Congreve*, New York: Twayne, 1971.

Peters, Julia Stone, *Congreve, the Drama, and the Printed Word*, Stanford: Stanford University Press, 1990.

Sieber, Anita, *Character Portrayal in Congreve's Comedies: The Old Batchelor, Love for Love, and The Way of the World*, Lewiston, NY: Edward Mellen Press, 1996.

Thomas, David, *William Congreve*, New York: St. Martin's Press, 1992.

John Dryden

Harth, Phillip, *Contexts of Dryden's Thought*, Chicago: University of Chicago Press, 1968.

——, *Pen for a Party: Dryden's Tory Propaganda in Its Contexts*, Princeton, NJ: Princeton University Press, 1993.

Hume, Robert D., *Dryden's Criticism*, Ithaca, NY: Cornell University Press, 1970.

Miner, Earl, *Dryden's Poetry*, Bloomington, IN: Indiana University Press, 1967.

Rawson, Claude Julien, *John Dryden (1631–1700): His Politics, His Plays, and His Poets*, Newark: University of Delaware Press; London: Associated University Presses, 2004.

Winn, James A. (ed.), *Critical Essays on John Dryden*, New York: G.K. Hall, 1997.

Winn, James Anderson, *John Dryden and His World*, New Haven, CT: Yale University Press, 1987.

Zwicker, Steven N., *Politics and Language in Dryden's Poetry: The Arts of Disguise*, Princeton, NJ: Princeton University Press, 1984.

George Etherege

Huseboe, Arthur R., *Sir George Etherege*, Boston: Twayne, 1987.

Kachur, B.A., *Etherege & Wycherley*, New York: Palgrave Macmillan, 2004.

Mann, David D., *Sir George Etherege: A Reference Guide*, Boston: G.K. Hall, 1981.

Thomas Otway

Munns, Jessica, *Restoration Politics and Drama: The Plays of Thomas Otway, 1675–1683*, Newark: University of Delaware Press; London: Associated University Presses, 1995.

Warner, Kerstin P., *Thomas Otway*, Boston: Twayne, 1982.

Samuel Pepys

Taylor, Ivan E., *Samuel Pepys*, Boston: Twayne, 1967.
Tomalin, Claire, *Samuel Pepys: The Unequalled Self*, London: Viking, 2002.

Rochester (John Wilmot, Earl of)

Burns, Edward (ed.), *Reading Rochester*, New York: St. Martin's, 1995.
Thormählen, Marianne, *Rochester: The Poems in Context*, Cambridge: Cambridge University Press, 1993.
Vieth, David M. (ed.), *John Wilmot, Earl of Rochester: Critical Essays*, New York: Garland, 1988.

John Vanbrugh

Berkowitz, Gerald M., *Sir John Vanbrugh and the End of Restoration Comedy*, Amsterdam: Rodopi, 1981.
Bull, John Stanley, *Vanbrugh and Farquhar*, New York: St. Martin's Press, 1998.
Downes, Kerry, *Sir John Vanbrugh: A Biography*, New York: St. Martin's Press, 1987.
McCormick, Frank, *Sir John Vanbrugh: The Playwright as Architect*, University Park: Pennsylvania State University Press, 1991.

William Wycherley

Marshall, W. Gerald, *A Great Stage of Fools: Theatricality and Madness in the Plays of William Wycherley*, New York: AMS Press, 1993.
McCarthy, B. Eugene, *William Wycherley: A Biography*, Athens: Ohio University Press, 1979.
—— , *William Wycherley, A Reference Guide*, Boston: G.K. Hall, 1985.
Thompson, James, *Language in Wycherley's Plays: Seventeenth-Century Language Theory and Drama*, Tuscaloosa: University of Alabama Press, 1984.
Vance, John A., *William Wycherley and the Comedy of Fear*, Newark, NJ: University of Delaware Press; London: Associated University Presses, 2000.

Index